DIGITAL VIDEO
SOLUTIONS

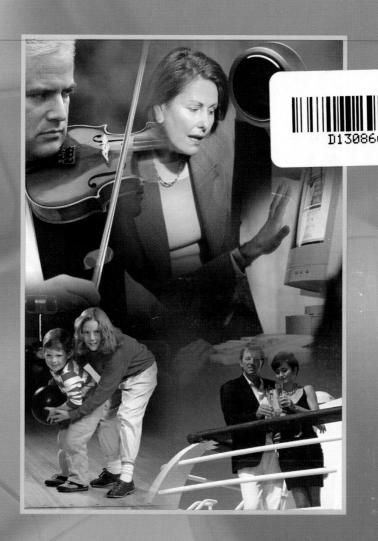

Winston Steward

Digital Video Solutions

Credits: Senior Editor, Mark Garvey; Production Editor, Rodney A. Wilson; Technical Editor, Travis White, *Ulead*; Cover and Interior Design, Stephanie Japs, Cathie Tibbetts, and Kevin Vollrath, *DOV Graphics*; Indexer, Kevin Broccoli, *Broccoli Information Management*.

Publisher: Andy Shafran

Library of Congress Catalog Number: 2001092000

ISBN 1-929685-53-X

5 4 3 2 1

Muska & Lipman Publishing

2645 Erie Avenue, Suite 41

Cincinnati, Ohio 45208

www.muskalipman.com

publisher@muskalipman.com

About the Author

Winston Steward is a freelance author, videographer, musician, and Web designer. He lives with his family in Los Angeles, California. He has written over a dozen books on almost every aspect of computer technology.

Dedication

To my family: Barbara, Larisa, and Trevor, and to friends who have been so supportive...especially, my best friend Louna, and to all future filmmakers everywhere who have yet to pick up a camera.

Acknowledgments

Special thanks to Andy Shafran, Mark Garvey, and everyone at Muska & Lipman for pitching in to make this book the best. And thanks to my agent, Margo Maley Hutchison, and to Louna, for listening to me even when I make very little sense.

Introduction

Welcome to the world of digital video. Prepare to exercise your creativity and have lots of fun.

In this book, you'll learn about digital video from end to end—from how your digital camera works to shooting, editing, and producing top-notch work. The video camcorder lets you tell a story. You'll learn how to storyboard scenes, plan an effective voice-over, and anticipate problems that could prevent you from obtaining the footage you need. I'll show you how to recognize good camera work and effective angles, as well as how to frame shots. We'll also discuss how to make sure your work is in focus, properly lighted, and has good, clear sound.

We'll explore video editing tools at length. You'll use software to cut, paste, and blend your footage into the story you want to tell. There are toys galore to explore here, and this book acquaints you with most of them. You'll learn about adding music, voice-over, and soundtracks as well. Video, like music, is all about emotional timing. The right music enhances your video's mood and setting like nothing else. We'll look at some great creative family fun you can have with the video camera. You'll learn simple but clever editing tricks, stop-motion and time-lapse filming, and using narrative to create an enjoyable piece of family memorabilia.

Finally, on a more business-like note, you'll also learn how to develop professional video-based presentations, school curricula, and trade show kiosk exhibits. You'll learn how to use movies in your Web creations, creating interactive, video-based Web sites.

After your work is perfected, you'll want to share it with the world. Your video must be compressed into a format and standard that can be viewed by your intended audience. It can remain on your computer monitor, be sent across the Internet, or saved to DVD, disk, or tape.

What You'll Find in This Book

The goal of this book is to teach you how to *do* things. Through clear, step-by-step tutorials, you'll learn how to use video-editing software to achieve great results. You'll also learn lots of shortcuts, fast solutions, and quick tips for creating better projects. I'll show you how to avoid needlessly duplicating your efforts and help you avoid pitfalls common to the medium. The color illustrations throughout the book will spark your imagination and lead you to explore your own video creativity.

When you're done with this book, you'll be a different person. Here's how:

▶ You'll know more about how your digital camcorder works, and you'll know how to get the best results while using it.

▶ You'll be able to watch your raw footage and have editing ideas pop into mind.

▶ You'll open a video editing program and not be mystified by its screens, controls, and buttons.

▶ And, finally, when it's time to send your video here, there, and everywhere, you'll know how to do it.

Who This Book is For

This book is for owners of digital video cameras who are ready to jump into this exciting new medium. It is for those who want to capture special family moments, vacations, and events on film. It's also for those with professional or semi-professional aspirations. If you are creating videos for business, children's education, distance learning, product descriptions, medical filmwork, Web deployment, or aid to the disabled, this book will guide you to attaining the required skills. It's also for anyone interested in just having fun with the camera and doing something different for a change with friends and family. Why go see a movie when you can make one?

If you've not purchased a digital video camcorder yet, rest assured that this book will give you many reasons why you should. They are exciting, amazing tools. With this book as your resource, you can be sure your camera won't just sit on the shelf. You'll put it to more use than you ever imagined.

How This Book is Organized

This book contains twelve chapters.

▶ Chapter 1: "Digital Video: Imagine the Possibilities." You'll quickly be introduced to digital video and its creative possibilities and get a glimpse of all that we'll cover. This chapter offers examples of kinds of projects and skills you'll learn about in the rest of the book.

▶ Chapter 2: "Understanding and Working with Digital Video." You'll learn how digital video differs from non-digital and a little bit about the technologies it encompasses. You'll understand the remarkable feat that makes it possible to work with a medium as enormous as film on your desktop computer. You'll be amazed at the tools that are now available at your fingertips. We'll also discuss equipment requirements for shooting and editing digital video.

▶ Chapter 3: "Taking Great Videos." You'll learn about camera technology in general and how video differs from still camera work. We'll also take a tour of your digital camcorder's dials and buttons and learn how to adjust the settings for the best possible shots. We'll talk about lighting, focus, depth of field, and how to put every aspect of your filming environment to work for you as you create your movie.

▶ Chapter 4: "From the Camera to the Computer." You'll learn how to transfer digital video from your camcorder to your computer, where it can be edited. We'll discuss FireWire technology and the options you have for transferring your film. We'll also get started with video capture software. Using programs like Ulead VideoStudio, you'll discover how video is actually captured and stored on your computer and how it becomes editable. We'll cover tips for capturing the right amount of video, so your hard drive doesn't get overloaded.

▶ Chapter 5: "Planning and Shooting Your Video." We'll cover how to film various event types and how to plan ahead for all kinds of environmental factors. We'll discuss scenes, camera movement, and how to set up the action so that the story you want to tell will really get across. You'll learn how to be in the right place at the right time with your camcorder and how to get the shots you want.

▶ Chapter 6: "Basic Video Editing." You'll learn how to create and organize a great video project. Just like a professional editor, you'll learn how to build a movie by combining your best footage. I'll show you how to create transitions, add text, combine still images with your footage, and add a little music to your video as well.

▶ Chapter 7: "Going Further with Your Video." We'll move beyond the basics and discover creative ways to combine video clips and advanced track editing. You'll also learn how to add multiple audio tracks to your footage and how to use professional video filters of all types. With today's tools, if there's something missing from your original footage, you can probably add it.

▶ Chapter 8: "Making Magic: Video Special Effects." Defying gravity and transporting characters to new environments is only the beginning of what you can do with the amazing video special effects we'll cover in this chapter. You'll learn to use video masking and overlay technology similar to that employed by professional studios.

▶ Chapter 9: "Making Great Business Videos." Videos are a way of communicating with the world about your company or product that goes far beyond words. Videos can be used as educational tools, tutorials, product displays, VIP interviews, and more. We'll talk about what makes a good business video, as well as how to develop and polish your message. You'll also learn how to enhance your video's message using powerful video layout tools such as PowerPoint, Adobe Acrobat, and Macromedia Flash.

▶ Chapter 10: "Publishing Video on the Web." You'll learn what it takes to successfully get your videos on the Web. You'll learn what makes a good Web movie and how to create one. We'll discuss streaming video, setting up a Web page so that your video plays back as soon as someone opens it, and Web-friendly video formats like QuickTime. You'll learn skills for taking control of your movie's online appearance in many ways.

▶ Chapter 11: "Special Events, Family Fun, and Educational Projects." You'll learn how to film weddings and special events like athletic competitions and recitals. We'll talk about making sure your event footage captures everything special about the moment. Kids can have lots of fun in the digital video realm as well, and we'll try out some kid-specific projects. Finally, we'll take a look at enhancing educational projects with digital video, and you'll learn how your camcorder can become a powerful learning tool for children.

▶ Chapter 12: "Exporting and Organizing Videos." Exporting your video requires careful consideration. We'll discuss how to create a final video in just the right format for your target audience. You'll learn to create video DVDs as well. And, finally, we'll cover what to do with all your video footage, how to keep track of it, and how to archive the raw footage that you won't be needing for the time being.

1

Digital Video: Imagine the Possibilities

What is Digital Video?

Welcome to the world of digital video! With your digital camcorder—and the computer hardware and software you'll learn about in this book—you are on your way to extending your artistic, creative flair in directions you've probably never even dreamed of. Digital video is a marriage between the power of film and the indestructibility and convenience of digital information. When you film a video, you are capturing light and sound from the world around you. Each frame freezes a split second of movement, light, and color into an exact replica of a passing moment. When filming with a digital video camera, the same rules of exposure, color, and aperture apply just as if you were filming with a standard film camera. However, since digital video is stored in binary, computer-friendly form, it offers many advantages over traditional film. This book is all about exploring those advantages and creating top-quality videos.

The Creative Possibilities

Filming your digital video is just the beginning. Your movies are like putty in your hands. It's like this: If you see a special effect in a feature film at a theatre—a fade or blend, trick of light, or unlikely combination of onscreen elements—you can almost certainly do something similar using the software we'll explore in this book. The programs you'll learn in this book are tools powerful enough for professional video editing, but soon you'll be well on your way to mastering them. Your videos can be combined and overlaid, re-colored and brightened, and edited in many ways. Anything from simple home videos to elaborate corporate presentations can be improved to enhance their creative value or add a touch of professionalism.

Following are some examples of all you can create with digital video, using tools you'll learn about in this book:

Weddings

Nothing captures important wedding-day moments like video. Weddings are a ceremony of motion, and if you plan ahead and edit carefully, your movie can virtually recreate the event in a vivid and interesting way. In Chapter 11, you'll learn how to video weddings and special events to make sure you get good footage you can weave into something compelling (Figure 1.1).

Figure 1.1
Each wedding is unique. Create a video that truly tells its story.

Family Fun

Figure 1.2 shows a video trick the kids will love. Using stop-motion filming, the little girl makes her older brother turn into a stuffed animal. One simply films her waving the magic wand, while the boy stays in place. Then the camera stops, and the boy is replaced with a stuffed animal. Filming resumes. If nothing is changed except for the replacement, the magic wand illusion is quite believable.

Figure 1.2
Good old stop-motion video fun for everyone.

Videos for Education

Videos can be used to shed light on complex processes, supplementing instruction provided with helpful diagrams and pictures. In Figure 1.3, you see an online product tutorial explaining the highlights and main features of a product diagram. The visitor clicks the instructor in the video, and the explanation begins.

Figure 1.3
The small figure appearing at the top is a video that, when clicked, describes the product.

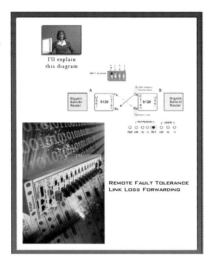

Videos for Marketing

Videos are great tools for market enhancement. You can create virtual tours and display real-life situations as well as product close-ups and cutaways. It's easy to keep people's interest when you can show what you are offering rather than just talk about it. Figure 1.4 shows a real estate virtual tour; the three short movies do the house much more justice than a few pictures. You'll learn to create documents like this for the Web or distribute video clips with a little flourish using Adobe Acrobat (as shown in this figure).

Figure 1.4
A virtual tour of a house for sale.

Web-Based Videos and Hyperlinks

Videos can add a nice touch to a Web page. With a little imagination, even those tiny, fast-loading "postage-stamp" videos can be effective. Figure 1.5 shows an example: The small image of the girl playing the violin is actually a video, tinted blue. The still shot above the movie, tinted brown and blurred, is taken from the same movie. The still was extracted from the movie before it was shrunk down to its current, Web-friendly dimensions. The movie begins playing back after a few seconds, allowing the visitor time to view the page contents.

Figure 1.5

The smaller image of the violin player is actually a video clip that will begin playing automatically.

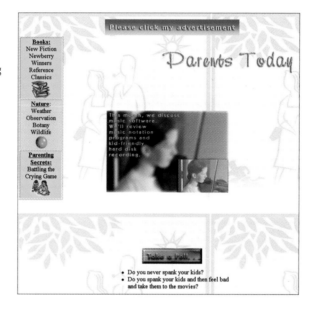

Combining 3D Art with Your Videos

Programs like Ulead Cool 3D provide simple tools for creating shapes and objects. Artwork is rendered in 3D, objects can move and twist, and their actions can be saved as a movie. You can then blend this movie with another video, and the 3D objects you created in your art program will appear to interact with your "living" video subjects. Figure 1.6 shows an example: Cool 3D was used to create moving 3D text against an animated backdrop. The objects can move, shrink, and rotate, because they are part of their own movie.

Figure 1.6
Ulead Cool 3D lets you
create small videos with
3D objects that you can
import into your main
project.

Music and Sound Effects

Music overdubs can transform a video into a dynamic multi-sensory experience. Using programs
like Ulead Media Studio or Adobe Premiere, you can switch video scenes on a single beat of a
soundtrack, zooming in for a close-up view of an audio track and determining exactly where the
track change should take place. In Figure 1.7, a marker indicates where the beat is, so that
footage of a single guitarist will switch to a new view. You'll get acquainted with some of the
newest audio mixing tools. You'll have total control over your tracks, applying music filters and
effects and changing volume and track placement.

Figure 1.7
You can create a video
transition that occurs
on an exact beat in a
music clip.

Movie Compositions

Overlapping still images can enhance even a simple video, transforming it into a work of art. In the example below (Figure 1.8), the only moving video is the girl, who is looking out the window and gesturing. The car image is overlayed, and the other partially transparent and masked images interact with the video. This was all done in Ulead MediaStudio 6 using keyframes. Keyframes are simply markers that specify the movement path of objects in your video composition. Similarly, the music video montage below was assembled in After Effects, using still shots and a single clip. You'll learn to create multimedia experiences like these in Chapter 8.

NOTE

If you've created images with layers and filters using PhotoImpact, Paint Shop Pro, Photoshop, or any other graphics tool, imagine making those layers resize and change position over time. You can create a path for their movement and make them dance and interact with other layers and special effects.

Figure 1.8
These layered images and videos move around the canvas using keyframes.

Digital Video Camera Features

There's a lot going on in the controls of a digital camcorder. Manufacturers design them to be sleek and stylish, but all those button panels provide access to many advanced features. What follows are descriptions of some of the basic controls of a typical digital camcorder. While this list is not meant to replace a thorough reading of your camcorder manual, let me introduce you to the buttons you'll probably be pressing most often.

Basic Features and Specs

You may want to get your camcorder out and take a look at it while walking through this list:

Record button

There should be a prominent red (or at least partially red) button to begin recording. When pressed, this button records frames of video, starts the tape motor, and saves the recorded frames onto the tape or DVD-RAM disk.

Record Indicator Light

There should be some sort of glowing indicator to show when you are currently recording. It could be a red light near the Record button or a big friendly REC viewable in the LCD or viewfinder.

Rewind/Play/Fast Forward/Pause

Quickly locate the Rewind, Play, Fast Forward, and Pause buttons. Your workaday videography will always involve recording, rewinding, viewing, setting Pause, and then recording where you left off. Pause is used frequently as a standby mode, in preparation for recording, playing back your tape, or uploading your video to computer.

Switching Between Record and Play Mode

After recording video, it's important to quickly play back your footage. When you view an instant playback on your LCD, you'll see things you didn't see before. Lighting conditions show their true colors on playback, and you can determine whether to keep filming or make adjustments before continuing. To this end, you'll need to become skillful at quickly switching between record and playback. Find out how to move conveniently between recording footage and viewing your results, then fast-forwarding to where you can record again. Figure 1.9 displays the rotary mode button on the Canon Elura 2. Notice how you can switch between various playback and record modes by turning this single dial.

Figure 1.9
The Canon Elura 2 has a
convenient rotary dial
for switching camcorder
modes.

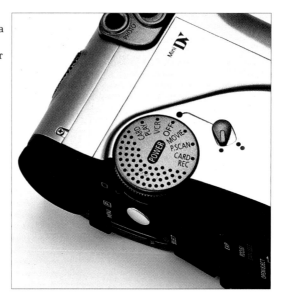

LCD

An LCD (liquid crystal display) is the flip-out screen that displays what you are recording and acts as your playback screen. When in standby (the camcorder is paused, ready to record), the LCD displays what the lens sees. An LCD can range from 2.5 inches to 4 inches and flips into place like the lid of a cigarette lighter. LCDs provide a bright, flattering view of what your lens sees. Most scenes look good in an LCD. To avoid surprises in the editing room, keep these points in mind:

▶ Scenes that look dark through the LCD are, in reality, even darker. Your video will probably look darker than what you see through the LCD.

▶ If you see glare in your LCD, you'll see even more glare in your video.

▶ Anything that looks slightly hazy and out of focus in the LCD will look unacceptably so when you play the tape.

Therefore, rerecord anything that looks even remotely "off."

Viewfinder

As in traditional cameras, place your eye at the viewfinder to see what the lens sees. Good camcorders display what the camcorder is truly capable of recording. Areas where light is too intense for the camcorder to record properly will glow in a kind of unpleasant nuclear white. If a region is too dark, the viewfinder, bless its heart, will display it as such before you start tape rolling and suffer the bad news later.

Viewfinder Diopter Lever

Beneath the viewfinder is a small lever to compensate for nearsightedness and farsightedness. This allows the visually impaired to shoot without glasses.

Tape or Disk Insert Bay or Carriage

The MiniDV tape or MiniDVD-RAM disk has to be inserted. The process is both electrical and mechanical. That means you should not try to pry the carriage door open. Find out where the button for opening the carriage or bay is located. In most units, the camcorder must be powered on in order to insert the tape or disk.

Battery Slot or Bay

You'll need to know how to insert your battery. See if there is an indicator letting you know that the battery is seated properly in the slot or bay and that the unit is powered. There may be an audio indicator or visible "Power" light of some sort.

Battery Charge Kit

Your camcorder's battery will not arrive fully charged. You'll have to charge it up before taking the camcorder out and getting some real footage. To begin, plug in the charger and locate the indicator on the battery charge unit. This is a light that lets you know the battery is, indeed, charging. The indicator may be a blinking green or red light or a steadily glowing diode. Just make sure you learn the difference between "still charging" and "ready to go." When the battery is fully charged, you're ready to start filming. Your battery will likely keep your camcorder charged for about one-half to three-quarters of the time advertised. Use of the LCD rather than the viewfinder and frequent On/Off/Standby activity quickly deplete your battery. Most digital camcorders use lithium ion batteries. Unlike NiCad batteries, which require complete depletion of charge before they can be adequately recharged, it's perfectly fine to recharge a partially charged lithium ion battery.

CAUTION

Do not place a cold battery (a battery that has been below 40 degrees for some time and feels cold to the touch) on the charger. Wait for the battery to return to room temperature. Charging a cold battery reduces battery life.

The Zoom Controls

You'll want to locate your video's zoom controls (shown in Figure 1.10). They'll come in quite handy, and you'll want to learn quickly how to zoom in and out without having to move your fingers too far from the record button.

A word about "optical zoom" vs. "digital zoom": Optical zoom is considered "true" zoom. A mechanical process, optical zooming is performed by manipulating lens components. Most digital camcorders offer between 10× and 20× optical zoom amounts. Digital zoom is pixel manipulation—computer trickery. When you digitally zoom, the camcorder is figuring out

which part of an image you are trying to make bigger and pumps up the pixel count in that image area. Digital camcorders frequently provide 80× to 300× digital zoom. Using digital zoom too much results in blotchy, pixilated videos. It may look OK on your LCD at filming time, but you won't like the results later on the bigger screen.

Figure 1.10
A button-style zoom control. "W" indicates "wide" and "T" indicates "telephoto."

Time-Date Stamp

Setting the time and date on your camcorder not only stamps the continually updated information at the bottom of the video, it allows you to synchronize your video with other time-related devices. For example, you can synchronize the video with advanced audio equipment.

TIP
Enabling time-date stamping is not the same thing as continuously running that information on your tape. So make sure you do not leave the time-date display on, except perhaps at the very beginning and ending of the film. There's no reason why anyone would want to watch the time scrolling by throughout the entire video.

Switching between EP and SP Mode

MiniDV tapes allow you to choose between two recording modes: SP provides higher recording quality, but shortened recording time per tape; EP creates slightly lower quality videos and longer tape time. Locate the menu on your camcorder to set this option.

Locating Important Menus

Beyond the basics discussed so far, most digital camcorders provide extensive options, which are displayed in menus. These menus are usually accessed electronically and are visible on the LCD or in the viewfinder. Some options will be available in a panel hidden by the LCD, accessible only when the LCD is in viewing position (see Figure 1.11). You'll want to learn to access this main menu panel quickly, so you can make desired adjustments without fumbling.

Figure 1.11
On some camcorders, menu buttons aren't visible until you open the LCD.

CHAPTER 1

Microphone

Your digital camcorder has a stereo microphone, an area mic that will pick up every nearby sound. In a later chapter, we'll discuss digital audio editing for your videos, but for now remember one thing: If you will be doing any type of direct audio recording, such as interviews and live music, you'll need to purchase an external mic. Your digital camcorder has an input for one.

Output and Input Ports

If you are simply going to film video and edit it on your computer, all you need is a FireWire port. Note that a single FireWire port can be both input and output. Also, all digital camcorders have analog outputs, allowing TV playback and recording video to VHS tape via your VCR. However, if you want to save VHS tape material onto your camcorder's MiniDV cassettes or disks, your camcorder will need an S-Video or standard analog input, sometimes called A/V In.

Still-Picture Capabilities

Most digital camcorders function as a still-picture camera as well. Frame for frame, though, a digital camcorder's image is not on par with pictures produced by digital cameras. Decent digital cameras produce pictures with two to three times as many pixels as an individual video frame produced by a digital camcorder. To take a still picture, you press a separate button; on most models, you'll find it right beside the video Record button, making it easy to grab a still shot while filming. And, yes, some digital camcorders let you take a snapshot while filming video. Depending on the camera, still images may be on the MiniDV tape itself or on separate, removable media.

Non-Essential (but Nice) Features

The following are not features that will make or break a camcorder. They can be convenient and helpful—or end up unused or misused. If you don't yet own a camcorder, take a look at these extras and see if having them in your machine may make your life easier in some way.

Remote Control

A remote control unit lets you include yourself in the video, film subjects unawares while your camera is unattended, and save footage onto your computer without having to scrunch back behind the computer and press the camcorder Play button. Many menu-based features are available from the remote control, and some are even more accessible via remote control than they are on the camcorder because they are not buried inside multiple layers of menu options, which camcorders frequently use in order to save space.

Audio or Video Insert

Sometimes you may want to add a music clip or voice-over to your video without having to rerecord your scene. Likewise, at times, you may want to keep the audio track the same, while punching in new visual footage. Video Insert and Audio Insert, respectively, let you do just that. This feature applies to editing the tape while it is in your camcorder. Video editing after uploading to the computer is something else—we'll cover this in detail later in this book.

Video Effects

Many camcorders allow you to add basic special effects such as image stretching, transitions, and curious image distortions. This book teaches you how to edit videos extensively, utilizing much more control than you'll have with a camcorder's onboard options. Also, editing video in your camcorder alters the original footage. Once the attack of the cutes subsides, you'll wish you hadn't put little starbursts on your one and only record of this year's vacation. PC-based editing, however, never alters your original digital tape.

Audio Sound Effects

Similar to video effects, audio effects add cute digital sounds directly to the tape. You can add a car-crash when a drop-dead pretty girl appears on the screen or arena-like applause when someone says something clever. Just as with video effects, the experiments should be saved for non-destructive PC-based editing.

Saving Video as MPEG

MPEG is a favorite file compression scheme, allowing movies to be saved at a fraction of their "raw video" format size. Hardware MPEG compression is superior to software-based, allowing a cleaner compression of the images. Some digital camcorders let you save your video as MPEG right onto tape. You'd want to do this only if your purpose is to make quick videos for e-mailing or the Web. But for those so inclined, letting your camcorder compress to MPEG on the fly can save lots of editing steps.

High-End Gear

Currently, consumer-grade digital camcorders cost between $700 and $1,600 dollars, each containing pretty much all the basic features described above. When you reach the "prosumer" level, the price takes about an $800 jump. What do you get when you pay more than $2,000 for a camcorder?

3CCDs

Basic digital camcorders have a single CCD (charge-coupled device), the mechanism that converts incoming images to colors, each with a specified voltage. The hallmark difference between consumer and prosumer digital camcorders is the presence of two additional CCDs, with each of the three CCDs assigned to a primary color. On this grade of camcorder, colors are noticeably richer than with their single-chip cousins. This is not to say that single-CCD color is not adequate; on the contrary, it's usually quite good. Three-CCD camcorders create film with colors that are near flawless in their rendering. One should feel compelled to purchase a 3-chip digital camcorder only if professional, broadcast-quality video is a requirement.

Better Lens and Extra Lens Capabilities

Professional videographers often complain that standard digital video camcorders have "soft lenses," meaning lenses that are not crafted as flawlessly as they could be. Precision lenses truly make a difference in image sharpness, and each of the major camcorder cobblers introduces its own special lens technology in its higher-priced models. Along with improved lens quality, you're also purchasing the ability to easily add more lenses, such as telephoto or wide-angle (see Figure 1.12).

Figure 1.12
An example of wide angle and telephoto lenses.

Wide Angle

Telephoto

NOTE
Many entry-level or mid-priced digital camcorders do not support standard lens sizes, so purchasing additional lenses can be a problem. Professional or semi-professional lenses can spell the difference between an OK video and something you could potentially sell.

Better Still-Image Technology

You'll find more advanced still-image technology on the upper-priced digital camcorders. Although very few digital camcorders can take digital photographs on par with digital cameras, high-priced digital camcorders start to poke their heads into the 1-megapixel range. The better digital cameras take pictures in the 2- to 3-megapixel range.

Accessory Hot Shoe

More expensive digital camcorders have a hot connector at the top of the unit for attaching an optional external microphone or a high-powered light for filming in less-than-optimal lighting conditions. These extras help dress up the camcorder into something approaching a professional unit.

Other features you'll find in high-priced models include better microphones, more cabling options such as crossover cables for audio editing, S-Video Out and In, and a larger LCD. Important for professionals, the lens is usually removable and extra professional-grade lenses of many types are available for most upper-priced units.

Camcorder Extras

The items below don't come with your camcorder, but if you spend much time shooting videos, you'll find most of these very helpful at one time or another. They are available at photography stores, via mail, and on the Web.

Tripod

Many shots are greatly improved by the use of a tripod. Tripods provide a stability of vision that allows the viewer to forget about the presence of the camera for a while. For a novice filmmaker, handheld video shooting tends to look jittery, even in spite of gallant efforts otherwise. Tripods provide a consistent horizontal plane from which to film, adding continuity to the video project. They are especially important for night filming, where low shutter speeds are a must. In such cases, shooting without a tripod will almost certainly result in a jittery picture.

Filters

Filters screw in atop the video lens and are applied and removed as needed. They cost between $30 and $50 each and must be purchased for the specific lens size of your camcorder. Filters alter the lighting quality in natural ways (Figure 1.13 and Figure 1.14). Made of specially treated glass, they are effective without being artificial looking.

Figure 1.13
Filming from the air looking out the window just about requires a polarizing filter.

Figure 1.14
Neutral density filtering at work.

Before Neutral Density Filter   After Neutral Density Filter

Lights

Digital video is a very light-sensitive technology. If you plan to do a good deal of indoor filming and want to have a reasonable amount of control over how well lit your subjects are, look into purchasing a couple of standard photography lights. In the absence of well-controlled lighting, faces move in and out of the dark with maddening regularity, limbs recede into shadows, and video generally looks Hitchcockian. In Chapter 5, we will discuss effective lighting in some detail.

Camcorder Upkeep

A digital video camera represents a substantial investment in a piece of sensitive high-tech equipment. You will get more years and more fun out of your camera if you take good care of it. Following are a few tips for good camcorder care:

► **Avoid temperature extremes and condensation.** Owners of digital equipment are always told to avoid temperature extremes. Indeed, condensation, below-freezing cold, and extreme heat can cause real damage to the unit. The warning bears repeating here, though, because you are most likely to take your digital camcorder on vacations—and what do many vacation spots have in common? Temperature extremes.

▶ **Avoid jarring and bumping.** Always carry your camcorder onto the plane with you when flying. A bump in the head on the baggage rotary will not do your camcorder any favors.

▶ **Cleaning the lens (don't).** The consensus among the experts is not to let the lens get dirty in the first place. You may purchase a clear or polarizing filter for your lens to protect it from dirt and dust. Fingerprints and scratches from rough paper will permanently damage your lens. However, if you do need to clean it, visit a camera store and purchase a little lens-cleaning kit that will probably feature a can of compressed air and a special brush. Do not blow on your lens yourself. The moisture is bad.

▶ **Cleaning the viewfinder and LCD.** Remember that no image data passes through the viewfinder or LCD, so a fingerprint smudge on either surface is an irritant, but it won't appear in your video. You may clean your viewfinder using special lens-cleaning solution and soft tissue. To clean your LCD, use a damp soft tissue or gentle cloth or use gentle, non-soapy cleaning solvent. Apply very little pressure to the LCD. It is not made for rough handling.

Crossroads

Now that you've been introduced to your video camcorder and all it can do, in the next chapter you'll learn more about digital video—what it is, and how it differs from other film mediums.

2
Understanding and Working with Digital Video

In this chapter, you'll learn how digital video differs from analog and what is required for filming and editing in the digital realm. We'll touch on how to incorporate some of your old analog video into your digital moviemaking. You'll learn what is unique about the digital video medium and why your digital camcorder is such a remarkable device. We'll also look at digital audio as it relates to your video-making. And we'll consider the different video file types you'll be dealing with and the technology that makes your video movie projects small enough to transport.

The Digital Difference

Digital video springs from the marriage of two historic technologies:

▶ TV, film, and video, which have their roots in waveform, or what is called analog technology.

▶ The personal computer, with its digital language of ones and zeros.

The following section is divided into two parts. The first describes the analog and digital realms and how they converge when you create a video project. Next, we'll talk about video compression, the technology used to convert video files into something usable on your PC. We'll also cover the names and file types you'll be referring to in your day-to-day video editing.

Analog vs. Digital

Videos and PCs have their roots in two separate technologies, and when you transfer and edit digital video, you merge the two, at least temporarily. The distinction comes into play at two steps in the video editing process:

▶ Transferring video from camcorder to computer for editing.

▶ Saving your final project for distribution.

If you understand the basic differences between analog and digital video, your final video output will be of much higher quality.

The Analog World

TV, film, and video capture light and sound as they fluctuate along a wave, recording gradations in light intensity and brightness, gradual shifts in color, and subtle changes in sound amplitude and frequency. These changes are recorded along a continuum. We refer to this as analog recording.

The analog method of storing visual and audio data parallels the human experience. Our eyes process fluctuations in color and brightness very smoothly, enabling us to see millions of shades of color. Because our ears hear sound as wave-like patterns (analog), we can process a huge array of volume and timbre combinations, and we can distinguish subtle changes in a sound's quality and character.

Figure 2.1 displays an audio track in Ulead Media Studio Pro. Later in this book, you'll learn how to edit video in sync with the peaks and valleys of wave modulation. The world of sight and sound comes to us in a ceaseless ebb and flow. Because we perceive all sensory phenomena as waveform combinations, our sensory "palette" of color, brightness, and sound is infinite. Your life is analog and, therefore, not boring.

Figure 2.1
An audio waveform as displayed in Media Studio Pro's track list.

Waves and amplitude measurements are also the language of electronics. Television, analog video, and film process information as fluctuations in electronic signals, mirroring how we see and hear the world itself. A gradual change in voltage is recorded on tape and reflects a slight variation in color, brightness, or sound quality. Visual and audio equipment is calibrated to record the subtlest oscillations in light, color, and sound.

The Digital World

As you no doubt have heard, digital is different.

A digital video camera records what the lens sees and the microphone hears in binary computer code (see Figure 2.2)—the language of computers. The digital video camera's advantage is its ability to make a non-destructible permanent record of all the data passing through. A digital video camcorder takes millions of samples of the analog world as seen and heard through the camera and stores them in indestructible, unchanging code. The feat is remarkable, because a camcorder generally records at about thirty frames per second. (In Europe, video records at a rate of twenty-five frames per second.) The amount of digital information stored on a digital video (DV) cassette is mind-boggling, since all the shades of color, nuances of sound, and fluctuations in lighting that your camera sees and hears must be converted to their digital equivalents and saved onto the cassette or disk inside your camera.

Figure 2.2
The same sound wave displayed in Figure 2.1 can also be represented in binary code. The more "1s and 0s" used to record, the more accurate the "digitized" file will sound when you play it back.

How Digital is Superior

So why is digital better? What can you do with digital cameras and technology that you could not do with analog?

▶ **No Generational Loss**. If you copy the video stored on your digital cassette or CD, the copy will be as good as the original. Digital replicas do not become less accurate when copied. Also, generally speaking, movies stored on digital cassettes or CDs will not deteriorate. VHS recordings are stored on oxidized tape, just like music stored on the cassette tapes you (used to) play in your car. Over time, the oxidation wears away, and the quality of the recording becomes noticeably diminished. Since digital video cameras store recordings as binary code rather than as voltage impressions on oxidized tape, your movie will look the same two years from now as it does today.

NOTE

In the analog world, any type of video transfer causes a step down in display quality. This is called generational loss. Generational loss would occur when you upload your video to your computer, render your project as a final movie, make a copy of your movie to a CD or tape, or download your video project back to your camcorder.

▶ **Digital Audio**. One of the supreme advantages of digital video is its ability to record (and maintain) CD-quality audio. Before uploading your video from camera to PC, your editing software gives you the option of maintaining your audio track at 100 percent quality, no compression. Not only that, but audio you add to video during editing can be maintained at digital quality. This means that the audio you ultimately send out with your finished project can be the same quality as the original recording, without degeneration.

▶ **No Static**. When you transmit digital data, if the data is received at all, the movie will look good. There is no "fuzziness" or variability in reception quality. As long as the code arrives on the other end, everything will be fine. However, as anyone who has had to fight with static and dial in a station with poor reception knows, the same is not true for analog.

▶ **Progressive-Scanned Image**. PCs are capable of displaying a complete frame of video at once (rather than using interlacing technology, an earlier method of displaying video). Videos filmed using progressive scanning will have sharper color, and the image will appear sharper when displaying film of a fast-moving subject. A video with fast-moving subject matter will be less likely to blur or look like a comb has been dragged across it.

NOTE
When you film fast-moving subjects without using progressive scanning, interlacing will show (see Figure 2.3). Your image will look like a comb has been dragged through it.

Figure 2.3
A video filmed without progressive scanning shows the effects of interlacing.

▶ **Non-Video Data Layers**. Digital video can carry much more data than just a video signal. A digital video can be embedded with viewer preference information, viewing options, hyperlinks, and all kinds of interactivity that has not even been thought of yet. Digital video transforms movies into an interactive technology.

▶ **Superior Transfer of Colors.** Another digital plus is that the post-transfer color quality of your video will be inherently better. When transferring data from camera to VCR, or TV to VCR, analog video systems use a single wire to transmit all the color, brightness, and luminance information, leading to blurry colors and indistinct images, especially after you've made a copy of your original video. Even newer video systems that attempt to overcome the problem still suffer from a loss of color quality during transfer (see Figure 2.4).

Figure 2.4
Video dulled in color and quality from too many transfers.

What is Compression?

Now that you understand some of the differences between video and digital technology, you can appreciate the roadblocks that prevented digital video editing from coming into its own. How, for instance, could video makers transport and transform the data between camcorder and PC without altering the content (and thereby making it incompatible with TV broadcast)?

Video files are huge. There are color model and dimensional differences to consider, too. TV screens, movie screens, and computer monitors are all different proportional sizes. What is the technology that will shepherd your video through all these format and standardization requirements, managing the differences between how video is recorded and the digital domain of the PC?

The Development of Compression

A number of professional agencies and engineering groups have worked for years to develop various types of video compression. If you've worked with computer images, then you are probably already familiar with compression. You may know, for example, that JPEG images are very small and viewable on the Web, where file size is a major consideration. TIFF images are larger, but viewable on both Macs and PCs. There are many image compression schemes, and something similar had to be developed for digital video. However, video compression had to provide much more drastic reductions in file size while retaining as much of the quality and native formatting as possible. This was, and still is, a very tall order.

To be played back properly under various formats, digital video requires more than just a simple compression system. After being made smaller for transport and editing, video must also be decompressed carefully, according to its architecture and original format. The term "codec" stands for compression/decompression, and it refers to a class of compression schemes that make it possible to play back otherwise prohibitively large movies under many circumstances. When you compress your video, you'll see lists of various compression types. Figure 2.5 shows the QuickTime compression list. These options are available if you choose to recompress your movie using the QuickTime Pro viewer.

Figure 2.5
The QuickTime Pro
Viewer's compression
options.

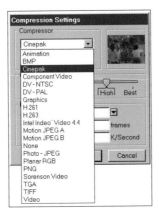

Compression Schemes

The table below briefly describes MPEG (Moving Picture Experts Group) compression schemes. The name MPEG is derived from a group of industry experts commissioned to standardize compression technology for movie playback on the PC and other platforms. Each new MPEG version represents an advance in the ability to create movies small in size that still look and sound good.

Table 2.1
Compression Schemes

Compression Scheme	Quality	Typical Use
MPEG-1	Poor. Very small movie size.	Developed in the early 1990s to facilitate digital movie technology for the PC. Quickly superceded by MPEG-2.
MPEG-2	Creates movies that look decent at a reasonable file and screen size.	Still in use today, used for CD, computer, and Web-based deployment of digital movies.
MPEG-4	Capable of creating full monitor-sized movies of near-DVD quality (Figure 2.6). Introduces layer technology, allowing innovators to add interactivity to their movies.	Rendering DVD movies for computer deployment, game creation, e-commerce, and other applications of hyperlinks and interactivity.

Figure 2.6
Higher frame rates and screen sizes are easier to handle with MPEG-4 compression.

CHAPTER 2

Codecs

A Codec is a coding method that facilitates the distribution and smooth playback of digital movies. Digital movie creators apply a codec when saving their movie for playback on various systems. For playback, viewers must have the same codec installed on the computer. Some codecs are shipped and installed with devices such as Windows Media Player. As more efficient codecs are introduced, they can be downloaded by the public.

Table 2.2
Codecs

Codec	Quality	Typical Use
Indeo	Produces movies that are small enough for the Web but that look good on playback.	Digital movie creators often use Indeo compression for quality movies that will be played back from a hard drive.
CinePak	Decent movie quality at CD data rates.	A common choice for movies that will be played back from CD. Playable on both PCs and Macs.
Sorenson	Good quality movie. If you save your movie with Sorenson codec, allow plenty of time for the operation.	Standard codec used with QuickTime movies, thus movies are playable on both Mac and PC.
DV-PAL and **DV-NTCS**	Very high-quality movie.	Used for transferring video clips from camcorder to computer.
H.261	Decent quality movie that plays back well over telephone lines and ISDN connections.	Used for teleconferencing video or movies played back across telecommunication lines.

File Formats

Let's take a look at two popular video file types or formats that can be played back on your computer or elsewhere. They'll provide video controls, screen size choices, and other options associated with the "look and feel" of the video player. When you are ready to complete your video project, you can save your video creations as a file type, and anyone who has the specified player can play back your video on their machine.

▶ **AVI**. AVI (Audio Video Interleave) files are the standard video file types used in Windows (see Figure 2.7). The AVI architecture is open, so video designers can include many types of compression and playback options to suit their projects' needs. However, this means that not all Windows Media players will be able to play every type of AVI file. As the native Windows file format, AVI has built-in popularity.

Figure 2.7
An .AVI movie played back in Windows generic Media Player interface.

▶ **Quicktime**. QuickTime (Figure 2.8) is a favorite video format because it is cross-platform, meaning that QuickTime videos can be played on both PCs and Macs. QuickTime videos compress well and retain their high quality even at small file sizes, making them useful on the Web. The QuickTime file type is .mov.

Figure 2.8
A QuickTime movie.

CHAPTER 2

Video Streaming

Video streaming is an Internet technology that allows live events to be broadcast over the Web. Also, with streaming, movies appear on the screen without the viewer having to wait for the entire movie to download before viewing. The following table looks at three video streaming movie types.

Table 2.3
Video Streaming Movie Types

Streaming Type	Background	Typical Use
RealMedia (RM)	Developed by RealNetworks. The movie creator targets a specific audience based on playback speed. Viewers may visit RealNetworks to download the player.	Creates either a Web-based or server-based streaming movie. Web-based movie begins playback before download is complete. Server-based begins playback as soon as viewer opens Web page. Server-based deployment requires special server equipment.
Windows Media Format (WMV)	Developed by Microsoft. The movie creator targets a specific audience based on playback speed. Viewers may visit Microsoft's site to download the player. If configured correctly, Windows will attempt to download the right codec automatically. (Figure 2.9)	Creates either a Web-based or server-based streaming movie. Web-based movie begins playback before download is complete. Server-based begins playback as soon as viewer opens Web page. Server-based deployment requires special server equipment.
QuickTime (MOV)	Developed by Apple as a tool for video developers to provide advanced playback options to wide audiences.	Movie begins as the viewer indicates playback. Playback continues as portions of the movie are downloaded. Larger file size and better quality movie, generally speaking, than other two streaming types.

Figure 2.9
A WMV movie
displayed in Windows
Media Player.

A Word about Digital Audio

How is audio recorded on your digital camcorder? Similar to the way in which digital video creates binary samples of the visual world, digital audio records a digital snapshot of an audio signal thousands of times every second. Audio sampling rates vary; the more times per second a sound is sampled, the more accurate will be its reproduction when played back. We'll learn more about digital audio recording and editing in Chapter 7.

NOTE

You'll find that the audio portion of your digital video does not contribute much to file size. Taking a compression axe to your audio will not gain you much in video file size reduction.

Tools for Working with Digital Video

The creation of a digital video project can be divided into four basic steps: shooting (the actual recording of the images), transferring (getting the images into your computer), editing (selecting, manipulating, and reordering your images with the help of software), and distributing (outputting your finished video in a format that meets your needs and the needs of your intended audience). Each step requires its own set of tools. Right now, we'll run through a quick overview of all of them.

Tools for Shooting

The Camcorder

First of all, you'll need a digital camcorder. Look closely at the word "camcorder." You can see it implies a hybrid of two machines: a camera and a recorder. The "camera" aspects of a digital camcorder (meaning the lens, the aperture, exposure settings, and so forth) are not that different from analog camcorders. Analog is the older technology for video recording. The difference, as we've learned, is that digital camcorders record the information as code, saving a more permanent, accurate, and non-destructive record of what the camera sees.

What does a digital video camcorder produce? A synchronized stream of recorded pictures and sound, saved in sequence. The term "video" is also a hybrid, combining "visual" and "audio" into one medium. Digital video, then, always includes an audio track. When filming digital video, you will be recording background noise, people talking, and your own voice barking out commands as you try to be Steven Spielberg.

Recording Media

As video cassette technology has advanced, the cassettes themselves are smaller than ever (see Figure 2.10). VHS cassettes can be recorded onto by analog camcorders and popped into a VCR for immediate playback. However, Mini-DVD cassettes can be preserved for years, with no loss in quality.

Figure 2.10
Each advance in camcorder technology has included a reduction in cassette size.

Following is a brief description of each video cassette type. Note that the vertical dimension of video is not measured in pixels, as it is on a computer monitor. Rather, a video frame is measured in horizontal lines, and a particular tape technology is capable of reproducing a specific horizontal line resolution.

▶ **VHS** is the familiar video format that brought personal movie viewing into millions of homes. VHS camcorders are the handbag-sized behemoths people take on vacations to memorialize special moments. After recording onto a VHS tape, you can take out the tape, pop it into your VCR, and play it back onto your TV. This is the ultimate in convenience, and with a little cabling, a similar feat can be accomplished with your digital camcorder. VHS tapes are about 7 $1/2 \times 4 \times 1$ inches. VHS tapes give you 250 lines of resolution. If you watch a VHS tape after seeing a digital video, which records at twice the resolution, you'll notice the lower VHS picture quality.

▶ **VHS-C** cassettes are smaller than VHS and provide the same 250 lines of resolution picture quality. The camcorders are more popular due to their convenient size. However, VHS-C cassettes contain less tape, resulting in shorter recording time.

▶ **Eight mm** cassettes are smaller than either VHS cassette (about 3 $1/2 \times 2$ $1/2 \times 1/2$ inches), and thus, 8 mm recorders are smaller as well. A special connector cable or TV port is required to play back an 8 mm tape, and you can play them back only from the recorder itself. Nonetheless, the format and size are extremely popular. However, just like VHS, 8 mm tapes produce a picture based on 250 lines of resolution.

▶ **Hi-8** cassettes and recorders capitalize on the popularity of 8 mm by upping the picture quality (400 to 420 lines of resolution). The difference is quite noticeable, and some professional videos are recorded on Hi-8 cassettes. However, to see the difference, you must play back the recording on a higher-resolution TV set that has an S-Video input. Still very popular because of the huge installed base of Hi-8 video equipment, Hi-8 recording was the predominant semi-professional video recording medium before the advent of digital.

▶ Sony's **Digital 8** cassettes provide near-digital quality recording (500 lines of resolution). Digital 8 recorders are also very popular, especially since older 8 mm and Hi-8 tapes can be played back in Digital 8 camcorders. Notice I said "near-digital." For reasons I'll explain shortly, digital video is still far superior for producing the highest-quality movie, especially if editing will be involved.

▶ **MiniDV** is a purely digital medium. About the size of a Tic Tac box, MiniDV cassettes have become the standard digital format for video recording. Since editing video involves at least two transfers of data (one to the computer for editing and another for creating your final output), a purely digital medium is very desirable. MiniDV cassettes record at 500 lines of resolution, and copies made onto MiniDV cassettes do not lose any quality whatsoever. Also, MiniDVs can record CD-quality audio.

CHAPTER 2

▶ **Mini-DVD-RAM.** A handful of manufacturers have produced camcorders that record onto Mini-DVD-RAM disks. These disks can hold about 4.7 gigabytes of data. The convenience of Mini-DVD-RAM disks is portability. You can simply remove the disk from your camcorder and place it into a compatible DVD player. However, that's also the drawback. The dust has not quite settled in the DVD format wars. You must be sure the DVD player in your computer will play back your Mini-DVD-RAM video. As DVD-RAM standards become agreed upon, this format will become hugely attractive.

Tools for Transferring

Let's discuss how to get video out of your camcorder and onto your computer. Digital video would be transferred via Firewire card. Non-digital video can be transferred using professional video cards with special connectors, as described below. The goal is to facilitate a smooth video transfer frame by frame, so that there are no "dropouts." Frame dropouts occur when the computer cannot save fast enough and "keep up" with the rate at which the camcorder is sending video.

FireWire Card

Digital camcorders require that your computer have a FireWire card for uploading video (see Figure 2.11). FireWire technology provides the data transfer rate adequate for uploading video from your camera to your computer. Your camcorder may also have a USB port, but this is probably primarily meant for transferring still pictures from your camcorder to your computer. Although on some camcorders, the USB port can be used for uploading digital video (of course, your computer must have a USB port), the video will upload slowly to the point of tedium, and you may notice frame dropouts.

Figure 2.11
A FireWire Card.

In Chapter 4, you'll learn how to install a FireWire card and other specifics about video transfer to your computer.

NOTE

The terms iLink, IEEE 1394, and FireWire all refer to the same installable cards, connectors, and general technology. For example, if your camcorder has an iLink DV interface, it will connect to your FireWire card. The terms are interchangeable. If your computer has an IEEE 1394 port, that's the same as having a FireWire port. If your camcorder has a small port with a tiny "I" next to it, that stands for iLink. That's where you connect the cable for uploading video to your computer.

Transferring from Older Media

Let's look at what's required to transfer VHS or Hi-8 tapes to your computer for editing. After all, just because you are now working in the digital realm doesn't mean your older videos should be off limits. With a little extra cable work, you can move your old analog video data either directly to your computer for editing or to your digital camcorder's MiniDV cassette or DVD-RAM disk. The exact methodology depends on your VCR, TV, and digital camcorder ports. We'll consider some common methods for doing this.

To begin with, if you have a Sony Digital 8 camcorder with a FireWire port, and if your older videos are recorded on Hi8 or 8mm cassettes, you can play back those cassettes and transfer the data to your computer via the FireWire port. However, if you don't have that technology available, what else would work? The best transfer method would involve using S-video ports. If you have a newer VCR or large-screen TV, it probably has an S-Video output port. Figure 2.12 shows a digital camcorder with labeled ports:

Figure 2.12
A digital camcorder with labeled iLink, S-Video, and Audio/Visual ports.

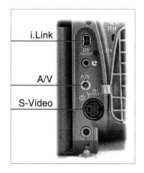

S-Video ports accommodate newer, higher-quality analog VHS technology. Newer televisions also have S-Video ports. The good news is that most digital camcorders have an S-Video port as well, as well as some video capture cards. (Check the back of your computer. Also, see Figure 2.13 for a look at the required S-Video cable.)

Figure 2.13
An S-Video cable.

Depending on your existing ports, you can do one of the following:

▶ Plug the S-Video cable out from the VCR directly to the S-Video port on your digital camcorder and play back your VHS tape in your VCR. Press "Record" on your digital camcorder and monitor the results on your camcorder's LCD. Now your old VHS recordings will be on digital MiniDV disks.

▶ Plug the S-Video cable into your television and run the output from your television to your digital camcorder. Then play back your VHS tape. You'll probably have to use the cable with three RCA plugs (see Figure 2.14) on one end and a single output on the other. For this to work, your digital camcorder must have an "Analog in" input. Don't forget you can use the TV to monitor the results. Again, your old VHS recordings will be on digital MiniDV disks.

Figure 2.14
You'll often use RCA plugs for analog video connections.

▶ If your TV has an S-video input, connect to your television using the standard analog three plugs (the red one, the yellow one, and the white one). Then, use your TV's S-Video out to connect to your digital camcorder's S-Video in. Play back your VHS tape.

▶ If your VCR has standard A/V out and your digital camcorder has A/V in, play back your VHS tape, going from the VCR out using the standard RCA-plug connectors on one end and camcorder A/V connectors on the other.

NOTE
If you purchased a high-end video card, perhaps for gaming or some other reason, it may have an S-Video input. This would save you some steps. You could simply transfer your older video from your S-Video-equipped VCR right to the computer.

Tools for Editing

To adequately edit digital video, you need a fast computer with a large, uncluttered hard drive, good video editing software, and an adequate storage medium (such as CD) to save your videos once you are done editing them.

Adequate Computing Power

Editing digital video requires a powerful computer. There isn't much you can do on your computer that will push its limits as much as digital video editing. Minimum requirements would be:

- ▶ 400 MHz processor
- ▶ 64 MB RAM
- ▶ 20 GB hard drive
- ▶ 32 MB video card
- ▶ Recordable CD-ROM drive (CD-R)
- ▶ 17-inch monitor capable of displaying 1078×780 Resolution
- ▶ A FireWire card

An ideal computer for editing digital video would include:

- ▶ Pentium III, 750 MHz processor or higher
- ▶ 256 MB RAM
- ▶ 80 GB hard drive
- ▶ 64MB video card
- ▶ Recordable DVD drive
- ▶ 19-inch monitor capable of displaying 1600×1200 resolution

Why the stellar requirements? Because all of your computer's major components are tested by some aspect of digital video editing. Here's how:

Hard Drive

We're used to evaluating hard drives on disk capacity. A big hard drive is better. However, one activity that truly taxes a hard drive is transfer rate. How fast can your hard drive absorb large amounts of data when you are loading something onto it? You'll find out when you upload a digital movie from your camcorder to your computer. Each frame has to be stored. If your hard drive can't accept data fast enough, your video capture software will report that a large number of frames have been "dropped." The software will let you know if the dropped frames will create noticeable gaps in playback. Newer, larger hard drives on the order of 40 to 80GB have faster data transfer and will serve you well in this regard.

Video Card

Your video card will have to perform at top speed to display all the frames in your movie. Most often, when you watch movie sequences in computer games, embedded in applications, or broadcast on the Web, those movies are very compressed. Compression minimizes the strain on your video; however, the video you upload from your camcorder is minimally compressed. Your video card must be up to the task of displaying thirty large frames per second of "raw" video footage. That's why I recommend at least a 32 MB video card.

RAM

Editing digital video can give your RAM a real workout as well. For example, most good video programs have "multiple undo." This feature allows you to step backwards through recent changes, undoing several recent edits. Undo works only if recent edits have been saved in RAM, so they can be easily undone. The more RAM you have, the faster you can render edits and undo things you've just done.

Processor Speed

What difference will it make if you have, say, a 750 MHz processor, rather than a 400? The main difference will be in how long it takes movies to render. After you are done editing your movie, it must be compressed to a form you can distribute. This final compression can take an hour or a day, depending on video length and processor speed.

Sufficient Storage Space

A five-minute video can take up hundreds of megabytes of storage space. Also, most video editing programs do not edit the actual movie. A copy is made so that you'll always have your original video to revert to. This doubles the storage space required for a digital video. Obviously, you do not need your older video work on hand indefinitely, taking up such gargantuan amounts of hard drive space. Even if you're archiving to CD-ROMs, which can hold a bit more than 600 MB of data each, you might find them proliferating faster than you'd anticipated. One solution is a recordable DVD drive. A recordable DVD can archive up to 4.7 GB of data. DVDs are a genuinely workable long-term solution for archiving your digital video projects. Plan ahead for something like this so that videos don't end up taking over your computer.

Video Editing Software

You'll also need video editing software. A large portion of this book is dedicated to that topic, but let's talk momentarily about why it is required. To begin with, you can't send anyone your raw video footage. You can play it back on your TV, but it would need to be reformatted and compressed to even place on a CD, let alone be e-mailed or used as part of a presentation. Secondly, raw video footage generally has lots of dead moments that will detract from your video's highlights. You'll need video editing software to cut those out and rearrange your video the way you want it. And, of course, you can't do any of the cool things shown in Chapter 1 without software. At a minimum, you'll want to add titles, cut to the best parts of your tape, and compress your final output into a form that can be viewed by your target audience.

Crossroads

Now that you've learned a bit about digital video and some of the related technology and formats, the next chapter describes camera and filming basics. You'll also learn camcorder controls that ensure good quality filming.

3
Taking Great Videos

In this chapter, we'll discuss the basics of how photography—any kind of photography—works. We'll learn what digital camcorders have in common with other cameras and how to apply that knowledge in your workaday videography. Best of all, we'll delve into a series of tips and techniques that will help you make great videos.

All Cameras, Great and Small

You will take better digital videos if you first understand basic camera components and how they work together to capture images. A digital camcorder is primarily a camera. It records fast-moving pictures and sound more accurately than all its predecessors, but it is still a camera. A digital camcorder uses the same principles of gathering and focusing light that every other camera does. When you look into your viewfinder and see what would be a perfect video if it weren't for the glare or the overcast haze muddying up everything, you will solve these problems using the same techniques that any skilled photographer would use. For this reason, let's spend a little time exploring basic photography principles.

All cameras, including video camcorders, take advantage of one nifty fact of nature: If you shine light through a glass disc that bulges in the middle, the light will concentrate at a point just in front of it (see Figure 3.1). If you take a lightproof box and make a tiny hole at one end, and then place your bulging glass in the middle of that box, you've got a camera of sorts. Point that hole at something for long enough, and a tiny representation of whatever you're pointing at will be reproduced inside the box, at the other end. If your bulging glass happens to be sending its bent light rays toward a piece of paper coated with silver nitrate (film), you've got a photograph.

CHAPTER 3

Figure 3.1
How a lens concentrates light.

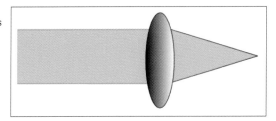

This is all courtesy of the concentration of light through the tiny hole, bent and rendered into a likeness by the bulging glass, and then somehow recorded.

Lens and Aperture

I am telling the story of your camcorder, and you have perhaps guessed that two major players have been introduced: The bulging glass is the lens, and the tiny hole is the aperture. When you buy a really good lens, you are paying for a glass bulge that has zero imperfections, a bulge that is perfectly shaped, "just so," without aberrations.

Similarly, a good camera aperture differs from your simple lightproof box in that you can specify exactly how wide the opening should be. Aperture diameter determines how much light should shine onto your film, allowing you to take good pictures in both brightly or dimly lighted environments. Aperture controls image brightness, which greatly affects image quality. Too much light, and the image is overexposed—color is washed out. Too little light, and the image is dark, underexposed. Figure 3.2 shows a Canon Elura 2 camcorder lens. The aperture, partially open, is the black area in the middle.

Figure 3.2
Viewing a lens, the aperture (opening) looks like a dark hole.

It turns out that there is more fun to be had inside your light box. The lens inside the box can be moved around to improve the quality of your image. We call this "adjusting the focus," and here's how it works.

Light and Distance

If you ever played "shadow bunnies" in class by placing bunny-shaped fingers in front of the projector when the teacher wasn't looking, you may have noticed that when the kids near the front of the class held up their fingers, they cast the sharpest-looking bunny shadows. Front-row kids projected smaller bunnies with very precise edges. This is because the light was hitting the front-row hands very close to where the shadow of the hand would be projected (the classroom wall or movie screen with the boring movie on it). Similarly, when you focus your camera to record an image that is close to the camera, you move the lens so that it is close to the film. This brings the closer image into focus.

The shadow-bunny makers near the back of the class made huge bunnies with fuzzy edges. That's because their hands were far from the wall where the shadow would hit. The farther light has to travel, the more it spreads out. If you increase the space between your bunny-shaped fingers and the wall, the light shining around your fingers becomes diffuse by the time it gets to the wall.

Lenses are like that, too. If you bend the light far away from where you are going to be projecting it, you will get an out-of focus image, unless the object you are photographing is quite far away from your camera. Having something "in focus" is all based on proportion of distance.

Focus and Image Projection

The bunny-example teaches us that if the thing you are projecting is close to where its image appears, it will be very small. But if the thing you are projecting is far from the wall (or film, or any surface), the image will be very large by the time it finally gets there. The same thing happens inside any camera: If you move the lens to the point at which all the light shining through it is perfectly collected and shined onto your surface, your image will be in focus.

Now that we are grownups, we do not play hand-bunnies. We turn a focus knob on a camera and say, "Ah, that's it," and press the Record button. The lens has one spot at which its collected light will shine against something and make a perfect image with no fuzziness. What you are doing when you move your camera's Focus button is finding the spot from which it can shine its best image onto your recording medium. Figure 3.3 shows a focus ring on a Canon GL-1 video camcorder.

CHAPTER 3

Figure 3.3
Adjusting focus moves the lens closer or farther from its projection target.

Shutter

The other basic mechanism that determines how light interacts with film is the shutter, a device that opens momentarily to allow light into the camera for the purpose of exposing the film. A photograph (or frame of video) does not stay exposed to light indefinitely. Exposure of just a tiny fraction of a second can completely alter your image. Generally speaking, in bright sunlight, a very high shutter speed is used, resulting in the shutter being open for perhaps 1/250th of a second or even less. High shutter speeds are important for photographing fast-moving objects.

For example, if you expose a piece of film to a fast-moving car for 1/60th of a second, do you think the car will be in pretty much the same position at the end of your exposure time as at the beginning? No. The car will have moved several feet. Capturing fast motion requires an exposure short enough so that the filmed object won't have noticeably moved during the entire exposure time. Figure 3.4 displays a fast-exposure photo of an explosion. We can see the shards of glass only because the image was frozen into such a short time frame that there was virtually no movement.

Figure 3.4
A fast shutter speed lets you see glass shards in this explosion, rather than just a blur.

But what about movies and video? Don't they record constant motion? No, they don't. Videos are short, fast exposures—frozen frames. You see movement because the exposures occur in rapid succession. Filming constant motion while never closing the shutter would result in a blurry mess.

Slower shutter speeds have their place as well. If you are filming at night, your camera needs to absorb all the light it can, so the shutter needs to be open for quite some time. For dark or indoor filming, a shutter speed of 1/15th of a second is common. If you film at even slower shutter speeds—1/4th of a second, for instance—your hand is likely to shake during that time. Figure 3.5 shows a video filmed at night, using a low shutter speed. Tripods, which solidly hold a camera in place, are required for low shutter-speed filming.

Figure 3.5
Night video filming, with its required low shutter speed, produces interesting results.

Shutter and Aperture Work Together

Shutter speed is always adjusted with regard to aperture. For example, a high shutter speed may indeed gather enough light if the aperture of the camera is open wide enough. Or a low shutter speed, which carries the risk of gathering too much light and creating a washed-out image, may look just fine if the aperture is open only slightly. That's because the aperture size determines exposure just as much as shutter speed does. They balance each other out.

CHAPTER 3

Have you ever seen a photograph of a stormy night sky full of lightning (see Figure 3.6)? Photos of that nature are taken with the shutter open for perhaps thirty seconds and the aperture open quite wide. Just about the only available light would be the lightening. Over thirty seconds, you're apt to see quite a bit of it and, courtesy of the long exposure, you get all of it. The light is gathered into the wide-open aperture to create a dramatic vision of a wild sky.

Figure 3.6
A long shutter speed allows the filming of multiple lightning flashes.

Field of Focus

Let's return for a moment to how aperture is measured and its unique effects on an image's appearance. Understanding aperture allows you to use selective focus as a tool for enhancing your video footage and create videos that are richly saturated in color.

First of all, aperture measurements are designed so you can make your adjustments in steps. Adjust your aperture "up" and you'll let in twice as much light as previously. Adjust your aperture "down" and you've cut the light in half. This is done to make it easy to work with aperture and shutter speed simultaneously. For example, if you change your shutter speed from 1/60th of a second to 1/120th, you've cut your image's light source in half. You'll have a much darker picture. However, to avoid that result, just move the aperture measurement "up" one step, which doubles the available light.

Each aperture measurement is called an f-stop, and all good cameras have f-stop dials allowing you to move through several aperture diameters. Typical cameras have f-stop settings of 1.4, 2.0, 2.8, 4.0, 5.6, 8, 11, 16 (see Figure 7). Higher f-stop settings create smaller aperture diameters. So, for example, when you "stop down" on a camera, you are increasing the aperture diameter. "Stop up" means to decrease aperture diameter.

Figure 3.7
A camera's f-stop dial.

Whether working with photographs or video footage, a relatively higher f-stop (making the hole for light smaller) increases the field of focus. What does this mean? Have you ever seen a video where only the main subject closer to the camera was in focus, while the background was a bit blurry (see Figure 3.8)?

Figure 3.8
A narrow field of focus emphasizes the foreground of this image.

Decreasing the field of focus sharpens the foreground even when the "background" is not that far back. The field of focus is a measure of how far back into your picture everything will look sharp. A narrow field of focus means that only the objects near the front of your picture will be in focus (see the diagram in Figure 3.9).

Figure 3.9
Field of focus diagram.

Wide Field of Focus   Narrow Field of Focus

A deep field of focus will make everything in the picture, foreground and background, look very sharp. When you make your camera's aperture smaller (increase the f-stop), you'll bring more of your picture into focus. The background will begin to look clear. Of course, your picture will start to look too dark unless you increase the shutter speed as well.

CHAPTER 3

So, are f-stop and shutter speed adjustable on consumer-level digital video equipment? For shutter speed, the answer is yes. Aperture, on the other hand, is not directly adjustable. Most digital camcorders automatically adjust aperture as needed, providing automatic settings for hard-to-film environments such as twilight or sand and snow. Only professional and semi-professional digital camcorders allow you to manually adjust aperture.

Top Tips for Better Videos

What follows are some specific ways you can improve your video footage. There are steps you can take to making sure the colors are right, things are in focus, and the action flows smoothly. Your camcorder has controls for achieving these ends, and we'll see how to apply them when needed. It'll be helpful to know which button to press in which situation.

Movement and Speed

The world we video seldom stands still. Here are tips to make sure you get all the action without shaky, blurry, or distorted images.

Image Stabilization

If you find that your videos are a bit shaky, and your involuntary hand movements are obvious on video playback, you can use Image Stabilization to minimize the effect. The hand is not always the best camcorder support system. You'll find especially that the more zoom you have to use, the shakier your video can become. Distance magnifies even subtle hand movements. Happily, there's something you can do about it.

Image Stabilization, a button control on your camcorder, works by locating the highest-contrast portion of the image and stretching that to fill the whole frame (see Figure 3.10). This is a very popular control that really works. Mild to modest amounts of hand shaking really are removed when you film with image stabilization. Note, however, that a small portion of your video resolution is used to provide "stretch room" for image stabilization. Therefore, video with image stabilization will be at a slightly lower pixel image quality.

Figure 3.10
Image stabilization
at work.

Progressive Scan

If you are filming fast-moving activity, such as a car race or basketball game, use your camcorder's Progressive Scan setting. This directs your camcorder to film an entire frame of video in one exposure, rather than the interlacing method that would be used to accommodate the world of broadcast. Available in mid- and upper-range camcorders, some camcorders will offer Progressive Scan as a shutter setting called Sports. That's because of its predominant use in filming fast action.

Shutter Speed

Not all digital camcorders allow the selection of specific shutter speeds, but if yours does, it can be nice to have the control. Manually adjusting shutter speed allows you to specify how much time light should saturate the CCD before moving on to the next frame. Typical digital camcorder shutter speeds range from 1/15 sec. up to 1/1,500 sec. Here are some ways to use manual shutter speed to your advantage:

> ▶ Use fast shutter speeds for fast-moving objects or in bright light.
> ▶ Use slow shutter speeds for maximum color saturation, dimmer light, or to create a slight blurring special effect.

Bright and Dark Filming

We can't always film in ideal lighting. These tips are specifically for settings that are overly bright or too dark. Your camcorder has preset features that can produce marvelous results in these situations.

CHAPTER 3

Automatic Shutter and Aperture Adjustments

When it comes to adjusting for difficult lighting, your camcorder does have some worthwhile tricks up its sleeve. Below are popular automated settings that are common to almost all digital camcorders.

Night Shot

If you want to film at night, use your camcorder's Night Shot feature. Many newer digital camcorders will let you film in near-total darkness. Depending on how dark the environment is, the resulting video will have very little color and appear black and white. Also, you'll need a tripod to reduce shakiness, because dark filming requires low shutter speeds and very wide apertures.

Snow

Are you filming in snow, or against the backdrop of a very bright lake, or in an area with lots of reflective glare? Use your camcorder's Snow feature. The Snow setting is helpful in reducing direct glare from surfaces in general. That's because filming in glare, a camcorder's sensitivity to brightness works against it. The lack of available contrasting colors leads to bleached-out videos and huge patches of unpleasant glare. The Snow filter works like a Polarization Filter; in fact, your camcorder may refer to it as such.

Sand

For filming in bright sun at the beach, use your camcorder's Sand feature. Like Snow, the Sand setting reduces glare from an over-bright backdrop, this time filtering out the yellowish hues of intense sun against sand.

Spotlight

If you are filming a character in a spotlight, or in an area where the background is quite dark, use your camcorder's Spotlight feature (see Figure 3.11). Filming in high-contrast environments can drive your camcorder crazy. Since areas in view are both extremely dark and light, the camera is not sure what aperture and shutter speed to employ. The Spotlight feature will prevent your subject from looking like a video of a white blotch.

Note that Spotlight filming is easier if your hand is not shaking. Also, try to keep the camera focused exactly on the subject in the spotlight and leave it there. This allows the camcorder to fully adjust to lighting around the intended target and not the dark periphery.

Figure 3.11
The Spotlight setting tries to clarify what is visible in the brightest area of the footage.

Zebra

When you think a portion of a scene you're filming may be overly bright, confirm your suspicion by using your camcorder's Zebra setting. If your camcorder has a Zebra feature, this is a good way to avoid blotchy glare.

Zebra creates a visual indicator that your camera is focusing on an area with too much brightness. When it's on, look into your viewfinder or LCD and you will see rows of clear "marching ants" filling the segments that are overwhelming your camcorder's color sensors. You can then change your camera direction somewhat to even out the light. You'll find that even small amounts of shifting can even the light disbursement, improving your video color range.

Color Improvement

If you want to obtain the best video color values, try these tips:

Twilight or Dawn Filming

If you want to get the deepest and richest colors possible out of your video, film at dawn or twilight. You'll need to use your camcorder's Twilight or Evening setting, however, or else your film will be dark. Since the Twilight feature works by drawing out the maximum available light, your film may be a little hazy or yellowish (see Figure 3.12). Avoid this by positioning your subjects in the most evenly, well-lighted area available.

How does the Twilight feature work? Like night filming, using the Twilight setting will open your camcorder's aperture and decrease shutter speed, but not nearly as extremely. Depending on available light, you may not need to use a tripod.

CHAPTER 3

Figure 3.12
Digital video shot at twilight.

White Balance

If you are filming indoors, or in a muted light environment, and find your colors are muddy, you may need to adjust your white balance. This is a common camcorder control that adjusts the color range for the video you are currently shooting.

Your camcorder probably has a White Balance button. What you'll do is bring along a perfectly white piece of cardboard into your filming environment, point the camcorder at it, and press the White Balance button. You are, in effect, telling your camcorder, "While we are in my grandmother's kitchen, with its fluorescent lights and avocado green paneling, this piece of cardboard represents 'white.' Just deal with it." The camcorder adjusts its entire range of color values, and the results will be that every Formica table and Holiday Inn place mat in grandmother's kitchen will now be bursting with color. Here's why this step may be necessary:

One hallmark of the digital camcorder is its extreme sensitivity to the widest range of color values. Film an off-white kitchen wall and it can look downright muddy. That's because the camcorder's color sensor (the CCD) knows very well what white is, and we're sorry, that kitchen wall is not it. Your camcorder doesn't care that the kitchen wall is *more or less* white, relative to other color values in that room.

Human vision can adjust to relative color values. So, when you walk into an environment, your eyes adjust their perceived color range according to what's in the room. When you see "white" in that environment, your eyes are not straining to locate some mathematical value that calculates out to exactly white.

The white balance feature is your chance to tell the camcorder what "white" is for that particular environment. The camcorder can then rework its entire spectrum of colors based on its new information about the color white.

NOTE

Over a long day of filming, numerous white balance adjustments may be necessary. If you are filming outside for hours and hours, moving from midday sun to dusk, for example, you'll need to readjust white balance as the available light changes. Likewise, if you take your troops outside grandma's kitchen to the balcony to watch the fireworks from outdoors, you'll have to get a new white balance reading.

Crisp, Clear Videos

Getting good crisp video mostly involves understanding focus and knowing when and when not to use your camcorder's auto-focus feature. However, using controls such as Sharpness and using aperture to adjust field of focus can make a difference as well.

About Auto-Focus

If your video is out of focus for the first few seconds of filming, it could be because it takes a little time for the auto-focus feature to figure out what it is you are trying to film. To fix this problem and still use auto-focus, look closely into the viewfinder or LCD before recording, and make sure the focus point is settled exactly on your action point. Then you can begin filming. A digital camcorder tries very hard to impress you with its automated skills. Focus it at a nearby object, look in the viewfinder or LCD, and you'll see the object gradually come into focus. The camcorder will always attempt to determine what you are trying to film and change to optimize the image in every way possible. Now point your camcorder at something far away, and you'll notice the same process. The aperture and lens position will adjust to make the image you are pointing at look focused and properly lit. Most often, it is fine to allow your video camcorder to create the optimum picture. However, auto-focus takes time. That's why you may have to wait a couple of seconds before filming.

Manual Focus

If you are finding that auto-focus keeps changing its focus while you are filming, not quite keeping up with your movie action, you may have to switch to manual focus. There are three steps to this:

1. Take a minute to learn how to override your camcorder's auto-focus feature.
2. Then, you'll have to adjust the focus yourself before filming.
3. Now that auto-focus is off, you're on your own. While recording, you'll be adjusting the focus yourself as your focal point of action changes.

CHAPTER 3

NOTE

Here's a setting in which you may want to use manual focus: When focusing on an object far away, first zoom in on your object, then turn off Auto-Focus. Then, zoom back out to take in more of the entire scene. Then, hit the record button and film your video. The camcorder will retain its main focus on the far-away object while including the foreground. If you had done this with Auto-Focus on, the camera would simply have refocused as soon as you zoomed out.

Creative Depth of Focus Use

Figure 3.13 shows a fun video trick using high shutter speeds and a shallow depth of field. The tiger is behind a fence; however, filming with a fast shutter speed and shallow depth of focus that was intentionally focused right on the tiger virtually ignores the fence. It looks like the tiger is free.

Figure 3.13
The tiger is behind bars, but the high shutter speed and shallow depth of focus causes the camcorder to virtually ignore the fence.

Sharpness

If you are filming areas with jagged lines and would like them to appear smoother, increase your camcorder's Sharpness setting. This feature is sometimes used to minimize face wrinkles and make the subject look "younger" on film. It works by compensating for blur and makes patterns of color look more even.

Crossroads

Now that you've learned some of the ins and outs of shooting video, and a bit about how cameras work, you're ready to start making movies. In Chapter 4, you'll learn video capture—how to effectively transfer video footage from your camcorder to your computer.

4

From the Camera to the Computer

In this chapter, we'll talk about moving video from camcorder to computer, ending up with a digital movie you can edit. You'll learn how to open a software interface for monitoring your movie while it is uploading and choose a video format for your project. This is called *video capture*. You'll use video capture software to limit movie file size so your computer doesn't grind to a halt every time you try to make a simple edit and use the software to divide your video into manageable scenes that can later be brought together if you choose.

When you're done with this chapter, you'll know how to select a video transfer solution adequate for your needs, install a FireWire card, choose a video format for editing, and view your raw, unedited video on your computer.

While there are alternatives, FireWire is the preferred method for uploading videos, because it facilitates fast transfer of large amounts of data. Generally speaking, PCs do not come off the shelf with FireWire cards installed, so before uploading video, you'll have to open your computer and insert a FireWire card into a PCI expansion slot. This process will be explored in some detail in this chapter. However, if, for some reason, installing an internal card is not an option, there are other, limited solutions. We'll discuss those as well.

NOTE

There is no need to install the FireWire card until you've shot some video with your camcorder. You don't need to worry about opening your computer or installing programs until you've gone out and had some fun filming. After you have footage and are inspired by its potential, come back here and walk through the installation steps. Note that the video capture techniques discussed in this chapter—choosing a video format, determining frame rate, error tolerance, and monitoring your upload progress—are fairly universal among all popular video editing programs. You'll not need one specific video capture program.

We'll also talk a bit about proprietary bundle packages that include both software and hardware. These packages insure compatibility. Even though the technology among all FireWire cards is fairly universal, the differences that do exist sometimes affect video format. This means that the FireWire card that came with your scanner may not produce video compatible with the video editing software you bought on special at the computer store. Purchasing a package such as Pyro ProDV, Pinnacle DV500, or AIST Movie Suite—all of which include a FireWire card and software—means that compatibility is guaranteed.

Transferring Video without Installing a Card

Before we discuss installation of a FireWire card, let's consider a video transfer option that does not require opening the computer and installing a card.

Video Upload via Connection Bridge

The SCM Microsystem company "Dazzle" makes a small unit that you cable between camcorder and computer (see Figure 4.1). The interface allows you to upload videos via USB port or A/V "composite" inputs.

Figure 4.1
How a connection
bridge works.

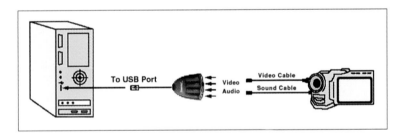

Dazzle offers several units, and all are helpful, depending on the interface you currently have on your computer. Since your main interest in such a feature would be to avoid opening your computer and installing a card, you'd want to use the Dazzle converter that uses your existing ports. The best would be a USB solution. USB is fairly fast, and almost all newer computers have USB ports. Therefore, the Dazzle Video Creator would work nicely, connecting from your camcorder's A/V ports to your computer's USB port.

The Dazzle Hollywood Bridge offers broad connectivity, allowing you to connect analog and digital camcorders to your computer via A/V composite connectors (see Figure 4.2).

Figure 4.2
Dazzle Hollywood
Bridge.

These solutions are convenient but have the following drawbacks, each related to speed and file size limitations of non-digital transport media:

▶ With any current Dazzle product, the biggest movie you'll get is 352×288 dpi. That's because USB and A/V ports are just not up to the task of moving large-frame video. It's a matter of practicality—you wouldn't want to wait that long. This limitation, however, will not cramp you at all if your target is Web viewing or e-mailing video. Unless everyone in your audience has DSL or a T3 connection, you'll not want to e-mail or post online a movie larger than 352×288 psi.

▶ The second drawback is speed. Uploading movies via USB or composite cable will take far longer than FireWire transport. But, again, if a Web-based audience or e-mail video is your main interest, you'll not be creating large movies but, rather, uploading only the best bits and, from there, editing to an even smaller final product.

▶ Finally, since the transport method is not digital, there will be generational loss. You'll probably not notice the loss in quality after a single transfer, but if you make copies of your final product to send around town, that'll cost you three generations. The accumulated loss will be noticeable at that point.

Nonetheless, for those who want to edit small to moderate amounts of digital video and avoid opening their computers, Dazzle bridges are an adequate solution.

CHAPTER 4

Video Upload via Professional Video Card

You can avoid installing FireWire if your computer already has a top-of-the-line video card, one with S-video or A/V inputs. Otherwise, for the rest of you who want to go entirely digital, a date with a screwdriver is in your future.

Let's talk for a minute about how a FireWire card differs from a video card:

A video card connects your monitor to the computer, determining image and text quality on your screen and the number of colors used. Video cards used by graphics professionals and computer videographers cost hundreds of dollars, but they provide quality 3D image and rendering options that are well out of the realm of computer graphics and video hobbyists. Computer imaging systems used by professional animators can cost more than a very nice car.

The video cards used by professional and semi-professional digital artists will have video capture capabilities. These include composite A/V inputs, as well as S-Video input and output. The pluses and minuses of these technologies have already been discussed.

A FireWire card, however, is not a video card. It does not hook up to your computer monitor or serve any purpose other than to provide connectivity to a digital device such as a camcorder, hard drive, or scanner.

NOTE
FireWire card installation and setup is far less conflict-prone than any peripheral device I've ever installed. The technology is simple, fast, and, importantly, it doesn't seem to interfere with other computer processes, which can cause lock-ups and the need to reboot. In short, this will be easier than it might seem.

Working with FireWire

In this section, we'll talk about why FireWire technology is so well suited for video, and then move on to how to obtain and install a FireWire card.

FireWire is a high-speed interconnection standard that is comparatively simple for a manufacturer to implement. FireWire can connect up to sixty-three devices, using cable lengths of up to fourteen feet. It represents the best of many worlds: It is low-cost; does not require a Device ID, DIP switch, or jumper setup; and uses a single cable for both input and output. Best for us, FireWire was developed with high-speed data transfer in mind. For this reason, every digital camcorder has a FireWire port.

FireWire's large dual data lines allow data transfer rates of 400 MB per second (see Figure 4.3). Compare this transfer rate to the much-heralded USB technology, which transfers data at about 12 MB per second.

Figure 4.3
FireWire's large, dual data lines provide amazingly fast transfer rates.

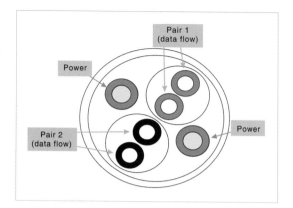

Not only is FireWire's data transfer rate up to the task of digital video, it has headroom to spare. As technology develops for creating video with multiple data and audio layers, FireWire will still be able to handle the load. For one thing, FireWire allows for asynchronous data exchange, meaning that data speed is not diminished because another device or data source is simultaneously uploading or downloading. FireWire is ideal for any high-speed peripheral, including music devices and hard drives. One huge plus is that when you plug in a device via FireWire (including a digital camcorder), you need not restart your computer. No resetting is necessary.

FireWire cards do not come with your digital camcorder. You may purchase them separately from the computer store or as part of a complete software/hardware digital video editing solution. Additionally, if you've installed another peripheral device such as a FireWire scanner or external hard drive, such devices sometimes come with their own FireWire cards. Often, the best solution is to purchase a FireWire card bundled with a software package.

NOTE

Although FireWire is a somewhat universal technology, and multiple devices can, indeed, share the same FireWire connection on the back of your computer, many FireWire cards are proprietary. They may work well only with the scanner or hard drive or video software that came bundled with the card.

The cable required for connecting a digital camcorder to your computer is usually smaller at one end than the other. In most configurations, the 4-pin plug (smaller end) connects to the camcorder and the 6-pin plug connects to the computer.

Before You Start

Before you install the card, please note the following:

Have your Windows system disks handy. If, during the installation process, you are asked to provide your Windows CD or disk and realize you were not provided this when you bought your computer, your required setup files are probably located in this path: C:\windows\options\cabs.

Immediately after installing your FireWire card, you'll be able to plug in your digital camcorder, open a video capture program, and begin saving movies. For this reason, you may first want to install your video editing program of choice. However, we don't closely examine video editing programs until Chapter 6. To jump the gun and install a program now, just make sure it has video capture capability and supports FireWire. You'll be fine.

So, where exactly does this card go? It fits into one of your computer's expansion slots, which are thin bays designed to hold the circuit boards for devices such as a tape drive, a scanner, a sound card, or a FireWire card. Your computer has several types of expansion slots. The two main types are ISA and PCI.

▶ ISA (Industry Standard Architecture) slots are longer, usually made of dark, formed plastic with squeeze-connectors inside the slot. They represent an older technology and are used for standard sound cards, modems, and network cards. Cards for ISA slots have more connection points than PCI cards.

▶ PCI (Peripheral Component Interconnect) slots are shorter and are most often made of off-white, formed plastic (see Figure 4.4). They represent a newer technology and are often used for "next-wave" sound cards and other higher-end devices.

Figure 4.4
PCI expansion slots are smaller and usually made of off-white plastic.

As cards go, the FireWire card is relatively short, and you will insert it into a PCI slot.

Inserting the Card

The following instructions for FireWire card installation are not meant to replace the manufacturer's manual, safety guidelines, and specifications. This is a general "how to" that you'll probably find helpful as a documentation supplement.

With your FireWire card handy, do the following:

1. Unplug your computer from its power source, unplug all cabling, and move the tower (the main computer without the monitor) to a well-lighted location. You'll be removing the computer case and will need enough light for seeing everything inside clearly.

2. Remove the case from your computer. This may be a matter of unscrewing the sides and sliding the cover away from the main tower or using the screwdriver as a wedge to separate the case from the tower. When the cover is removed, you'll have access to the expansion slots.

3. From the side, look in and locate a blank PCI slot inside your computer. If possible, choose a slot without any cards installed directly above it. The extra gap will make it easier to manipulate the card into the thin space provided.

4. Remove the corresponding expansion slot protector cover strip from the back; Figure 4.5 shows the back of the PC with most expansion slot covers in place. You can pry this off using the screwdriver end like a wedge. Be careful not to allow the expansion slot protector to scrape against other cards inside the computer.

Figure 4.5
Metal expansion slot covers must be removed before inserting a card.

5. Unpackage the FireWire card and locate the single screw required for installation.

6. The connector end of the card will be facing in, or down (see Figure 4.6), towards the back of the computer. These connectors must make firm contact with the inside of the slot.

7. Without touching the gold connectors, grasp the card by both sides longways and orient the connectors forward into the slot. On the other end of the card, the single screw hole must line up with the back of the slot (the slot brace). This screw hole is near where the cable will attach (see Figure 4.6). View the other installed cards as an example.

Figure 4.6
Position the card firmly inside the slot, connector side first.

8. After orienting, firmly insert the FireWire card into the slot.

9. Screw in the screw. Make sure the FireWire card is sitting firmly in the slot.

10. Note how the FireWire ports appear facing the back. Close the computer and plug in all cables again. You may plug the FireWire cable into the computer now, if you like.

11. Turn on the computer. The FireWire card will probably be detected immediately. Windows will begin building the driver database and start installing components from Windows source files, usually without any prompting. However, if requested, you may have to insert your Windows CD or provide the path to where source files are stored (usually C:\windows\options\cabs).

After Windows installs the FireWire drivers, you'll receive no indication that your computer has changed. There will be no new program icon on your desktop or Start menu. The next step is to install video capture software, or a complete video editing package that includes capture software.

Camcorder Meets PC and the Fun Begins

Now that the hardware is installed, your computer is plugged back in, and the FireWire cable connected, you can plug in the camcorder. The following steps get your camcorder and computer ready for video upload:

1. Conveniently position your camcorder where you can reach its Play/Forward/Rewind/Pause controls and view the LCD.

2. Plug the FireWire cord into the camcorder and turn it on. You don't need to have video capture software installed to do this.

3. Make sure your recorded MiniDV tape is in the camcorder, and set the unit to Playback mode.

Video Capture Software

You'll spend the rest of this chapter learning about video capture software, what it is, and how it works. You'll learn to use video capture software to successfully upload video footage to your computer and assign compression and other formatting options.

First, what does video capture software do? It captures and formats the video frames you want to transfer to your computer. Figure 4.7 shows the Preview screen from Ulead's Video Capture, which comes bundled with Media Studio Pro. Happily, you can preview your video before uploading, and, I must say, the digital video looks quite good on a computer monitor. You can use your camcorder's Play/Pause/Forward/Rewind buttons to get a good, flattering look at your footage before you start sending your movie upstream—and perhaps avoid the dead bits that will amount to a big waste of hard drive space unless you find a way to leave them out of the soup.

Figure 4.7
Ulead Video Capture's
Preview screen.

Video capture software helps you divide your movie into segments, a great feature for pinpointing areas for special attention. Dividing your movie into easily editable segments also smoothes the editing process, since you'll not be required to render changes to a 300 MB file. You can also rename these movie segments and save them as stand-alone videos. Video capture software allows you to determine compression amounts, limit your movie's file size and length, and set error tolerance. For example, if the program has dropped too many frames, you can stop transferring and fix the frame uptake problem.

Let me point out that video capture can be a component of a complete video editing program or a stand-alone program. As an example, Ulead VideoStudio has video editing tasks laid out in a logical sequence at the top of the screen, and Capture is near the beginning (see Figure 4.8). On the other hand, Ulead Media Studio Pro is a suite of video-editing applications, of which Video Capture is but one.

Figure 4.8
Ulead VideoStudio logically sequences editing tasks along the top of the screen.

Video Capture: Basic Steps

Although each program organizes video capturing tasks a little differently, the task is essentially the same. Here's a fundamental walk-through for capturing video to your computer:

1. Plug the FireWire cable into your camcorder, then into your computer—camcorder first because some capture programs will try to open before you are even ready for capture.

2. Using the LCD on your camcorder, locate the first few frames of the video you want to upload. Play these and press Pause. This is so that your video capture program will have something to view when it opens rather than blank space.

3. Start your video capture program. Some programs will display your paused video frames immediately. Others require you to activate the capture Preview Mode or Input Type before displaying frames.

4. If necessary, specify the Device Type you are using—for example, MS 1934—and set Device options such as Record Pause Time.

5. If necessary, set Capture options such as Frame Drop Error tolerance, file size, and time limits. Below are important settings you want to make sure are in place before you actually begin recording:

    ▶   **Dropped Frames**—Most capture utilities let you specify that recording should automatically stop if too many frames have been dropped. That's because dropped frames indicate that your computer cannot keep up with the recording. You indicate that if a certain percentage of frames has been dropped, recording should cease. I recommend between 1 and 3 percent. More than that, and the dropped frames could be noticeable.

    ▶   **Time**—Some capture utilities let you limit how many seconds of video are filmed at once. This is a great safeguard. If the phone rings and you are recording madly for minute after minute, your 40 gigabyte hard drive— that you could never imagine filling beyond 10 percent—will suddenly be boiling over. By specifying that recording should automatically stop after a certain number of seconds, you'll prevent your video from taking over.

    ▶   **Disk Space**—A safety feature similar to the above. Filming stops after the movie has reached a specified file size. Use this setting to keep your movie segments manageable and easy to edit.

6. Pay special attention to file saving location, the place where this movie will be stored on your hard drive. Choose or create a more convenient location than the folder offered to you, if you like.

7. Set compression options, such as NTSC DV or QuickTime (Figure 4.9 shows this in Canon Home Video). These options determine frame rate, movie dimensions, audio quality, and other options.

Figure 4.9
Compression choices in Canon Home Video.

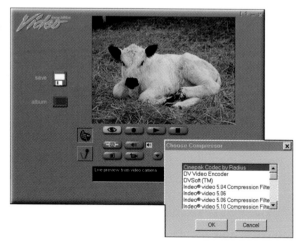

8. Preview your movie, determining the parts you want to upload and those segments just as soon forgotten.

9. Enable Automatic Scene Detection. On some programs, you'll run this after upload.

10. Mark Record In and Out points, if this feature is available in your software.

11. Make note of where the Record button is on your software interface. Begin recording, noting file size and elapsed recording time as the frames roll by.

12. When finished, press Stop. Note that the movie is already saved. There will more than likely be no "Save Movie?" option offered. It is done.

13. More than likely, your saved movie is now on the Preview screen. Click your software's Rewind control button and play your recorded movie. Enable Automatic Scene Detection if you want to save segments of your movie separately from the main film.

Common Video Capture Software Features

What are some features common to all good video capture programs?

Pre-Recording Preview.

When your camcorder is connected via FireWire and is detected by the software, playing the video on your camcorder displays the movie within your program. At this point, the software playback area is simply a monitor. No size or frame information is measured or displayed.

Digital Video Device Options

You'll be able to select your digital device type from a list of choices. Most often, your device type will be MS 1394 Device Control, the "1394" indicating the use of a FireWire connection (see Figure 4.10). Device-specific options such as delays between when you press Record and the software actually beginning to record or software-initiated stop-and-start enabling will be set via Device Options.

Figure 4.10
You must usually choose MS 1394 Device Control from the capture software's Device list.

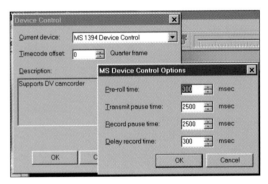

Compression Options

All good video capture programs present you with several compression choices before recording. These will limit frame size, frame rate, and audio quality and provide other space-saving options as well. Figure 4.11 displays one of many possible compression configurations in Ulead Media Studio 6.

Figure 4.11
When capturing video, Ulead Media Studio 6 provides many compression options.

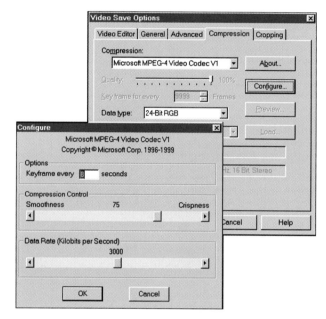

Renaming and Save File Location Options

All capture programs let you choose where your video file should be saved (Figure 4.12 displays this option dialog box in Ulead's video capture). After you're all done with your captures, you'll open your video from this location in an editing program and start editing. Renaming video segments helps you keep track of each section's significance.

Figure 4.12
Ulead's Video Capture
Save Options.

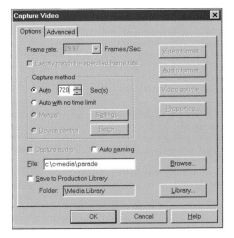

Direct Monitoring of the Recording Process

When you are ready to begin video uptake and save your movie to your computer, you'll press the Record button. As your camera plays frames, your computer will be hard at work as well, compressing, displaying, and saving high-quality digital video (see Figure 4.13). You'll want to monitor this process, keeping track of file size, dropped frame amounts, and elapsed recording time.

Figure 4.13
During video capture,
you can monitor
recording as it occurs.

Playback of Recorded Movie

After recording a video segment onto your hard drive, you'll want to view the results. Where exactly did you jump in and jump out of recording? Is your computer chugging on all cylinders just to play back your video? These surprises will not be evident until you play back your recorded result. All video capture programs let you view what you've just recorded.

Variations on the Video Capture Theme

Each program has a slightly different approach to uploading and saving your video. Initiating video capture especially varies from program to program. Here's how a few of the prominent programs handle these chores:

▶ In some programs, you create a video project before capturing. As shown in Figure 4.14, in Ulead VideoStudio, you create a new project, specifying a folder for all videos and images associated with this project, and then you capture or import your video.

Figure 4.14
VideoStudio's Capture options.

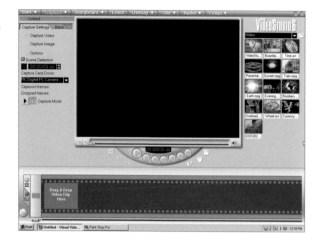

▶ In other programs, such as Video Wave 4, the Capture feature is available as soon as the program opens (see Figure 4.15).

Figure 4.15
VideoWave allows you
to capture immediately
upon opening.

▶ Canon Home Video is a convenient getting-started video editor that comes with
some Canon digital camcorders. Using it to capture video, you would choose
New > Capture (see Figure 4.16), and if your camcorder is plugged in via
FireWire and playing video, Canon Home Video will display it. Next, you would
press the Compression button to set compression options (see Figure 4.17), and
press the Record button to begin recording.

Figure 4.16
Capturing video using
Canon Home Video
editor.

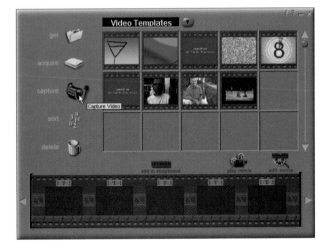

Figure 4.17
Canon Home Video lets you set compression options in a simple dialog box.

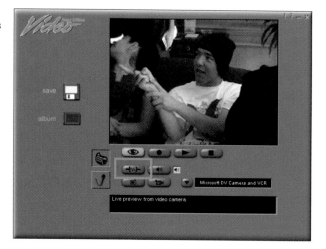

A Closer Look: Ulead Video Capture

Let's look a little closer at Ulead MediaStudio Pro's dedicated Capture program, Video Capture.

1. If you open the program without your camcorder plugged in via FireWire, you'll be prompted to turn your unit on so it can be detected.

2. After a wait, the movie will display in the preview area.

3. If you do not then see the movie, click the eye icon at the top, then click Capture > Video (or press the Record button down below the preview area).

4. Initiating recording will open the Capture Video dialog box (see Figure 4.18). Here you can choose file location, elapsed time, and frame amount limitations.

Figure 4.18
Video Capture's capture dialog box.

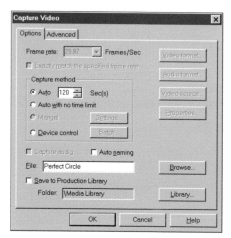

5. Click OK, and when the final prompt appears indicating that recording will now begin, press OK.

6. Like many programs, while recording is occurring, the number of dropped frames, frames recorded so far, and elapsed time will appear at the bottom of the Preview Window (see Figure 4.19).

Figure 4.19
During video capture, elapsed time, frames recorded, and frames dropped are available at the bottom of the screen.

7. Press Escape to stop recording. Your movie is automatically saved.

A Closer Look: VideoStudio's Batch Capture

One very convenient system for capturing bits and pieces of video from a MiniDV is VideoStudio's Batch Capture feature. Using it, you play back your video, and when you see a segment you want to begin recording onto your computer, press F3. When you want to stop recording, press F4. You'd do all this while watching the playback. The video will not stop and start—the program is merely marking your In and Out points. Again, while playing, if you see another segment you want to capture, press F3, and when you want to stop recording, press F4. When you are finished viewing and marking segments for recording, press the Batch Capture's Record button. The program will then capture only your marked segments.

Here's how to use VideoStudio's Batch Capture:

1. Before filming your video, turn on your digital camcorder's timecode feature and, without removing the lens cover, record the entire tape. You are "striping" the tape with the timecode without a break.

2. Rewind and begin filming as you normally would.

3. Making sure your MiniDV tape is rewound, connect your camcorder to your computer and start Ulead VideoStudio.

4. Click Capture at the top of the screen. On the left, you'll see two tabs. Click the Batch tab; you'll then see the Batch Capture features.

5. Click the Play button, and your tape will begin playing. You are not recording but, rather, previewing areas for marking.

6. Use the F3 and F4 keys as In and Out buttons, as described above.

7. You'll see the Batch Capture Task List begin to fill with the In and Out points of your desired segments for capture.

8. When you are finished marking, select any or all the items in the list, using Ctrl and Shift just as you would in Windows Explorer.

9. Press the Batch Capture Record button, and VideoStudio will selectively capture only those segments you want to capture.

Other Video Capture Features

The options listed below are common to some, but not all, video capture programs. If these features seem particularly helpful to you, you may want to hold out for a program that has them.

Preview Window Size Option

Would you like to watch your captured video at 720×480 dpi? Or how about the usual CD-ROM playback option of 352×240? Most, but not all, capture programs let you select a playback size (see Figure 4.20). One benefit to a large movie is the ability to view previously hidden detail. However, your audience may not be seeing your movie at such a large, flattering size. For this reason, you may want to view your movie at the same size as your intended audience.

Figure 4.20
Selecting a preview and playback window size.

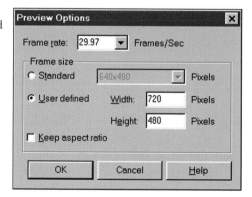

Record In and Out Markers.

In professional video editing, you set a timed entry point or physical marker indicating where you want recording to begin. This eliminates the need to press Record at rolltime with exact precision—not everybody's cup of tea. Also, you can set an Out point, rolling back and forth and zeroing in on exactly when you should stop recording.

About half of the video capture programs you'll encounter in the marketplace let you select Record In and Out points, which is quite convenient. Figure 4.21 shows Ulead's Video Capture markers. With that program, just press F3 to mark your Record In and F4 to mark Record Out. Then rewind your tape and press Record on the software interface. Recording won't really begin until your marked In point, and it will end automatically at your marked End point. However, please note that you can always trim your video in the editing phase. You'll not lose much time by having to perform precise editing at a later point.

Figure 4.21
Setting Capture points with Ulead Video Capture.

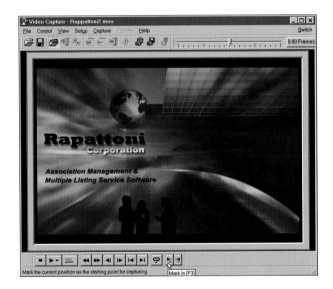

Automatic Scene Detection

Earlier, I mentioned uploading your video a segment at a time. Shorter video segments are easier to edit, and our first experiences with the camcorder tend to be a bit episodic anyway. Some programs make the scene-breakdown process easier by providing Automatic Scene Detection. This feature divides movies at obvious scene breaks. Figure 4.22 shows Scene Breaks as thumbnails in Video Wave 4. For example, when you switch from filming a party to some shots of night life, Scene Detection splits the movie at the change point, resulting in two separate video clips. Scene Detection continues to divide the entire uploaded video at these obvious breakpoints.

Figure 4.22
VideoWave's automatic
scene detection feature.

At times, Automatic Scene Detection splits scene portions that actually belong together. That's
why good programs like Ulead VideoStudio let you override the scene breakpoint by specifying
"Join" with the previous video clip (see Figure 4.23). Some programs also make it very easy to
build a video project—a storyboard—by grouping video segments (see Figure 4.24). You can
rearrange your video shoot and add interesting transitions this way, if you like.

Figure 4.23
VideoStudio lets you
join videos that were
split into separate
scenes during capture.

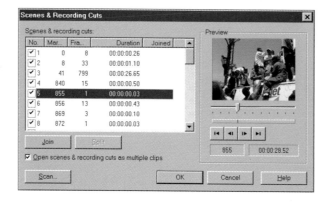

Figure 4.24
Storyboarding in Ulead
VideoStudio.

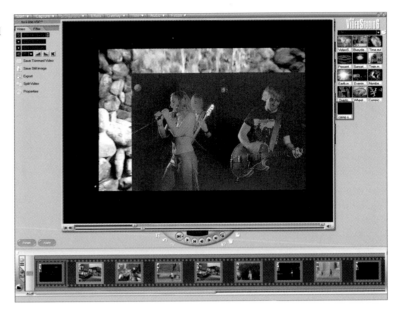

Saving to a Library

While all video capture utilities save the movie to disk, most also save the video to a program folder and automatically create a video thumbnail for quick access. This means you won't have to hunt high and low when you want to use your video clip in a project. Thumbnail views of your video make it easy to combine video segments into a project, creating composites and transitions.

Audio Record Options

Sometimes, the audio portion of your video is as important as the visual, especially if there's music involved. At other times, the audio need not be uploaded at all, or certainly not uploaded at full 16-bit 44 MHz quality. Some video capture programs let you specify audio quality before uploading or even leave off the audio track entirely, if you are so inclined. Most capture utilities include an audio setting as part of an entire compression specification, and these work well enough. You can always alter the audio later during project editing.

Formatting and Compression at Upload Time

After uploading, your video has been changed somewhat. Your movie has been transformed from raw video data into a project-specific format. Your movie now exists as a file on a computer. Guiding this process, you'll have control over video compression and formatting options and an opportunity to set these specifications before the actual uploading begins. Among other video characteristics, you'll specify compression amount, dimensions, Frame vs. Field formatting, frame uptake rate, and audio quality.

Let's discuss the significance of some of those adjustments.

Compression

Your choice of video compression is one of the most significant decisions you'll make at upload time. Too much compression, and your video quality suffers. Too little, and your computer chokes every time you try to make a simple edit. So, when you transfer your movie to your computer, I would recommend compressing it only to a small degree, working with small video segments while editing and combining the segments near the project's conclusion. Right before distribution, you can decide to compress more, if you like.

Dimensions

Video dimension choices depend on your project's intended audience. For example, video that will be primarily displayed on your PC will conform to computer monitor dimensions. For such requirements, you'll notice a 640×480 dpi dimension option, typical for PC movie viewing. If your video is destined for the big screen, you'll need to work in Wide Screen format. Look for the 16:9 dimension option in your capture program's compression choices. Use 320×240 dpi for CD-ROM-based projects, videos embedded in PowerPoint presentations, and teleconferencing across a LAN or telephone connection; and 720×480 for telebroadcast or a VCR-bound project. Video projects for European distribution should conform to PAL standards, and they should be formatted at 720×576dpi.

Video Data Rate

Data Rate targets your video for specific transfer capabilities. For example, online video projects require a low data rate, since even DSL or other high-speed Internet options cannot support full-quality high-speed video transfer. CD-ROM-based projects also require a relatively low data rate (1100 to 1600 kilobytes per second). For VCR or broadcast video, data rate should be very high to ensure the highest possible quality.

Field or Frame Formatting

Field-based video (video that interlaces one field of lines, then another) is used for broadcast or VCR-bound projects. Frame-based is used for everything else.

Audio Compression

If the video you are uploading has music on it, maintain the audio quality at 44 MHz, 12- or 16-bit stereo. If the video has spoken word in which clarity is an issue, you can drop the quality to 22 MHz, but no further. That's because by the time your project is distributed, you'll start to lose sibilance (the clarity of high-frequency sounds, such as the letter "s"), and interviewees will sound thick-tongued. If your video has crowd voices and incidental "Great to be here!" exclamations from the peanut gallery, then go ahead and compress down to 16 MHz, but no further. In my opinion, audio compressed at 11 MHz sounds muddy and is not worth keeping.

Compression Templates

You'll not be left alone to make sense of format choices without further guidance. As Figures 4.25 and 4.26 show, video compression settings are often grouped in one specification and presented to satisfy a particular requirement. These are organized as templates—although not always referred to as such—and they are easily applied, depending on need. Choosing a compression template saves you picking through each selection. For example, if you know you'll be sending your movies around on a CD, then choose one of the CD options.

Figure 4.25
A "template," or group of video compression settings.

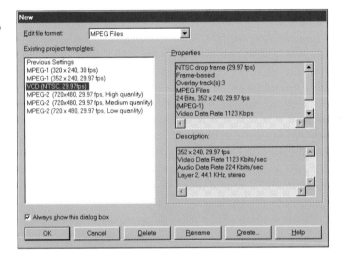

Figure 4.26
Compression settings are combined to fit a particular specification.

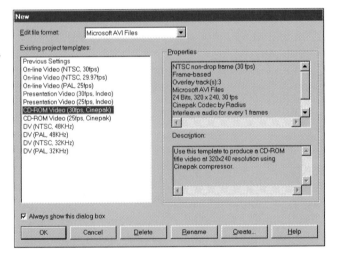

Post-Recording Chores

After recording and previewing, open the folder where the movie was saved and play back your captured video in a standard movie viewer such as Windows Media Player or QuickTime Viewer. This format pretty much represents how the world would see your movie. While you are in the folder where your movie is stored, view its file size (right click on it and choose Properties). You may want to keep tabs on how much disk space your movies use, especially if you do several "takes," and treat yourself to a particularly productive afternoon or two.

This step is especially important when you've allowed Scene Detection to carve up your movie into manageable segments. The original movie is not erased. You'll be amazed at how much hard drive space is used by saving a large, main movie and then saving the segments as well. Perhaps later, after your project is completed, you can go back and do some erasing. Remember, you still have your DV tape as your ultimate back-up.

You've now uploaded and converted a raw video segment into a format you can edit. In the following two chapters, you'll learn how to shoot good video and create compelling movies that actually tell a story. The second half of this book deals exclusively with digital video editing.

Crossroads

You've learned how to export video from your camcorder to your computer, where it can be edited freely. In the next chapter, you'll learn how to shoot good quality video, making sure the footage you capture on your camcorder is something you'll want to keep.

CHAPTER 4

5

Planning and Shooting Your Video

Whether you're filming a swim meet, a wedding, or a multimedia project for your history class, every successful film project begins with a good plan. In this chapter, I'll teach you how to save time and improve your results by applying a little forethought to your projects. Next, we'll dive right into the fundamentals of making good videos. You'll learn how to get the best possible footage, how to anticipate your needs, and how to work around impediments to good video. We'll discuss specific types of shots, how to frame video action, and how to effectively utilize lighting.

Thinking Ahead

Your movie can look quite professional, crisp, clean, compelling, and like something people will want to see again and again. Getting good video is all about planning, which involves bringing two of everything (especially batteries and other supplies), anticipating bad weather, and making backup plans in case key players don't show up. Remember that people are counting on you to capture lots of special moments. Keep in mind all the key moments where that camera will be needed. Remember that it is easier to cut film later than to make up for something you forgot to film. Let's consider some other key points to consider before filming begins.

Scenes and Movement

Every movie is actually a collection of scenes. Movie scenes are not that different from camera snapshots, except that they record a bit more of any given moment. You'll find that your most appreciated videography will be scenes that have a very clear purpose: A family member walks up to the podium, collects an award, and gives a short speech. Everybody gathers around the birthday cake to sing and blow out candles. Someone you've not seen in years approaches you from across an airline terminal, getting closer. Some scenes have natural beginnings and endings, while others will require you to film specific elements to make clear what is happening and why.

Also, consider subject positioning. People often refer to the "all-seeing camera eye," but in reality the camera only sees exactly what you put in front of it. When filming, be conscious of who is in front, who is in back, the subjects' relative heights, and whether people in the camera view are being partially obscured in an unflattering way. Remember people move, and before you reflexively follow their movement with the camera, consider holding your camera position until some natural moment of closure happens, then stop filming and reposition your camera to take in the new action point.

The Shooting Environment

Every movie is made within certain environmental constraints. It is helpful to plan ahead for these. Here are some to look out for:

> **Approaching Dusk.** If you are filming in the afternoon, time is not on your side. When evening strikes, your lighting requirements will change, and you'll have to adjust your filming technique accordingly. If you are filming indoors, you'll be battling against dark corners or furniture that seems to swallow all your light and render subjects too dark as well.

> **Filming Outdoors.** When filmed in bright sun, light-skinned subjects will tend to look washed out unless you make sure very little reflective light is hitting your camera. Also, outdoor filming tends to absorb sound. People will be harder to hear.

> **Sports Events.** If you are filming an event with fast-moving subjects, use a high shutter speed if your camera has an adjustment for this, or use Progressive Color filming so that your frames are filmed 1 to 1, and not interlaced.

> **Minimizing Noise.** If you are filming an event with lots of environmental noise and your subjects are more than a few feet away, try to use an external microphone, or reposition yourself to minimize the surrounding sounds, if at all possible.

Telling Your Story

Video is storytelling. Even if your video work is simply chronicling family vacations, you are building a plot, an entertaining sequence of events that people will watch again and again. When you dragged your camcorder up to the redwoods for a family vacation, you didn't just want movies about trees. Things happened that made people laugh, cry, or think. As a student of digital video filming, this video storytelling is a skill that can be yours. Here are some tips to make your video storytelling more compelling:

> Every movie should tell a story in an interesting way. The opening should set the tone, give an indication of what the audience will see, and create interest, perhaps by alluding to an element of surprise.

> A movie should have a clear beginning, middle, and end. When filming a local sporting event, what marks the passage of time? What inning are we watching? What is at stake if someone strikes out? Find a way to pace your movie. Anticipate the ending, and hint at some possible outcomes.

> Even movies that simply record important events like sports or special occasions should have a little bit of something compelling about them. Try to film little telling details that will make viewers laugh or give them something to think about. Try to capture moments that are a bit unique.

> Every movie will have central characters involved. Return to those main characters from time to time with your camera, and let the audience know what is important about them. Is it a little girl's birthday party? Is she getting anxious about presents? Or perhaps a little bored and exhausted with all the company? Use the camera to convey those emotions.

Working Like a Pro

Keep in mind that just because you might be new to this doesn't mean your video has to be amateurish. You can surprise yourself and others by how professional your video will look. You can capture the most telling moments at the right camera distance—not too close, not too far— and quickly set up the best shot when you only have a moment to spare. You'll now learn some of these techniques.

Camera Movement

No one wants to go home at the end of the filming day with a tape full of abrupt motion, out-of-range subjects, and unintended close-ups. Here are some steps to getting footage you'll be happy with.

Stabilize Your Camera

Start with good, stable filming technique. Newer digital video cameras weigh very little and they're very easy to move unintentionally. Audiences don't need to be reminded that their window on your world weighs less than a pound. A solid, immobile view is appreciated. You may want to use a tripod, or you can eliminate jittery motions by using your camcorder's Image Stabilization feature.

Benefits of Tripod Use

Allow me to sing the praises of tripod use. Note that tripods allow you to reduce shutter speeds, making it easier to film indoors in dimmer light. Also, tripod use lets you clearly define your camcorder's position. That way, if you note your tripod's exact position, height, and angle, you can stop and resume filming with some precision. If you need to return to this view and obtain more footage, reproducing your tripod's exact setup will give your footage some continuity. This is important, because you don't want your audience to be jarred by the sudden realization that the view suddenly got lower and angled differently than before.

Note also that using a tripod means you can turn off Image Stabilization. This is nice, because image stabilization sets aside a portion of your CCD for its electronic centering, meaning that your images are just a shade less color-rich than they might be otherwise.

Camera Movements and Positions

The following are names for common camera positions that change your view of the subject, or movements that either follow your subject's path or change your view of the subject while stationary.

- ▶ **Pan Left and Right.** Panning comes from the same root word as "panorama." Panning is a right or left camera movement, taking in the area immediately to the right or left of the straight-ahead camera view. When panning, you rotate the camera on its vertical axis.

- ▶ **Tilt Left and Right.** Tilting the camera to the left or right alters the slope that the subject is being viewed on. You'd not do this very often, except, for example, to exaggerate the angle of a subject standing on a hill, or to reorient an object being held at an obscure angle, such as in industrial or medical filming.

- ▶ **Upward Tilt.** Placing the camera at a relatively lower position and tilting the camera upward will make the subject appear larger. Exaggerated upward tilting disproportionately increases the size of the upper part of the subject.

- ▶ **Downward Tilt.** Placing the camcorder at a relatively higher position and tilting the camera downward makes the subject appear smaller. Exaggerated downward tilting can obscure the lower part of the subject.

- ▶ **Dolly Forward and Backward.** Named after a camera transport device for movie sets, dolly means to physically move the camera forwards or backwards, rather than to zoom. Physically reorienting yourself and the camera will, most often, provide a better picture than simply zooming. To minimize the jerkiness that occurs when walking, you can be seated in a swivel chair and have someone gently move you forward or backwards. Rolling motions are far less disruptive to viewers than filming while walking.

▶ **Truck.** The Truck shot is a circular motion around the subject. It lends grandeur and importance to the subject. It is almost impossible to shoot unless you have some sort of amphitheater to film around and have drawn a 360-degree circle, or you have a circular structure to walk on as a guide.

Long Shots, Medium Shots, and Close-ups

When you shoot video, be conscious of the subject's relationship to his or her environment. Keep in mind what the audience has seen so far. Audiences like to be introduced to the subject and environment. For an audience, the details of a person's actions won't make much sense until the context is known. Perhaps you've noticed that a head shot looks more agreeable if some background is shown (Figure 5.1). Extra-close shots (Figure 5.2) are used more for "edgy" advertisement photography and music video filming.

Figure 5.1
Head shots, even in video, leave lots of background around the head.

Figure 5.2
Use extra-close shots for more avant-garde, artistic filming.

CHAPTER 5

Below are examples of camera shots. The names are based on their relative distance to the subject. There really is no hard and fast distance measurements rule you can apply here. The shot names are based on how much of the subject is shown.

▶ **Long Shot.** This shot establishes the relationship between the subject and environment. It's the "big picture" shot (Figure 5.3).

Figure 5.3
A long shot establishes the subject in the environment.

▶ **Medium Long Shot.** Shows the subject in the environment, but closer in. The entire subject, head to toe, is shown. Use this shot if the subject is moving or changing positions (Figure 5.4).

Figure 5.4
A medium long shot shows the subject head-to-toe—typically used if the subject relocates.

▶ **Medium Shot.** There's a trick to displaying "half a person" without making them look as though they've been cut in half. You do not want an even slice of "just the torso" and up. Show some lap and a bit of lower body to create continuity (Figure 5.5).

Figure 5.5
Leave a little lap, and avoid the cut-in-half look when filming torso-up conversations.

▶ **Close-up.** Shows the upper forehead to the upper chest. Note that it's perfectly fine to cut off a bit of the top of the head. People are interested in eyes and facial expressions, not bald spots. A bit of chest is helpful to avoid a "talking head" look. Use this shot for interviews and close conversation, when the person's face and words are the main interest in the video (Figure 5.6).

Figure 5.6
Use the close-up to accent speech or facial expression. This is a good, comfortable face view.

▶ **Big close-up.** This shot shows the top of the head to the chin. Big close-up shots are used to display nuances in the character's emotions. Use sparingly; don't linger on a Big Close-up for longer than necessary (Figure 5.7).

Figure 5.7
Big close-ups should be used sparingly

CHAPTER 5

▶ **Very close-up.** Very close-up shots show the eyes and mouth only. Use this shot to display more subtle or secret emotions, or emotions that involve only the eyes, such as temporary shock that is quickly hidden, or a fearful glance that is quickly covered up. Again, do not linger on a very close-up shot for longer than necessary (Figure 5.8).

Figure 5.8
Use a very close-up shot to quickly accent emotions.

Framing a Shot

One of your most powerful tools as a videographer is to determine where a figure should appear on your screen. You need to frame your shot. For example, you can control who appears in the upper left of your image, who appears in the lower right, and where they will go next. We'll start with some basic shot framing rules.

The Rule of Thirds

Imagine your camcorder LCD is a tic-tac-toe board. Using two horizontal and two vertical lines, the screen is divided into ninths. You always want your subject's eyes to be near where the tic-tac-toe lines meet. You don't want a subject's eyes to be in the exact center of the shot or in one of the blank areas where no lines touch. The tic-tac-toe lines intersect away from the center, and away from the edges. These are natural guidelines for subject positioning. In the examples in Figure 5.9, the subject's eyes always fall on one of the lines. Notice that no one's eyes are at the center of the image.

Figure 5.9
Using the Rule of Thirds to avoid center-frame orientation.

The Rule of Thirds prevents the following shooting errors:

▶ A subject sitting in the middle of the screen gets boring. We think we've seen it all very quickly (see Figure 5.1, above).

▶ A subject with eyes toward the edge of the screen looks like it should be leaving—so why isn't it gone (Figure 5.10)?

Figure 5.10
A single face should not be positioned at the edge of the frame.

Subjects placed along the Rule of Thirds intersecting lines imply room for other screen subjects, which tells the eye to keep looking, that something is about to happen.

Film a tall person with a short person by placing the tall person along the upper right line intersection. Place the shorter person along the lower left line, and have them face each other. You'll be amazed how composed your shot looks (Figure 5.11). There's still room on either side of the subjects, but neither of them is crowding the center.

Figure 5.11
Use the Rule of Thirds
to frame subjects of
varying heights.

Leaving Room for Text and Overlays

The Rule of Thirds is especially important if you plan to add text, video, or still image overlays to your movie. Placing a subject at that lower right intersection gives you room for a text label or graphic at the upper left.

The Rule of Thirds makes it easy to place thought bubbles and other items where sequence matters (yes, you can use thought bubbles in video). For example, in Figure 5.12, the subject's head is placed along the lower left lines, and the thought bubble is placed more towards the right. In cultures where one reads from right to left, this is natural sequencing. We'd view the subject first, then be introduced to their thoughts.

Figure 5.12
Thought bubbles should
appear to the right of
the subject.

Filming Groups

Pay attention to the Rule of Thirds when filming groups. In this group shot, notice how clearly the exact center is avoided (Figure 5.13). That's because the faces are moving along the lines according to the Rule of Thirds.

Figure 5.13
A film of a group is more appealing if you avoid placing someone in the exact center.

Head Room and Nose Room

Viewers have unspoken expectations when watching the human face on film. Watch a movie, and you're likely to spend more time watching a face than any other form. If viewers cannot put their wishes into words, here are some rules for celluloid faces (see Figures 5.11, 5.12, and 5.22 for visual examples):

▶ Don't show a close-up unless there's a good reason. Why do I want to be so near that person?

▶ If a person's head is very near the top of the screen, viewers will feel an unnatural closeness, like they are trapped in a room together. If you leave adequate room around the subject's head, viewers will feel like the subject is part of the entire scene, and they'll look forward to what you introduce next.

The Z-Axis (Video Depth)

Another major consideration in shot framing is the Z-axis. You may have noticed that thus far we've discussed subjects moving from right to left (along the X-axis, horizontally), and up and down (the Y-axis, vertically). A good videographer can also make depth apparent. That's the Z-axis, the "front" and "back" of what you are viewing.

Avoid Aligning Subjects Horizontally

The most obvious tool for creating Z-pop (adding depth to your video) is to avoid lining up characters horizontally. (Thanks to character alignment, the image in Figure 5.14 has lots of depth. Notice the shadows around the praying hands and faces.)

Figure 5.14
When filming several people, avoid horizontal line-ups.

Horizontally aligned characters bring to mind police line-ups and look very posed. This can be done intentionally, though, such as in the movie poster for *The Usual Suspects* or on the Cheap Trick album cover, *Caught in the Act.*

Allow a Little Bit of Shadow

Lighting plays a big role in creating images with depth. When getting ready to film, look in your LCD and arrange the lighting so characters look solid, not drawn or flat. A little bit of shadow provides this (Figure 5.15).

Figure 5.15
Shadows add depth to an image.

Lighting and Environment

Digital video is very light-sensitive. What look to our eyes like small changes in lighting are, electronically speaking, actually very significant fluctuations in luminance. Therefore, a tiny turn of the head or camera, and someone's face is suddenly in a shadow or appears bleached out and ultra-white. Maintaining a consistent lighting environment while filming video is one of videography's greatest challenges. In some ways, filming indoors is preferable. This is because of predictability. By positioning several professional lights so that the figures are always evenly illuminated, you can control shadows and limit those sudden blotches of nuclear white that occur when filming a white sweater in direct sunlight.

To avoid unpleasant surprises at the end of the day, film a few frames in the current lighting environment, rewind, and view them on a monitor. Look especially at skin tones, at people's arms and faces as they move across the screen. Watch for unevenness, shadows, and bright-white blotches. Note the location of the problem, and consider what can be done lighting-wise to fix it. Try changing the angle of the camera slightly, moving the shot just a little to the right or left. If you are indoors, try repositioning the light beams for more evenness.

Avoiding the Flat Outdoor Video Look

After filming in bright sunlight, you may find, upon playback, that everything looks bright and crisp but is without depth (Figure 5.16). After you've worked with your camcorder for a while, you'll start to notice the "look" of video. Turn on your TV and channel-flip for a while, looking briefly at what's on the screen. Movies have a richer color depth that will become more apparent to you. Then switch to a golf game or talking head interview recorded onto video. You'll notice immediately the over-bright colors and lack of shades, no sense that one object is behind another. It looks flat. That's because digital video is so light sensitive that it is very easy to overwhelm a camcorder with too much light. Your camcorder will therefore automatically use a very narrow aperture and high shutter speed. This is a recipe for a flat image with super-high contrast, no shadows, and no color subtleties.

Figure 5.16
The video on the left was shot in too much light. The video on the right has more color depth.

How do videographers avoid this? By filming in subdued light. Film at dawn, at dusk, with a cloud cover, or against a large wall or structure that shields you from direct sun to at least some degree. Filming at dusk or on a cloudy day makes for especially rich colors. Also, in very bright situations, use a Neutral Density Filter. This, too, will get rid of some of that unforgiving brightness and allow your camcorder to capture more shades of color.

We've already discussed some environmental concerns in the planning section, above. Outdoor shooters need to remember that daylight doesn't last forever, and outdoor video shot at noon will not look the same as footage shot at four or five o'clock in the afternoon (Figure 5.17), especially in fall or winter. A heavy coat of clouds significantly changes the look of your film.

Figure 5.17
Video shot in the same environment at different times of day will have different light qualities.

Filmed in Bright Daylight   Filmed at Dusk

Other Environmental Hurdles

You also need to think about the effects of human traffic flow. If you are filming outdoors, can you stave off pedestrians while the camera is rolling? Can you find someplace that is a bit deserted at certain times of day, without having to wait until night?

You may need to consider audio interference as well. Quiet dialog may not work well with freeway noise and cars honking. In such situations, move upwind from the traffic, or consider external mics that can be pointed directly at the audio source. High wind will affect audio as well. Beach filming creates a layer of surf noise that you simply cannot do anything about. Your subjects will shout over the surf, not whisper. If you don't want sounds o' the beach, consider overdubbing your audio later.

NOTE
For high-quality audio, consider using an external microphone. On-board mics can be noisy, and they tend to pick up extraneous sounds in your shooting environment. With an external mic, your audio can be more accurate and more selective.

Where to Film

If you can choose where to film, think elevation: stairs, raised walkways, public outdoor stages, arches, 360-degree amphitheaters, and any other locales that provide a variety of height relationships. Figure 5.18 shows some examples from my city. Notice the various heights, elevations, and angles that are possible. As you drive around your own city, think of locations that offer such advantages.

Figure 5.18
When checking out filming locales, look for a variety of elevations, angles, and backgrounds.

CHAPTER 5

Locale Framing Tips

Look for creative framing opportunities wherever possible. Is your subject wearing red? Drive around and keep your eyes peeled for a building with a large black background. Do you have a building in town with an interesting cross-grid design near the front, a large rough stone, or a repetitive beehive pattern? Drag your subjects to these locals for filming, if you can. Do not film subjects in front of murals, unless you are drawing attention to them. Background patterns are nice, but they must be subdued, not distracting.

Contrasting Colors

Encourage your subjects to wear clothing that will contrast with the background. Will you be filming against blue? Get your subject to throw a bit of orange into their wardrobe. Purple and yellow work well together, but do not encourage red and green.

And finally, if you ever have the opportunity, film someone walking away into a tunnel with light at the other end. Use software to accent the light and amplify the colors as the subject slips into darkness. You may also film them emerging from the tunnel as well. The halo of light around the subject glows in quite a surreal way, especially when you use software to add a little rainbow of lens glare at certain points.

Common Mistakes

We'll end this chapter segment by discussing common video filming mistakes. These are all errors that arise from getting distracted by surrounding activity and neglecting what the camcorder viewfinder is telling you. If you can avoid these common mistakes, you'll have eliminated the telltale signs from your videos that scream, "Beginner!"

Interplay between Background and Subject

Videographers sometimes forget that items in the background can look "attached" to the subject. A circular graphic behind the subject's head can look like a bizarre hat. A bookshelf can look like it's emanating from the subject's ears. Film a few frames of your subject, then play it back and make sure none of this is going on.

Unnecessary Camera Movements

Novice videographers have a hard time resisting experiments with camera movements. If you find that your subject has relocated, go ahead and slightly change camera positions, but, later, edit out the adjusting camera movement. A scene break is fine, just cut out the moving.

Centering Subjects

Remember the Rule of Thirds when positioning subjects. Avoid the urge for symmetry when positioning subjects in your viewfinder or LCD. Remember that video is a moving medium, and using the Rule of Thirds helps keep people watching for what happens next.

No Background-Foreground Contrast

Be careful not to use a dark background with subjects wearing dark clothing. They'll get swallowed up by the similar colors. Also, avoid the white-on-white effect. Light clothing with light backgrounds will make your subjects indistinct.

Crossroads

Now that you know enough about camerawork to go out and film up a storm, in the next chapter, you'll discover editing software. You'll be amazed how much can happen with your video after you've shot it. In fact, after you understand a bit about video editing, you'll start coming up with editing ideas even while you are filming. Film is a very pliable communication medium. You're in for a lot of fun!

6

Basic Video Editing

In this chapter, you'll learn about basic video editing steps. These include trimming and combining video clips; adding audio, still images, and text; and using transition effects to sequence these components. The result of these efforts is called a video project. In a typical video project, you will combine perhaps three video clips from various segments of your MiniDV tape, record music over a portion of the combined clips, and add a text introduction and a couple of still images you'd like to particularly emphasize. You'll save this, perhaps as a mini-movie you can easily e-mail or as a more robust CD-ROM production.

How do you create a video project? The exact steps depend on your software. We'll be looking at several basic video editors in this chapter, but primarily we'll work step-by-step with Ulead VideoStudio.

Let's first go over the basic tasks for creating a simple video project. In Chapter 4, you learned how to capture video and save video files to your hard drive. We'll pick up at that point: You've captured clips from your camcorder, and you're ready to begin editing.

Video Editor Layout

Looking at your video editor's main screen, you'll notice these features:

▶ A preview window for viewing individual video clips (Figure 6.1) or project playback. Most editors use the same window for browsing through a movie you want to add to your project and for playing back your project in progress.

Figure 6.1
The Ulead VideoStudio
preview window.

> ▶ A control panel with VCR-style controls (Figure 6.1) for playing, rendering, fast forwarding, and rewinding video playback. Recording is a more elaborate process than the mere press of a button, and usually it's initiated through a menu.

> ▶ A library for dragging video clips onto the editing area (Figure 6.2). Often, the library can switch views to display video clips, images, transitions, and special effects. Any resources you need for your video project can therefore be close at hand.

Figure 6.2
The MGI VideoWave 4
resource library.

▶ An editing area for building your project. Video clips and other resources are dragged into a work area (Figure 6.3). Here they are sequenced, trimmed and cut, and combined as needed. The video editing area is where most of your work takes place.

Figure 6.3
The VideoWave 4 editing area.

▶ A workflow menu system for stepping through tasks logically. Building your project is a combination of adding and editing video clips and other media; trimming videos and adding transitions, music, sound effects, and voice-over; and, finally, exporting your project into a new file format for distribution. Each task requires unique tools for the job. Video editing programs provide quick access to these tools as you need them. Most try not to overwhelm you by showing you every tool at once. Rather, when you're ready to move on to the next phase of your project, you will click a menu button. A new screen will open, displaying the tools for that task. For example, Ulead VideoStudio sequences its editing areas according to workflow (Figure 6.4). In MGI VideoWave 4, users click along the left side of the screen to open new work areas (Figure 6.5). Sonic Foundry Video Factory tries to present all options in a single screen (Figure 6.6), thus your first impression of the work area can be a bit intimidating. Video Factory is powerful and closer to a semi-professional video editing program in both appearance and features.

CHAPTER 6

Figure 6.4
VideoStudio's menu
sequence across the top
of the screen.

Figure 6.5
VideoWave's menu of
"rooms" across the left.

Figure 6.6
Video Factory shows
you everything up front.

Video Editing Tasks

Regardless of the program you choose, creating a project involves a similar set of tasks that comprise basic video editing. In this section we'll discuss the key tasks involved in video editing.

Pulling Project Files Together

Before assembling your video project, you'll need to do some resource relocation. There are video clips, image files, and sounds that you'll want to use in your project. They need to be handy. Your video editing program probably has a library for storing resource files for your projects. Your materials need to be in that library.

In some programs, you'll be creating a new folder for your project and moving resources to that folder. In other programs, all resources will be available for all projects and you'll just have to move everything to that library folder using a browse menu. In any event, you'll need to bring your project materials close at hand before you get started (Figure 6.7).

Figure 6.7
In VideoStudio, resources from your hard drive are placed in the media library.

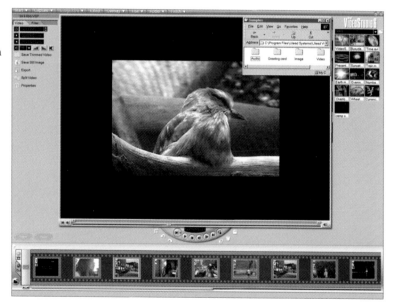

Some programs, however, simply present an Explorer-like interface of your hard drive right inside the program. You can scour your computer for any media you like. In such cases, you must set up your own folder for video project media and remember where it is.

CHAPTER 6

Adding Media to the Project

For adding and editing media, most video editors provide both a storyboard and timeline view. Each displays necessary tools and a unique view of your project.

Storyboard View

In a storyboard view, each video or image file is represented by a small thumbnail picture (Figure 6.8). You simply drag videos and image files onto the storyboard. Play back your project, and each item will play sequentially from left to right. Storyboards allow you to see your sequenced media at a glance. You can add transitions in storyboard view as well. Just drag a transition in between two media. Then, after editing, you'd press a "Preview Project" button, which compiles and displays your entire work in progress, transitions included.

Figure 6.8
Click a Storyboard thumbnail, and it appears in the Preview window.

Storyboard editing has limitations, though. You can't shorten or lengthen video clips in a storyboard view, and you cannot "stack" media on top of one another. For these tasks, a timeline view is required.

Timeline View

Most basic video editors provide a timeline view (Figure 6.9). A timeline view is necessary for isolating a small segment of video you want eliminated and cutting it out. In timeline view, video length is displayed, making it easy to trim footage from your video clip's beginning or ending. Some basic video editors also let you slice a segment from anywhere in your clip and either cut it or move it elsewhere along the timeline. Others allow you to drag the ending of a video clip to the right, towards a specific time marker on the timeline. As a result, your video clip will now repeat until the specified point on the timeline is reached.

Figure 6.9
VideoStudio's timeline view.

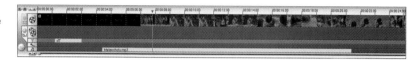

NOTE

Switching between storyboard and timeline view does not change your project, only your view of it.

Although most basic video editors do not allow you to play one video track while another is playing, most do allow concurrent audio tracks. Simultaneous multiple audio track playback is required if you want music accompaniment with voice-over and sound effects. If you're counting, you'll see that I just described three separate audio tracks.

A timeline view is essential for managing multiple audio tracks. Individual control over those separate tracks is important. To add sound effects at specific points in your project or have songs fade in and out when needed, you'll need to work with time markers. A timeline view is needed to adjust the starting and ending points of your various audio tracks, if you require them.

TIP

Use storyboard mode to view all your project clips at a glance, noting sequence, and dragging clips to a new location in your project. Use timeline view to trim clips, cut segments, and reposition audio track starting points.

CHAPTER 6

Adding Transitions

Transitions blend one video clip to the next using clever bits of visual geometry (Figure 6.10). They are initially rather irresistible, allowing you to bubble, fuse, bend, and rip your video clips together. But, like talking computer commands, the thrill wears off quickly, and you may notice that professional movies are very thin on special effect transitions. They do have their purpose, though, and every good video editor comes with plenty of snazzy transition effects.

Figure 6.10
Transition frames on display.

Project Rendering

Each time you add a component to your video project, you may want to preview the entire result. Once you add a still image, some video segments, and text overlays, you'll want to check out your work. Are the transitions too fast? Does the text just sit there and get boring? To really know what you've created thus far, you'll have to preview your project.

You may be thinking, "Fair enough. I'll press Play and I'll see my project." Not so fast. If you simply press Play right now in your video editor, you'll probably see the most recent video clip you added, and wonder what happened to all your nice transitions and text. Before a project can be played back, it has to be compiled. The project components must be rendered together as a whole. Your video editor probably has a separate "Render" or "Play Project" button that will start the compiling process (Figure 6.11).

Figure 6.11
VideoStudio's Play Project button.

Rendering your project is far from instantaneous. Depending on project length and computer speed, you can press Render, go make a pot of coffee, come back, and find you're still only 75% finished. All this just to preview a few transitions. However, in most programs, after an initial rendering, future updates will go faster. VideoStudio 6 has a tiny arrow beside the Preview button. For a fast but somewhat rough rendering of your project so far, click the tiny arrow and choose Instant Preview.

CAUTION
Adding lots of transitions dramatically increases video rendering time.

Trimming Video

A good basic video editor lets you easily trim video from the beginning and ending of the clips you add (Figure 6.12). As far as your project is concerned, a video clip is just a resource from which you can use and reuse frames and fragments as you see fit. You can drop in segments anywhere you like, repeat those segments, then jump ahead to an entirely different clip portion. It's the project that you render and send around town; the video clip is unchanged. Figure 6.13 displays a video project based on a single clip, with starting points and segments rearranged as needed.

Figure 6.12
VideoWave 4's Mark In tool.

Figure 6.13
These pieces of a project (below) are all drawn from the same library clip.

NOTE

When you add a video clip segment to your project, then later add a different segment, the program does not make a new copy of the video clip. That would be counterproductive. Your video project is a collection of commands that organize existing media, saving your various starting and ending points. The project file is small and does not make copies of the videos or images it uses in creation of your final product.

Adding Text

Another basic video editing task is adding text to your footage. For example, using Ulead VideoStudio's Text tool, you can choose font, font size color, text effect, and entry and exit points (Figure 6.14). Specific text controls are important. For example, you'll need to choose a font color that reads well against your video background and choose an entry point that makes sense with the storyline.

Figure 6.14
VideoStudio's Text
tools.

The Basics, Plus

The following features take you beyond just basic video editing. These will enhance or streamline
your editing skills and open up many possible creative avenues for your video project.

Saving a Video Frame as a Still Picture

You may want to extract a single video frame and save it as a still picture. Blending still images
with video lets you select which impressions should linger longer in the viewer's mind. Still
images add pacing to your project. Fading one image into the next with video interspersed can
provide a natural rhythm, especially if there's music that bounces along at the same tempo. Your
video editor undoubtedly has a method for extracting frames and saving them as still images.
Figure 6.15 shows VideoStudio's "Save Current Frame" feature.

Figure 6.15
You can click a button
to save the current
video frame as a
picture file.

CHAPTER 6

Adding Multiple Audio Tracks

A good video editor makes it easy to add multiple audio tracks. As mentioned earlier, you may want to add a voice-over, music, and sound effects. It'll be particularly important to control volume levels. Sound effects should not cut through at a distracting volume. And most importantly, the voice-over should be reasonably louder than the music. A good video editor not only lets you add audio tracks—it lets you manage volume levels as well (Figure 6.16).

Figure 6.16
Video Factory's timeline-based audio track features

Extracting a Video Segment

Earlier I mentioned the difference between a video clip and video project. Video clips are captured from your camcorder, and you combine them to create a project. The project does not alter video clips. If your video project makes your video look like scrambled eggs, the original footage from your camcorder remains untouched.

However, there are times you'll want to quickly render some segment of your project, or a video cut, saving that as a video. I don't mean rendering the segment as a project, or seeing a preview of that short bit of work. Rather, you should be able to save that segment as a standalone video that can be played back in any video program or player. You'll appreciate an "Extract Video" or "Save Segment as Video" feature very much.

Cut and Delete

Your video editor should have the ability to isolate unwanted frames and simply zap them out of the project. This feature is not as common as you might think. While almost all programs let you quickly set In and Out points for your clip, that's not the same thing as designating a chunk of video for the waste bin. Later in this chapter, I'll show you how to cut and delete video frames using Ulead VideoStudio.

Rendering a Fast, Small Movie

At times you'll want to create an e-mailable video without having to press lots of buttons. You should not have to wade through a lot of option screens just to save your project as a Web-sized mini-movie. Most basic video editing programs have something approaching a one-click "Web movie" or "E-mail Movie" feature (Figure 6.17).

Figure 6.17
Canon Home Video's e-mail video feature.

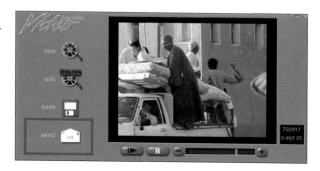

TIP

The above feature is great for sending a quick rendition of your project to someone who may want to view your progress or to yourself at another e-mail address.

Saving Your Custom Configuration

You'll want a program that lets you save a customized output configuration. Let's say you've clicked through various compression and formatting screens and come up with the perfect compromise between file size and quality, creating a version of your project that weighs in at 1.8 MB and still looks great. You'll want to save this output configuration for later use, so you can apply your settings to other projects. A good video editing program will let you do this.

CHAPTER 6

Creating a Video Project, Step by Step

Next, we'll step through the actual building of a basic video project using Ulead VideoStudio. We'll place two video clips on the storyboard, add a transition, and add a still image with a transition. Then we'll insert a blank color frame and use it as a backdrop for animated text. Finally, we'll add a voice-over, sound, and CD music, and we'll export the project to a video format.

Starting a New Project

We need to create a new project. This involves designating a folder for project resources and naming and describing the project.

1. First, click Start > New Project at the upper left of the VideoStudio screen. When the New Project dialog box appears, note the Working Folder at the top of the dialog box. This is the location where the project will be created and your project files stored. You can accept this location or designate a new one using the Location field. Note that many files may end up in this folder, so you'll probably want to designate a folder just for this project.

2. Later, at any point during your project, you can click the "Save" icon below the preview screen and save your project.

Figure 6.18
Setting project specifications.

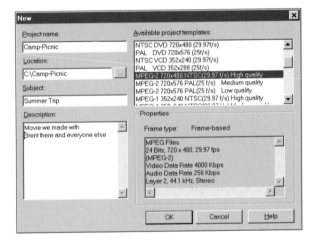

TIP

If you have a video on your computer that has the dimensions, frame rate, and other specifications that you have in mind, choose the Template From an Existing Video option in the Available Templates panel of the New Project dialog box.

3. On the right side of the screen, you'll see the Library, which contains VideoStudio's tutorial videos and other media files. When you create a new project, thumbnails of media files for that project appear in the Library. These will include any media files in your designated project folder.

Organizing Project Media

You'll need to have resources for your project close at hand. VideoStudio provides a complete library of transitions, special effects, color frames, and starter files to supplement your videos and images:

1. Click the dropdown menu above the library, and you'll see five sections: Video, Image, Color, Video Filter, and Library Manager. The first four sections are media types. Each section contains lots of media files to get you started on your creation.

2. To locate the folder where you've set aside videos and images for your project, click the New Media icon in the upper right-hand corner. Browse to the folder where you saved your captured video.

3. Click the Video. When you do so, the video's first frame will appear in the VideoStudio Preview screen. The video will also appear in the library for this project. Please note that it is not yet part of your project.

Adding Media to the Project

Now you'll drag videos and other media to the storyboard, incorporating it into your project.

1. To make the new video clip part of your project, drag it to the storyboard (Figure 6.19). At the top of the screen (not pictured), "Storyboard" will be highlighted, indicating you are building your project clip by clip as a storyboard.

Figure 6.19
The video clip is not part of the project until you drag it to the storyboard.

CHAPTER 6

2.   Note the control buttons located beneath the preview screen. After dragging your clip to the storyboard, preview it by pressing the Play button.

3.   To locate other media and make them available for this project, use the library's New Media icon at the upper right of the screen. Any images, sounds, or videos you select will appear in the library.

4.   To view all these files, use the drop-down menu and the slider on the right. Use them in your project by dragging them onto the storyboard.

Trimming Video Clips Using Shortcut Keys

If the video clip you inserted could use a little trimming at the beginning here's how to fix it:

1.   Press the Play button. Play past the point that has the problem in it.

2.   Mark this position as the In point by pressing F3. Your video clip now begins at the point at which you pressed F3.

3.   For your change to take effect, click Apply on the lower left of the screen (Figure 6.20).

Figure 6.20
When editing in VideoStudio, don't forget to click Apply.

If you need to finesse the In and Out points more precisely, and you want the clip to begin a few frames later or earlier than the point at which you pressed F3, do the following:

1.   Click the Control Panel's Previous or Next buttons (Figure 6.21). These advance or rewind your video one frame at a time (to advance or rewind multiple frames, keep pressing the buttons).

Figure 6.21
These buttons advance
or rewind your video
one frame at a time.

2. When you're happy with your In point, again press F3.

3. Again, click the Apply button. The project will now begin your video at your new In point.

4. If you want to trim some frames off the end of your video clip, press Play, and play the video right up to the point at which you want your video to end.

5. Press F4, and don't forget that Apply button. Everything after this point will not be used for the project.

TIP

Deleting segments from a clip used in a project does not alter the actual clip. You are merely specifying which segments should be used in this project's storyboard.

Adding a Second Clip to the Project

You now have one trimmed video segment in your project. Let's add another:

1. Click any video clip in the library, and drag it to the second frame in the storyboard area (Figure 6.22).

CHAPTER 6

Figure 6.22
To add additional clips, just drag them in from the library.

2.   To render this project and play it back, click the Play Project button. The two video clips will play sequentially, left to right.

Trimming Video Clips Using the Trim Bar

Let's trim this second segment using a different tool, the green trim bar right beneath the preview screen:

1.   Click and drag the left side of the green trim bar toward the right (Figure 6.23).

Figure 6.23
Editing a video portion using the trim bar.

2.   Stop at the point at which you want this video clip to begin.

3.   To make your change effective, click Apply, on the lower left of the screen.

4.   To fine-tune your video entry point, use the Control Panel's Previous and Next buttons.

5.   After each change, click Apply.

6.   To adjust this video clip's Out point, drag the right end of the green trim bar toward the left. This shortens the video clip, moving the clip's Out point to an earlier point.

7.   Again, click the Apply button.

You now have two video clips in your project, each with edited In and Out points.

Adding a Transition

To add a transition between the two clips, you need to access the Effects menu options by clicking Effects at the top of the screen.

1. Click the Effect label at the top of the screen. The library now displays transition effects (Figure 6.24).

Figure 6.24
To view transitions, click the Effect menu option.

2. While in the Library, each transition effect is displayed in motion, which previews the transition's action. In a transition preview, the letter "A" represents the first video in the transition. The letter "B" represents the second video, the clip that begins playing after the transition has passed.

3. When you click Effects and begin working with transitions, the space in between video clips is highlighted.

4. To select a transition, click the drop down menu at the upper right, which reveals many transition categories.

5. Select a category and a new set of transitions will appear in the library. Like most basic video editing programs, VideoStudio has gone all out to provide a large collection of these effects.

6. To add a transition to your project, drag it to the space between the two clips.

7. Press Play, and the transition will appear. You'll see the blend between the two clips take place. Until you render the project with the transition, it won't look very smooth in the preview screen. Keep in mind that transitions require lots of CPU power, so try to preview the areas right before and right after the transition.

CHAPTER 6

8. Edit your transition using the controls on the left. Especially consider modifying transition length. Default transition length may not be right for your needs.

TIP

Transition controls will be available as long as the transition is selected in the storyboard. If you click on the storyboard outside the transition, select it again by clicking. The controls for the transition will appear.

Adding a Still Image

Adding an image to your project is like adding a video. Images are dragged onto the storyboard. Any image in the library can be added to the video project. By default, an image added to the timeline will display for three seconds (this duration can be changed in preferences).

To modify image display time, click the image to select it, and then click inside the Seconds counter at the upper left. To adjust image display time to fractions of a second, click the digits to the right of Seconds, and type in a new number. Transitions can be added between still images and video clips.

To view your project so far, including the new image, click the black "Film" area surrounding the frames, and click the Play Project button. The project will render, then play back.

Saving the Project

Let's save our project. Do this from time to time so that your work won't inadvertently be lost because of computer trouble.

1. Click the Finish button at the upper right of the screen and choose the Save Project button at the upper left (Figure 6.25).

2. Or click the Save icon below the preview screen.

Figure 6.25
Saving a VideoStudio
project.

This action does not render your movie or create a file you can play on your VCR. It merely saves your VideoStudio project so that, if your computer crashes, you won't lose your work.

Adding a Color Background

Let's add a blank color frame and then add some text over the simple color backdrop. You can add text over video if you wish, but video footage, with its changing colors, does not make the best backdrop for text.

1. Click the Storyboard menu option at the top of the screen.
2. Click the Library drop down menu at the upper right.
3. Choose Color, and, when the Color panels appear in the Library,
4. Drag the medium blue panel to the available storyboard frame at the lower right (see Figure 6.26). The color panel's RGB values (Red, Green, and Blue) are displayed beneath each. The panel we want reads 68, 108, 145.

CHAPTER 6

Like images, the color frame displays for three seconds. While the color frame is selected (framed in red), you can use the option controls on the left side of the screen to alter display time and other settings. We'll be using the color frame as a text backdrop. Next, we'll drag a text message from VideoStudio's Text Library to the color frame. VideoStudio's preset text messages (called Titles) have preset duration and animation paths. These can be altered if need be.

Figure 6.26
Adding a color frame to the project.

Adding Text to Your Project

To add text to this color frame, you'll first place the text on the big "T" layer of the timeline. Then the text animation can be positioned right under the color frames, so that they'll display simultaneously.

The color frame we added for this text backdrop can be seen by dragging the slider at the bottom of the screen all the way to the right. However, because you did not "play" the project, but only scrolled to that end point, your editing will still occur at the beginning of the project. We'll move the edit point forward momentarily.

When you click Title, VideoStudio displays Title presets in the library. Note that you can also use the text tools that appear on the left to create your own message from scratch. You can type your own message, choosing font, font color, font style, and animation path.

For this exercise, we'll be using a preset text animation that moves from top to bottom, a simple "Thank You." You'll want to drag the preset text to a specific location on the timeline (Figure 6.27).

Figure 6.27
Adding a simple text
animation to the project.

Here are the steps for adding text animation. In this example, we'll fast-forward near the end and drop in the "Thank You." Note, however, that you can drop in the animated text anywhere you like along the timeline. It doesn't have to be at the end.

1. Click the Title menu option at the top of the screen. VideoStudio will change to Timeline mode.

2. Click the End button on the control panel. You've now changed the playback point to the very end of the project, and the text can be dropped in there.

3. Locate the "Thank You" title and drag it onto the Text layer of the timeline (indicated by a large "T") beneath the color frame.

4. Click the Library drop-down menu arrow at the upper right of the screen (it now reads "Title"), and choose Animation. You'll see a selection of VideoStudio's preset animations. Note the actions of the animation squares. They represent the animation style you'll be applying to your text. By clicking one, it will be applied to the title you just added to the timeline.

5. Upon playback, note that the preset text is yellow and the backdrop is blue. The text is quite legible.

Adding Sound Files

To add a voice or sound file to your project, you'll access the Voice layer of the timeline. You can drag audio files right onto the layer or record a voice-over from any point you wish.

To begin, click the Audio menu option at the top of the screen and choose Voiceover or Music. The project view will change to timeline. Dragging the scroll bar at the bottom of the screen does not fast-forward the playback point, it merely changes your view of the frames.

To drag in a sound or to begin recording somewhere in the middle of the video, you'll have to actually play the video to that point or change the playback point (Figure 6.28). Here's one way to accomplish this:

1. Type a minutes and seconds number into the green-numbered digital display at the bottom of the preview screen. (Just click inside the counter area and type a new number.)

2. Then, drag the thin Location Indicator bar to the exact point at which recording should begin, or just drag in a sound from the library to that exact point.

Figure 6.28
Playing back from a
precise clip location.

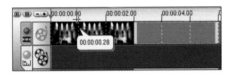

Working with Sound Files

You can record audio into your computer via a microphone. You can also drag audio files onto the timeline and adjust the audio file's playback start time by dragging the file to the left or right. Dragging the file to the right moves the start time forward. Dragging left moves the start time closer to the beginning of the video. Take care to click somewhere near the middle of the audio file and begin dragging, or else you'll change the file length rather than move it. Here are some tips for working with audio files:

▶ To play back your project from audio file start point, click the file, then press the Play button.

▶ To trim an audio file from its ending, click the audio file and drag inward from the right. The audio file shortens by truncating its ending. To trim an audio file's beginning, drag inward from the left.

NOTE
When you adjust audio file length, you do not alter the original audio file, only its usage in this project.

▶ You can adjust an audio file's overall volume by clicking the audio file as it appears in the timeline and then clicking the down-facing arrow that reads "100" on the left of the screen. Use the slider to move the volume up or down.

▶ To fade an audio file In or Out, while the file is selected, click the Fade In or Fade Out buttons in the Audio Options panel. The Fade buttons turn green when turned on. To activate your fade, click Apply. Please note that you cannot adjust Fade amounts.

Recording Voice-over

Voice-over is recorded on the audio track. Here's how it's done:

1. Plug a microphone into your sound card's microphone input.

2. In VideoStudio, click the Record button, at the upper left (make sure Audio > Voice is selected in the menu options at the top of the screen). A meter will appear for measuring your microphone input levels (Figure 6.29).

Figure 6.29
The VideoStudio microphone input meter.

3. VideoStudio does not offer microphone volume controls. Use your sound card's Line In and Mic In controls to adjust input levels. Set the input volume so that your normal speaking voice pushes VideoStudio's meter into the upper green, but not into the red. This is a good level that will give you plenty of volume without distortion.

4. When the meter is properly set, click OK. The record button at the upper left will glow red, indicating recording is taking place.

5. You need not record from the beginning of the project if you'd rather not. To begin recording later in the video, click the Rewind button and then drag the Location Indicator to where you'd like to record (or click inside the digital counter right below the preview window and type in an exact time).

6. To end recording, again click the Record button. The newly recorded track will appear in the Voice layer of the timeline. VideoStudio assigns it a name based on the entire project name. You cannot rename the recorded voice-over track.

7. You may drag the voice-over track to a new location along the Timeline by clicking in the track's center and dragging it right or left. Shorten the track from its beginning or ending by dragging inward from its left or right end.

Recording a CD Selection

To add music recorded from a CD, or to add another sound file that can play simultaneously with the voice-over track, do the following:

1. Click the Audio > Music menu option at the top of the screen. This activates the Music layer of the project's timeline.

2. After clicking the Music option, you can either drag an existing audio file from the library to the Music layer of the timeline or place a music CD in your computer's CD-ROM drive and record songs (click the Record button at the upper left). You can also record portions of songs.

3. Tracks you record can be moved, shortened, and faded in and out using the same tools as other audio tracks.

4. To preview your entire project so far, click the Play Project button.

NOTE

Like other VideoStudio project resources, recorded tracks will be added to the Library and can be used anywhere in the project just by dragging them to the storyboard or timeline.

TIP

You cannot drag an audio track from one timeline layer to another. If you want to play two audio tracks simultaneously, you must initially record them (or insert them) on different timeline layers. One must be on the Voice layer and the other on the Music layer.

Exporting Your Project

To output your movie—save it in a form that can be played back by others—click the Finish button, then click the Create Video Title button, in the upper left. If you click the film-roll icon, your video will be encoded with the same properties as your template. Choose the drop-down arrow beside the icon to select a different encoding template. Choose "custom" to specify all your own settings.

Cutting and Deleting Video Segments

As mentioned earlier, most basic video editing programs make it easy to adjust a video's In and Out points, but it's not at all obvious how to isolate and remove a video segment. I'll show you how to do this using Ulead VideoStudio.

Defining the First Cut Point

To mark the first cut point of your video segment, follow these steps:

1. First, insert a video clip onto the Preview Window, or the Storyboard/Timeline below.

2. Beneath the Preview Window are two scrolling bars. The top is the Trim Bar. The lower is the Preview Bar. Drag the Preview Bar forward to where you'd like to cut the video.

3. Click on Split Video (Figure 6.30). The movie clip will now be divided into two parts. You'll see the thick yellow boundary separating the parts.

Figure 6.30
Use this button to cut video segments.

Defining the Second Cut Point

Now we have to isolate the area to be deleted. This is done by cutting the second clip at the point where the "good" section begins.

1. Click inside the second video section. Locate the end of the point you want to remove (the end of the "bad" segment) by pressing the Shift key and clicking the Play button. Stop playing at the approximate point where the end occurs.

2. Zero in on the exact point by using the Previous and Next buttons on the Control panel.

3. Click the Cut button. You'll now have three video clips, and the middle clip is the one you want to delete.

Deleting the Clip Segment

The clip on the left and the clip on the right are the "good stuff." The middle clip is the data to be eliminated.

1. Locate the middle segment (the one to be eliminated) by clicking on it.

2. Right-click on the middle clip and choose Delete from the shortcut menu that appears (Figure 6.31).

Figure 6.31
Delete the middle segment, between the two thick yellow lines.

The unwanted segment will be gone.

A Step Further

Here are some tasks to master after you've saved your first project.

Zooming in on a Few Frames

Close edits require viewing a handful of frames at a time. For example, a song should start exactly when a particular on-screen event occurs. To facilitate this requires zooming. Zooming is also essential for cutting and trimming precisely. You'll be in total control over what your audience sees and hears.

Setting Preview Render Quality

If your video editor allows you to, locate and set Preview Render Quality for the highest speed and lowest quality. For your mid-project previews, when you are simply checking transitions, text visibility, and soundtrack volume, for example, you don't need a high-quality preview. Depending on the number of transitions, rotating objects, and special effects, rendering a high-quality preview could require one minute of rendering for each second of video. Choose low-quality rendering, unless you are specifically looking for visual quality.

CAUTION

When previewing a video, make sure you know whether you are previewing a video clip, a project, or a project portion. The preview screen is probably the same for both.

Editing Transition Speed

You'll also be spending time finessing transitions between video clips. At times, you'll switch to a new clip using a fast, barely perceptible special effect. At other times, you may want a dreamy, gradual fade. You'll be editing transition length using time markers, overlap indicators, or some sort of preference selection.

Setting Video Editor Preferences

A good video editor lets you set preferences. These may include preview window size, default save format, sound preview quality, and, most importantly, preview render quality.

NOTE

You probably don't need to change your video editor's default preferences until you've learned your way around the program a little bit. Most basic video editors walk you through your first few projects without requiring adjustments. After a little experience, you'll have a better understanding of the preferences you are adjusting.

CHAPTER 6

The Endgame

Now, to finish off your project, I'll show you how to create scrolling credits and end your feature with a quick "exit" effect.

Scrolling Credits

To end your movie with scrolling credits, you must create several frames of animated text and type a list of all the people you want to thank. Here's how it's done:

1. Create a color frame at the very end of your project, and extend the time for as long as you think your credits will require for display.

2. Then click Title at the top of the screen. VideoStudio changes to timeline mode. Click the End button on the control panel to change the playback point to the very end of the project.

3. Click the "T" icon on the left side of the screen. A box for typing text will appear.

4. The Option area at the left of the screen changes to show text editing options. At the bottom, click the option that reads "Pause" or "Static" when you hold your mouse over it. A menu of text animation options appear (Figure 6.32).

Figure 6.32
Text animation options appear when the left lower icon in text mode is clicked.

5. Click the Animation tab, and you'll see two cubes, Start position and End position. Each cube has arrows that represent an animation direction. Clicking the center of the cube denotes no movement. If you want the animation to pause between its Start and End position trajectories, click the Pause drop-down menu and choose a pause length.

6. After choosing a font and font color and style, type your credits as you want them to appear. Press Shift+Enter when you get to the end of each line. Create as many lines as you wish, since these credits will scroll from top to bottom, moving below the screen as they pass.

7. When you are done typing, click the Add to Timeline button at the bottom right of the text options screen. The text animation will appear on the timeline, inserted at the playback point.

8. Position the text directly under the color field, so that the color acts as a backdrop for the text credits.

The speed of the credits will be affected by the clip length. A longer clip allows the credits to roll by more slowly. For faster credits, use a shorter duration. To adjust duration, click first on the text animation and play it back (press Shift and Play to start playback where the text starts), then double-click on it to adjust the duration using the Seconds digit display in the text options. Finally, set the color frames duration the same as the text. Do this by editing the digit display with the color frame selected.

Creating an End Effect

Rather than simply allowing your movie to end when the frames run out, you can end your movie by displaying credits or by having a transitional effect that sends the last frames into blackness. There's actually a trick to applying a transitional effect to the end of your movie. You see, most programs only let you insert transitional effects between two clips. You can't just tack on a transition at the end. There's nothing to transition to. To sidestep this problem, simply add a few seconds of blank color frames to the end of your movie (black or white) and insert a transition between the final clip and the color clip. The end color is simply to give the Transition something to transition *to*. The last thing the audience will really "see" is the transition to nothingness.

NOTE

DIRECTOR'S CHECKLIST

When you're finished editing your movie, sequencing everything just the way you want it, you'll need a way to know that all is really as it should be. Render your movie one last time, and take special note of the following:

Good Source Footage: Are segments of your video too dark or too bright? Is action obscured or out of focus? Before combining footage into a project, clean up those clips or choose different clips later in the tape that don't have the same problems. Start with only the good stuff and build from there.

Transition Length: You've probably added transitions between your video clips. Are they a good length? Too long or short? Is the audience perhaps thinking, "All right already. Get on with it!"?

Voiceover/Music Volume: If you have a narrative track and songs, can the narration be heard clearly above the music?

Text Legibility: Displaying text against a video background is tricky because the background changes. An area of your screen that is dark one second may be light the next. What color text should you choose? Can you position your video in an area that changes minimally? Or, should you momentarily stop the video and display your text message against a solid color background, then return to the show? Text legibility and clarity are worth pausing the show for a few frames. Also, consider using drop-shadows and outlines to make your text "pop."

In and Out Points: Do your video clips only show what's necessary? Can you get rid of a little bit of the intro or exit a little sooner? Viewers will appreciate your taking the time to show only the best bits. Your video tape is surely full of great moments. Don't be afraid to ruthlessly cut to the chase and show only those.

Production Length: Is your show getting a little long? The mind can only absorb what the seat can endure. Also, if your project is destined for the Web or e-mail, small file size is a must. Ultimate file size of your project will be a mystery until you render at your final quality. However, you'll find that economy is always a good policy.

Crossroads

Now that you've learned basic video editing, in Chapter 7, you'll advance those skills and learn techniques that, until recently, were only available to video professionals. After working through this next chapter, you'll be amazed at what you can do.

7

Going Further with Your Video

In this chapter, we'll look at video software that can resize and rotate your video right on the screen, display two video clips simultaneously, and blend one clip with another. You'll learn how to insert video clip segments onto a timeline with exact precision, changing one clip to the next on an exact musical beat, for example. We'll explore creating and editing audio tracks, including changing volume levels, fading one audio clip into another, and adding audio special effects. We'll also look at video filters, which, among other things, can change your video's color value and add textures and lighting effects.

Most of the advanced work in this chapter will be done with Ulead MediaStudio Pro 6.5. MediaStudio Pro is a very powerful professional video editing tool that can be downloaded as trialware. Visit **www.ulead.com** or **www.hotfiles.com** to download it.

Advanced Editing and Ulead MediaStudio Pro

In MediaStudio Pro, up to ninety-nine video tracks can be added to a project; it handles multiple audio tracks as well. You can apply dozens of professional editing tools such as Alpha Matte for selectively blending videos and advanced audio editing support.

Let's explore the interface for MediaStudio Pro and create a new project. We'll add two video tracks and cross-fade additional audio tracks. We'll shorten and lengthen video tracks, adjusting a track length so that it will fit exactly in between two other video clips in an allotted time slot. We'll also take a deeper look at keyframes and learn how to move a video track around the screen along a motion path, as well as how to display two video tracks simultaneously. We'll end the chapter with a quick glance at video filters.

Before we discuss the common tasks and features of this class of video editor, let's consider some reasons users may need them:

▶ **Accommodate Larger Videos**. The video editors we reviewed earlier are not cut out to handle more than ten minutes or so of video. Nor can they deal neatly with the dozens of editing In and Out points that a larger project may require.

▶ **Multi-track Capability**. All but the most basic video projects will require working with several video tracks, the ability to layer more than two at once, and the ability to cross-fade multiple audio tracks.

▶ **Advanced Video Tools**. Color correction tools, masking, matte, and chroma key tools are examples of some features you'll only find in semi-professional and professional video programs. Also, the ability to freeze frames, stretch and shrink tracks, and alter track speed are very important.

▶ **Advanced Audio Tools**. Quite frequently, you'll want to add multiple audio tracks, correct their volume and equalization, and add believable audio special effects such as reverb, chorus, and delay. These tools are usually not available in basic video editing programs.

▶ **Advanced Track Zooming Capability**. Working on a timeline with advanced zooming lets you zoom close enough to view a single frame at a time, making cuts exactly where you want them, across several video and audio frames at once, and then zoom out far enough to view your entire video clip from beginning to end on a single timeline.

▶ **Advanced Video Export Options**. A video that must meet exact formatting requirements for broadcast will sometimes need advanced saving options that are not found in entry-level video editors.

THE MEDIASTUDIO PRO INTERFACE

MediaStudio Pro is a suite of applications, including Video Editor, the application in which we'll spend most of our time. All of your video composition work—cutting and pasting video and so forth—happens in Video Editor.

Out of the box, the MediaStudio Pro interface will look similar to the screen shot below.

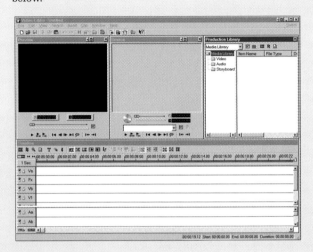

The MediaStudio Pro opening screen.

The opening screen features four windows:

▶ The Timeline, at the bottom, for adding videos, images, and audio files, and organizing their playback as you see fit.

▶ The Source Panel, for previewing and cutting video before you add it to the Timeline.

▶ The Preview Window, for viewing your work in progress.

▶ The Production Library, for accessing videos, music clips, transitions, and other media for your projects.

The MediaStudio Pro interface is very flexible. The windows within MediaStudio Pro can be resized and rearranged to match the way you like to work. As we work with the program in this book, you'll notice that the interface of my MediaStudio Pro screen shots varies somewhat from the program's out-of-the box appearance. I've rearranged the interface in order to show as much of the program's functionality as possible in my illustrations. Your interface will most likely not be identical to mine, but the functionality will be the same.

Creating a New MediaStudio Project

To begin a project with MediaStudio Pro 6, choose File > New and select a type of project from the list, based on the settings you want for your final movie.

The main MediaStudio screen is divided into rows. Video tracks are placed in the top rows, audio tracks in the bottom. Import a digital video, and both video and audio tracks will be inserted. The two track areas labeled Va and Vb are where the main video clips are inserted (see Figure 7.1—the Va and Vb tracks are highlighted).

Figure 7.1

The Ulead MediaStudio Pro 6 workspace, with video clips on Va and Vb.

Video edits usually flow from track A to track B. Video transitions are sometimes referred to as "A/B rolls," in that the contents of track A will roll into track B. For example, if you have a clip of a bridge on track A, and a clip of a butterfly on track B, the track A contents will play first. Specify the amount of overlap between track A and track B by dragging track B towards the left, so that it begins playing before track A finishes. Then, use a transition effect to blend track A and B for the amount of time that they are overlapping.

Other tracks—those tracks below track B—can be used as overlays, or incidental video material that moves in and out of the main production. In MediaStudio Pro, you can add tracks, so it's easy to pop in movie clips any place you like, while tracks A and B are used for the main video clips.

Adding Media to Your Project

To add video clips to the project, choose Insert > Video File, or drag a video from the Production Library, an Explorer-like interface at the bottom left of the screen (Figure 7.2). Click on the track you want to add the video to. Track Va is usually the first main track of any production. The audio clip will automatically appear on the corresponding audio layer as well.

Figure 7.2
To add a clip to a project, drag it from the Production Library to a track on the timeline.

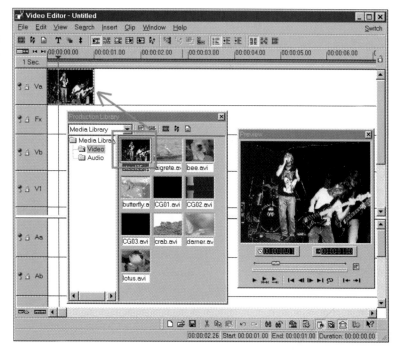

TIP

To see video displayed as frames, like the examples in this book, click the Display Mode icon at the upper left and choose Filmstrip Mode > 80×60.

By default, two seconds of video will appear on the screen. To view more of your clip (if it is more than two seconds long), drag the scroll bar at the bottom of the screen to the right. In Figure 7.3, the playback locator is positioned at the five-second point. (Figure 7.3 displays the audio track, too.) To learn how long your clip is, as well as its audio and video properties, choose View > Clip Properties.

Figure 7.3
The seconds indicator on the left specifies how many video frames will currently fit onto your screen.

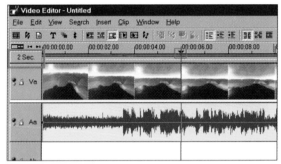

Still images and audio files are added to the timeline in the same manner.

To play back the video clip, press the Play button on the VCR-like control panel that appears beneath the preview window. Playback will initially be slow, because the clip is being rendered by MediaStudio. However, future playback will be faster, because the Smart Render feature only re-renders changes you made, not the entire clip again. For a quick but somewhat rough playback, click the drop-down arrow on the Preview button and choose Instant Preview. After rendering, playback begins automatically. To stop playback, click on the clip.

NOTE
You will not hear the track audio until the track has finished rendering. To render the clip, click the Play button on the Preview screen.

Zooming in on the Tracks

To view individual frames of your video more closely and, thus, perform more exact edits, click the Zoom tool at the top of the screen and click on the portion of the video you want to see more closely. Click repeatedly to continue moving in closer. To back up from this view, press the minus sign on the keyboard. To back up and see the entire video from end to end as it appears in the video track, click the menu that reads 2 seconds at the upper left of the screen, and click the Fit in Window option (Figure 7.4).

Figure 7.4
Choose Fit in Window to view your entire clip from beginning to end.

As you change your view of the clip, watch the Seconds ruler at the top of the screen and see how its scale changes to accommodate your view. If you have zoomed down to view a very few frames, the Seconds ruler will show each tiny fraction of a second. If you are taking a longer view, each marker on the Seconds ruler will represent multiple seconds.

The Clip Selector

When you click on a video with your mouse, you are using the Clip Selector tool. It is used to move clips along the timeline or drag them to new tracks. The Clip Selector (Figure 7.5) is also used to change the length of clips (Figure 7.6).

Figure 7.5
The Clip Selector tool is used to select, move, and resize video clips.

Figure 7.6
When positioned at the edge of a clip, the Clip Selector changes to a Resize tool.

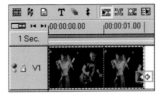

▶ Dragging inward on a clip from its ending removes a portion of the ending, shortening it.

▶ Dragging outward on a clip will have no effect unless you've previously shortened it. Then, dragging outward will restore a portion of the shortened clip.

▶ Dragging inward on a clip from the beginning shortens the clip from the beginning.

▶ Dragging outward towards the beginning after shortening will restore some of the clip length.

Previewing a Project Portion

If you make a change and only want to view that specific edit, MediaStudio 6 allows you to render and play back only a small segment of your project, if you wish. This lets you work closely with one segment of your video without having to continually render the entire project.

To select a portion of a video, do the following:

1. Hold the Clip Selector tool over the bar beneath the Seconds ruler at the top of the screen, until a tiny film icon appears (Figure 7.7).

Figure 7.7
When positioned "just so," the Selector tool changes to a film icon. Drag along the timeline to specify a playback segment.

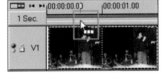

2. Click and drag from that point, forwards or backwards. Dragging selects video for playback, and the bar where you drag becomes blue.

3. To complete the selection, stop dragging the mouse cursor.

4. To play back only the selected area, click the second icon from the left on the Preview window (a tooltip appears: "Play the Preview Range").

Working with Project Cues

MediaStudio lets you mark the track with video cues. After setting a cue, you can click a button and go straight to that portion of video. Cues can be named, allowing you to later view a list of your marked cues, know what each cue represents to you, and fast forward there instantly. You may set as many cues as you like. To set a cue, hover the mouse cursor over the top of the video frame until a small round icon appears. Click once, and a tiny blue mark appears. That is your cue (Figure 7.8).

Figure 7.8
A cue appears as a tiny blue icon at the top of the timeline.

You should use cues to mark key transitions in your video. What's more, when you insert other video or audio clips, you can Snap To a cue. If you have the Snap feature turned on (Edit > Snap) and you place a clip on a new track near one of your cues, the video or audio track will snap into place exactly at that cue. This makes synchronizing music and video clips very easy.

In MediaStudio Pro, a segment with a cue at its beginning is called a Clip. You can use the Find Clip feature to look at a list of all your clips and jump to them instantly. These features are very important when you are editing a long project with many transitions.

The Scissors Tool

The Scissors Tool, at the top of the screen, simply cuts video (Figure 7.9). Click it on the video clip, and the clip will be cut in two at the point where you clicked. Each segment can be moved freely using the Clip Selector tool and dragged to a new track. For example, you can drag the second clip to the Vb track and insert a transition in between the two track segments to gradually fade (roll) from Video A to Video B. Unlike entry-level video editors, MediaStudio Pro lets you visually position each track and see the exact overlap amount for each video clip on the timeline.

Figure 7.9
Use the Scissors tool to slice a video clip where you click it.

Adding a Track to Your Project

Here's how to make a new layer (V4, V5, etc.) to place a clip on:

1. Choose File > Project Settings and click the Edit button.

2. When the Project Options dialog box appears, on the Video Editor tab, you'll see an Overlay Track option. The digit next to it indicates how many Overlay tracks (V1, V2, and so forth) you have available.

3. Indicate the number of tracks you want to have in your project by typing in a digit.

Let's talk briefly about transitions before moving on to audio/video editing and Moving Paths.

Adding a Transition

MediaStudio Pro has many preset transitions. Transition duration is set by specifying track overlap amounts on the timeline. When you create a transition in MediaStudio, a track is placed on Va and on Vb. The transition itself is dragged from the Production Library to the FX track, positioned right between Va and Vb.

NOTE

You can create transitions that start from Vb and end at Va, but you cannot use numbered tracks (V1, V2, and so forth) in transitions. Those are overlay tracks. Overlay tracks are extra tracks you can use to bring material in and out of your main movie. They can also be used for special effects.

I'll leave it to you to explore the dozens of transitions MediaStudio provides in the Production Library. We'll work with a simple transition that fades from Va to Vb. I'll show you how, by not overlapping Va and Vb, you can allow a quick "fade to black" between tracks, which looks very natural and film-like. Here's how to make a simple transition in MediaStudio Pro:

1. Place video clips on tracks Va and Vb. They should overlap for the amount of time you want the transition to occur (Figure 7.10). For example, if you want the transition to last a full second, have them overlap for a second.

Figure 7.10

Two overlapped video clips, with the Effects track between them.

2. Click the drop-down menu on the left side of the Production Library and choose Transition Effects.

3. Click the F/X folder, and when the animated icons for the Transitions appear on the right side of the Production Library, click and drag the Crossfade Transition icon onto the Fx track, between Va and Vb.

4. Position the Crossfade transition where the Va and Vb clips overlap (Figure 7.11). Drag in or out on the edges of the transition to resize it. The transition can be reduced or expanded to fill any time slot you wish.

Figure 7.11

Place the desired transition effect on the Fx track, positioned between the two videos.

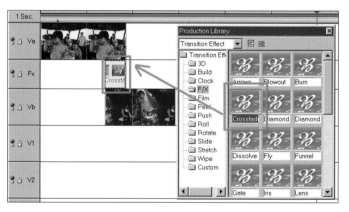

TIP

To allow a "fade to black" in which the screen goes momentarily completely black in between the video clips, reposition the video clips to avoid overlapping. The length of the transition will be unaffected by this. The moment of black will last as long as the gap between the video clips.

Adding multiple transitions between several clips on Va and Vb tracks can be easily accomplished with the aid of the program's Copy and Paste features.

Adding Audio Clips

MediaStudio Pro can incorporate audio files such as WAV, MP3, or AIF files, as well as audio segments of movie clips like QuickTime or AVI files. Keep in mind that your digital video tracks already have an audio track, and you may want to edit or apply filters to this existing track or replace or supplement it with other audio sources. Audio layers are positioned on the lower half of the MediaStudio Pro screen, in the tracks labeled A1, A2, and so forth. You may place an audio file on any track you wish.

To add an audio file, do the following:

1. Click the audio track you want to add a file to and choose Insert > Audio File. You can also choose a clip from the Production Library. Browse to the file you want to open and choose OK.

2. Then, click the track you want to add the file to. The audio file will be positioned there. If the audio file is quite long, you may not see its entire length, depending on your zoom amount and screen resolution and width.

3. Drag the audio clip anywhere along the track. Where you place the clip's left border determines when the clip begins playing back. Position the clip at the two-second mark and the audio will not begin playing back until two seconds into the video project playback.

The waveform peaks and valleys you see on the audio clip represent high and low volume levels in the clip. They are your visual cues for silences, kick drum beats, loud noises, and so forth. Audio clips can be shortened like video clips. This process does not change the pitch, but only truncates the clip length. Drag on a previously trimmed audio clip and its length will be restored.

The thin line running through the middle of each audio track displays that track's volume level (Figure 7.12). To change the volume of a track at a certain point, start by holding your mouse cursor over the line. When the cursor changes to a pointing finger, drag the line up or down at that point; the track volume will increase or decrease accordingly.

Figure 7.12
To adjust an audio track's loudness, drag on its volume line.

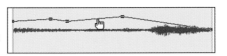

To increase or decrease an entire clip's volume, drag on the volume line at the very beginning of the clip, then drag the end volume to match your new beginning volume setting.

CHAPTER 7

Audio Crossfading

Crossfading occurs when you have two overlapping segments of audio and one fades out while the other fades in. MediaStudio sets crossfading automatically using the Crossfade tool (Figure 7.13). Click two overlapping audio tracks with the Crossfade tool, and the volume of the audio track that has been playing will decrease to zero, beginning its descent just as the second audio clip is introduced. Also, with the same click, the second audio track will begin playback at zero and reach full volume just as the first clip ends.

Figure 7.13
The Crossfade tool fades in one audio clip as the other fades out.

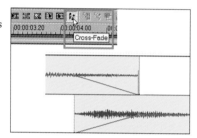

Later in this chapter, we'll look at MediaStudio Pro's standalone audio editing and recording program, called Audio Editor.

Moving Paths and Video Compositions

Moving Paths let you move video clips around the screen. A Moving Path is comprised of the points all around the screen that your video clip touches as it moves. Of course, the video clip would have to be smaller than the screen, so Moving Paths are used with clips that are reduced in size. And, of course, you'd have to create some sort of background that would stretch across the entire length and width of the screen. This background is the backdrop for your moving clips.

Thus, Moving Paths transform your video project into a canvas, and each video clip is a layer moving around that canvas. Your project is now a video composition. Moving Paths allow you to display two video clips simultaneously, either adjacent or overlapping. You'll learn to create video overlays in which one video or still image becomes the backdrop or "canvas" and the other video clip is in the foreground.

Working with Moving Paths

A typical example of simple video overlay is a video of a newscaster in the foreground describing a video being played in the background. In our example, we'll reverse those roles somewhat. We'll create a small video of a narrator positioned in the upper right hand corner of another video. Both these videos will be stationary. They'll not be moving across the screen while playing back. Thus, MediaStudio Pro refers to this as a Still Moving Path. Figure 7.14 shows the preview of the two combined clips, which are both also shown on the Va and V1 track.

Figure 7.14

The clip on V1 is overlapping the clip on Va.

Overlay Track Setup

When creating video overlays, the video positioned on top of other videos must be on a numbered video timeline. That means your overlay video must be on V1, V2, and so forth, not Va or Vb. The video on the bottom can be placed in Va or Vb. When creating multiple video layers (as we will do when we put a drop shadow behind a video overlay), the smaller-number timelines are the videos nearer the surface. For example, a drop shadow behind a video would be placed on V2, while the video itself would be placed on V1. The background video or image for the whole project would be placed on Va or Vb.

TIP

When creating video compositions involving several video layers, think of the lowest layer as your canvas. It can be a full-sized video, color frame, or still image. The other videos moving around the screen are not full-sized.

Creating a Video Composition

Let's create our first video composition:

1. To begin, place a background video on Va or Vb. Make this video something simple without bright colors or lots of movement.

2. Next, place the video overlay video on V1. You now have two videos, each on a timeline. One on Va, the other on V1. In my example, I chose a woman narrator, and the orientation of her video segment is actually quite narrow. In Figure 7.14, you can tell how misshapen it is by its appearance in the timeline, which forces the wider, full-screen orientation. However, we can use the Moving Path feature to restore the narrow width of this video, as we position it against the full-size

backdrop video. Using the Moving Path tool, the video on V1 will be reduced in size and repositioned. We won't be actually moving the video around the screen, so we'll not need to add or manipulate keyframes. We'll be adding a Basic 2D moving path to our video.

3. To open the Moving Path dialog box for the V1 (overlay) video clip, choose Moving Path from the drop-down menu on the left side of the Production Library. An Explorer-like menu of many Moving Path types will appear.

4. Click the 2D Basic folder and, on the right side, several moving path examples will appear. They're all fancy, and we don't need them. We want a simple "resize and reposition" tool.

5. Drag the 2D Motion icon (farthest to the left, up near the top in the 2D Basic folder) to the video clip on V1 (Figure 7.15). After you drag the icon to the video clip, the 2D Basic Moving Path dialog box appears (Figure 7.16). The left side of the dialog box displays Motion Control options, and the right side is the Preview area.

6. Type in new coordinates for your video clip's position, or just drag the small red box to a new location (the red box indicates your video clip's location). The adjustments you make on the left influence what you see on the right and what you see in your video.

Figure 7.15
To resize and reposition a video in a composition, drag the 2D Basic Moving Path to it.

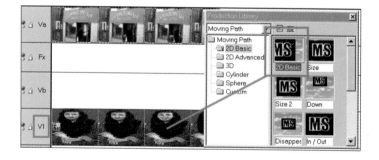

Figure 7.16
The Moving Path dialog box shows parameters for moving and resizing a video clip.

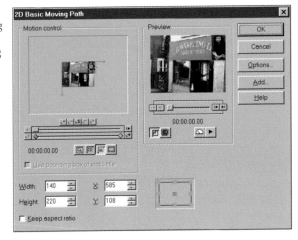

7.   After changing the video clip's location, click the Play button on the Preview area to play back your edited video.

Below, we'll take a closer look at what we accomplished.

Editing Clip Size and Position in a Composition

In this simple application of a Moving Path, you'll be positioning the size and position using the S (for Start) icon, and then setting up the same parameters after clicking the E (Ending) icon. If you wanted the video to end up somewhere else, or, for example, you wanted to shrink the video into nothingness, you'd set up different parameters after clicking the E icon. Let's make the preview more useful in this dialog box and adjust our video position and size. We'll make this video overlay very small and position it in the upper right corner of the screen.

1.   Click the True Preview button, the third button from the left of the four buttons appearing on the Motion Control side of the dialog box. You'll then see the video contents change as a result of your edits, rather than a black color square. Also, click the Layer button, the first button on the left beneath the Preview screen.

2.   Click the diamond-shaped icon at the far left of the screen (Figure 7.17), on the Motion Control side. The diamond appears red when selected. This is the opening Keyframe, and parameters you set now will apply to the video when it begins playback. You'll also notice that the "S" shown in the Motion Control screen also turns red, indicating you'll be manipulating the video's starting point.

Figure 7.17
To specify a video's size and position at its beginning, click the Keyframe icon on the left.

CHAPTER 7

3. Making sure the far-left diamond-shape is selected (red), in the Width and Height fields (Figure 7.18) of the Motion Control side of the dialog box, type 140 Width and 240 Height. The Keep Aspect Ratio option should not be checked, because we do want to change the dimensions of this video, not just resize it.

Figure 7.18
Change a clip's size and position using these parameter fields.

4. In the X and Y fields, type 585 and 108. This positions the video overlay up and to the right of the screen. Now since you've set these parameters while the Keyframe (the red diamond) at the far left (the starting Keyframe) is selected, what you've done is specify how the video should appear when it first begins playback. What we need to do now is set up the same parameters for when the video ends. When both your starting and ending points have the same parameters, you essentially tell the video to stay still, and not grow or shrink. If you set up the ending points with different parameters, the video would gradually change over time, until, by the time the ending is reached, the video would be of the size and in the position dictated by those parameters. First, we'll select the ending Keyframe, then type in the same parameters we used at the beginning Keyframe.

5. Click the diamond shape at the far right, under the Motion Control screen. It will turn red. Also, the E in the Motion Control box will turn red (Figure 7.19).

Figure 7.19
Click the Keyframe at the right to set the clip's ending parameters.

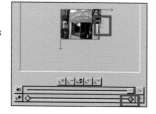

6. Type 140 in the Width and 240 in the Height fields.

7. Type 585 in the X and 108 in the Y fields. The video now has the same starting and ending parameters.

Adding New Paths with Keyframes

If you wanted the video to be somewhere else in mid-playback—or perhaps grow, then shrink again—you'd add a Keyframe in the middle of the video, then type new parameters into the Width/Height and X/Y fields. To add a Keyframe anywhere along the playback path, do the following:

1. On the left side of the dialog box, under the Motion Control screen, drag the playback bar to where you want to add a Keyframe. Dragging the playback bar to the right advances the video toward its end.

2. After dragging, click the plus sign icon with the tiny blue arrow on it, right above the playback bar. This adds a Keyframe. As you add it, it will be red, indicating it is selected.

3. When you add a Keyframe, a new tiny red rectangle appears in the Motion Control area, between the Start and End icons (Figure 7.20. In this figure, I made the narrator larger, so you can see how I could reposition her after making the new Keyframe). Drag that red rectangle to where you'd like the video to be when the video rolls by and hits that Keyframe. The video will move down to that Keyframe location before moving on to the End Keyframe location.

Figure 7.20
To create a new Keyframe, click the plus sign with the blue arrow tip.

4. You can also use the Width/Height and X/Y fields to specify size and location for this keyframe.

5. Using this same procedure, add as many keyframes as you like.

TIP
Remember, keyframes are only necessary when you change a video's direction as it moves along its path from beginning to end or if you want to alter its size at some point during playback.

After adding and setting parameters for your keyframes, press the Play button on the right side of the dialog box. You'll see your video and Keyframe settings in action.

After choosing Moving Path settings, click OK to close the dialog box, and then preview your movie. It will have to be rendered first, so click Play, and be patient while the movie renders. Then click Play again, and a rendered, smooth playback will begin.

Two Floating Movies and a Backdrop

Now let's take that first movie (the movie used as a backdrop), make it smaller, and place it at the lower left corner of the screen. We'll also place a still picture behind these two videos. That still picture will become our backdrop. We'll leave the video in the upper right hand corner where it is (Figure 7.21). This exercise is your key to making videos shrink and grow and move on your screen, creating dynamic video compositions.

Figure 7.21
The image on Va is the backdrop, while the two overlap videos on V1 and V2 move around the composition area.

Since the second video is now going to become an overlay (it will not be a backdrop video anymore), we need to move it to V2. Here's what to do:

1. Click on the first movie we added and drag the entire clip down to the V2 timeline.

2. Now let's add a still image to the project. We'll insert it on the Va timeline and drag it so that its length matches that of the existing videos. Click the Va timeline, which should now be empty, and choose Insert > Image File.

3. Browse to any image you want to use for this project. Since the image is a backdrop, choose something without mutli-color detail.

4. Once the image appears on the timeline, use the Image Selector tool to drag from the right end of the picture towards the right, making the length of the image clip the same as the videos.

When played back, the image display time will now match the video length.

Resizing the Second Video Clip

In order to appreciate the three-layered effect of these overlays, we need to make that second video clip smaller, which will allow the backdrop to show through.

1. Click the Production Library drop-down list, locate the Moving Path folder, and, when the Moving Path icons appear in the right side of the Production Library, drag the 2D Basic icon to the V2 timeline. The Moving Path dialog box will open.

2. Make sure the Start Keyframe is selected, then set the clip dimensions to Width 380 and Height 340.

3. Set the clip position to X 194 and Y 310 (Figure 7.22).

Figure 7.22
The size and motion parameters for the larger overlapping video clip.

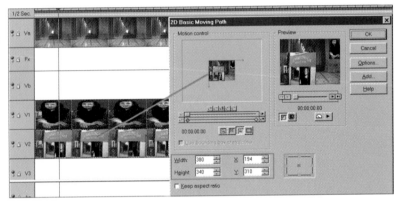

4. The clip will appear at the lower left of the screen and will fill a bit more than a third of the entire project area.

5. Repeat these same settings for the Ending Keyframe.

6. Click OK, and then click Play to render the movie.

7. When the movie is finished rendering, click Play again to play it back. You'll see the backdrop image behind the video clips, with one clip playing in the upper right and the other clip playing in the lower left.

8. You can make the video clips change position and move about the screen by going back into the Keyframe settings. Just make the start and ending parameters different and introduce a Keyframe with a new setting somewhere in the middle of the clip.

MediaStudio Audio Editor

As mentioned above, you can't open the Video Editor and start editing audio. Rather, when you install MediaStudio Pro, a separate program called Audio Editor is installed as well. You'll start this program by going to the Start Menu and clicking its icon, just like any other program. Note that Video Editor does not let you record directly in the program. To record live music or your own voice using a microphone, you will use Audio Editor.

Sounds are easily edited in Audio Editor. Since the program is dedicated to recording and editing a single track at a time, you've got plenty of room to zoom in closely and extract precise segments or apply special effects to those portions that need tweaking.

Recording with Audio Editor

Open the application by clicking Audio Editor in the MediaStudio Pro program group, in the Windows > Start menu. With Audio Editor, you can plug in a microphone or other input source and record directly onto hard disk. You may save your sound only as a WAV file (the standard Windows sound file type, WAVs are usually large) or as MPEG audio (smaller, especially customizable for Web playback). Sounds recorded in Ulead Sound Editor can of course be used for MediaStudio video projects. Figure 7.23 shows the Audio Editor interface with a sound already recorded.

Figure 7.23
Audio Editor's
workspace.

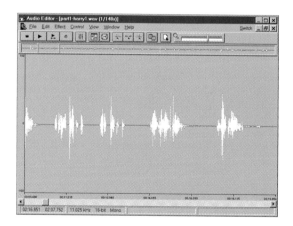

To record in Sound Editor, do the following:

1.   Make sure your sound source is plugged in and operative. Audio Editor does not provide a microphone or instrument interface. All inputs and recording capacity depend on your sound card. Audio Editor simply provides the recording interface, various views of the resulting sound wave, and editing and special effects tools.

2.   With your microphone or sound source at the ready, click the big red Record button on the Audio Editor interface. A Record meter will appear for adjusting input levels. As with all audio devices, you want a good high level without going "into the red."

3.   As you record, your sound wave will appear on the screen, indicating the volume fluctuations of your performance.

4.   When you are done recording, the sound waveform will remain on the screen, ready for you to edit or save. Please note that if you close the program before saving the file, the sound will be lost.

To save your sound, choose File > Save As, noting the save folder and file type. This sound will be available to MediaStudio Video Editor for your projects. To the left of the Zoom slider is a Drag and Drop icon. After saving your file, drag this icon to another open application on your screen (such as MediaStudio Pro), and the audio track will appear there.

Editing with Audio Editor

After recording, the sound waveform fills the Audio Editor screen. At the center top is a Zoom Slider (Figure 7.24). To zoom in on the sound, drag the slider to the right. To zoom out, drag to the left. If the recorded sound wave exceeds what can be seen on the screen, drag the Wave Navigator right and left to view the entire recording.

To select a portion of the sound for editing or deletion, just click and drag the mouse across a portion of the sound wave. If you press the Delete key, the selection will be deleted. Choose Edit > Cut, and the section will be cut. You can paste it elsewhere in the sound or even into a different file.

As you play back your sound, use the Cue tool at the top of the screen to mark significant entry points on your track (see Figure 7.24). You can then use the Previous Cue and Next Cue buttons at the top of the screen to jump to your cues.

Click the Effect menu to apply a sound effect to your entire track or to the current selection. You'll have many sound effects to choose from. These effects include echo, pitch and speed alterations, and reversing and inverting sounds. You can also apply an Amplify effect to generally increase the volume of a sound.

When you copy or cut a sound to the clipboard, you can do more than simply click on another area of the sound and paste it there. Figure 7.25 displays a selected region with a pasting option applied to it. Audio Editor has many useful and creative pasting options, including the following:

▶ Choose Edit > Paste > Insert to insert the clipboard contents where you've clicked.

▶ Choose Edit > Paste > Replace to replace the entire selected area with the contents of the clipboard.

▶ Choose Edit > Paste > Mix to mix the sound you are pasting with the existing sound. A dialog box will appear prompting you to choose mix levels for both the already existing and pasted sound.

▶ Choose Edit > Paste > Fill to fill the entire selected area with the sound you are pasting. The sound will repeat as often as necessary to fill the space.

Figure 7.24
With Audio Editor, you can zoom in using a slider, create Cues, and navigate to any position in your clip.

Cue Tools   Zoom Slider

Wave Navigator

Figure 7.25
Audio Studio's Paste options displayed with a selected clip portion.

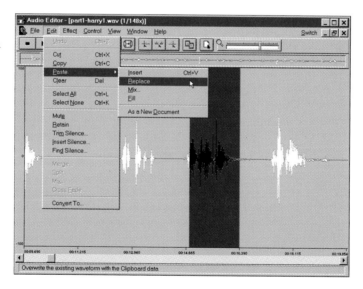

Tips and Tricks

Here are a few editing tricks that will help whip your project into shape. You'll learn about removing unwanted audio segments, adjusting video length to accommodate an audio track, and synchronizing audio and video clips precisely

Removing Audio Track Segments

Some audio clips may begin with "dead" space, a moment or two of silence before the sound begins. I'll show you how to remove that dead space so you can more precisely place the real starting point of the audio track. This should match up with an exact video frame. You'll find this necessary if you have a voice-over track that starts a little bit later than the visual and you need to trim off the empty lead-in.

Figure 7.26 shows an audio and a video track. They were recorded separately, but the audio got a bit of a late start. You can tell by the flat audio wave signal at the beginning. The voice kicks in a second or so later.

Figure 7.26
The blank space at the beginning of this audio track needs to be removed.

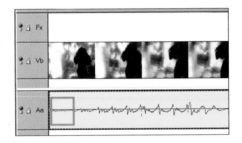

TIP

When micro-editing tracks, it's important to note the scale (in seconds) displayed above. Depending on your zoom setting, you could be viewing almost your entire video on the timeline, or only a handful of frames. Note the digits on the scale, which change every time you change the zoom. If the Seconds marker above a video segment you are looking at reads "0.00.00.03," for example, you are viewing a fraction of a second, and your zoom is very close. If the scale reads "10.03," your units of viewing are much larger, and you are probably viewing a few seconds of video at a time.

Your goal is to cut out the dead space before the audio starts, but not inadvertently remove part of the audio. You'll then want to scoot the audio so that it begins simultaneously with the beginning of the video. To perform this edit, zoom in very close.

1. Zoom in on the point at which the dead audio ends, and use the Cut tool to make a cut right at the end of the flat audio line, before the sound really starts (Figure 7.27).

Figure 7.27
Zoom in very close on the audio track's "dead" portion, and use the Scissors Tool to cut.

2. The dead audio portion is now a separate audio clip. Zoom out and click on the severed clip with the Video Selector tool.

3. Press the Delete key, and the clip will be gone (Figure 7.28).

Figure 7.28
After pressing the Delete key, the selected "dead" clip is gone.

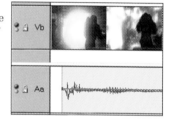

4. Using the Video Selector tool, click the remaining audio track and drag it to the left, where the video starts.

Adjusting Video Length

What if your video clip is a little short and, in order to synchronize it exactly with a particular audio segment or other video event, you need this clip to end a few frames later or a few frames earlier? Is there a way to adjust playback length so that the action stretches out or speeds up just a little bit, accommodating an exact synchronization? Yes, there is, and the answer is not simply to cut the video.

You can adjust a clip's playback speed and, thus, its duration (playing back a clip at a lower speed increases the time required to play it back). This is different from simply cutting a video clip, removing the end of the action. What I'm referring to is changing the speed of that action just slightly so that you have exact control over when it ends. Here's how it's done:

1. Line up the video and audio segments in question so that it is clear how much longer or shorter the video clip needs to be.

2. Click the video track to be adjusted with the Video Selector tool, and then right-click on it.

3. Choose Speed from the shortcut menu that appears.

4. Type a digit into the Speed field (Figure 7.29). The field currently reads 100, meaning that the track is now playing back at 100 % speed. Type a smaller digit to lengthen the track or a larger digit to shorten the track. A little goes a long way. A minor adjustment, bridging the difference of something like a half second, may only require an adjustment of one or two percent.

Figure 7.29
The Speed dialog box lets you adjust video clip length and frame speed.

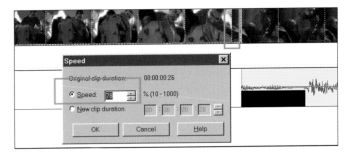

5. After you type in a new digit, click New Clip Duration. Click OK.

6. You'll notice the clip change length. To make the clip end exactly where you want it, you'll have to undo and repeat this process a few times.

You may find that no matter what percentage you type in, the clip is still a bit longer or shorter than you need. To fix this, you'll have to go back into the clip and add or remove some action. To add a little length, rewind the clip and find another segment you can isolate and stretch a little. To make a clip shorter, go back into the clip and find a few unimportant frames you can simply cut out.

A/V Synchronization

At times, you may want to position an audio clip to exactly match existing video. You could, for example, show a batter hitting a home run and simultaneously play a pre-recorded sample of the crack of the bat and the roar of the crowd. To line up the audio exactly with the bat impact, do the following:

▶ Trim away any dead space at the beginning of the audio track.

▶ Position the audio clip with precision by zooming in on the swinging bat video to access the exact point of impact.

CHAPTER 7

Dropping in Video Tracks

Let's try cutting a video track and leaving a gap of exactly a half second. Then, we'll drop a second video clip onto the Vb track, cut exactly one-half second, and paste the half-second segment into the blank space in the first video track. We'll then create a cue at the end of the insertion point, where the first video returns, and we'll add a completely new audio track at that cue point, using the Snap feature to make the edit precise.

1. Place a video on track Va, if you've not got one there already. The track should be around five seconds long.

2. Zoom in on the 2-second mark. Notice that as you click repeatedly and zoom in, the digits begin to display fractions of a second.

3. Click the Scissors tool and make a cut at the two-second and four-second marks.

4. On the toolbar at the top of the screen, make sure the No Ripple and Normal Trim options are selected. What we want to do is insert a video clip that replaces the segment we're about to remove.

NOTE

Ripple editing lets you insert clips while preserving blank video spaces. After you move a portion of the video clip, the blank space created by moving the clip will still be there. Also with Ripple editing, when you insert a new clip into that blank space, the space is not filled up by the clip you add. Rather, the space just moves to the left a bit. If you insert a clip and find you can't get rid of the blank space, turn off ripple editing. With Ripple editing off, you can insert a video clip and pull all the other video clips towards it, eliminating blank space.

5. Click the segment in between your two cuts, then hit the Delete key. A blank space appears between the two remaining clips. We'll fill that with a segment from a different video.

6. Select another video from your library of videos and insert it onto the Vb track.

7. Using the Zoom and Scissors tool, zoom in on the Vb track and cut a two-second segment of video (Figure 7.30).

Figure 7.30
After deleting, the blank space will be exactly two seconds.

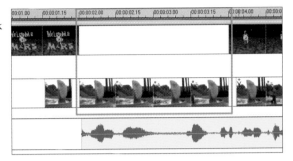

8.   When you're finished cutting, click the Clip Selector tool on the toolbar above, and then click and drag the second video segment to the space in between the clips on track Va. The fit should be perfect (Figure 7.31).

Figure 7.31
The other two-second clip is an exact fit.

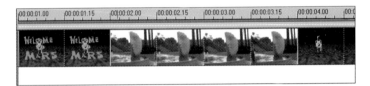

9.   Now let's place a cue at the insert point for the two-second video clip. Click the cue bar to insert a cue. Zoom in to be as precise as you need.

10. If there is an existing audio clip that is part of the two-second video you inserted, right-click on it and choose Split. This allows you to delete the Audio clip without deleting the video as well.

11. Click the audio clip that you have just liberated from its video and press the Delete key. There will no longer be an audio segment associated with your 2-second insert. Let's import our own audio segment.

12. In the MediaStudio Pro Production Library, click the drop-down menu at the left and choose Media Library.

13. Click the Audio folder.

14. Drag the bird.wav file to the Aa or Ab track.

15. Zoom in on the audio clip so you can easily cut and select a short audio segment.

16. Use the Scissors tool to isolate a two-second audio segment, cutting away the remaining audio on either side.

17. Making sure the Snap feature is on (Edit > Snap should be checked), drag the audio segment so it aligns with the cue you made at the beginning of the two-second insert point. If you drag the audio segment into the general area, the audio clip should snap into place, so it will play back at the exact point that the two-second video clip begins (Figure 7.32).

Figure 7.32
Because of the tiny blue cue mark, the audio will snap into place exactly where needed.

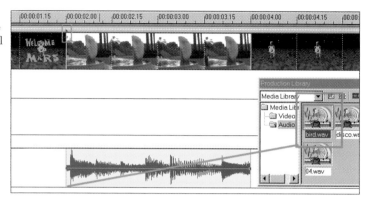

Video Filters

Filters are special effects that change your video's appearance, often quite dramatically. Video filters can be applied to an entire video, a still image, or a short video segment that has been cut from a larger clip. Most video editing programs offer dozens of video filters, ranging from color correction, lens adjustments, lighting and shape effects, or alterations that are just plain strange to look at. Let's take a look at some representative examples

VideoStudio Filters

Figure 7.33 shows the Mirror Filter, which creates a double-vision effect.

Figure 7.33
Dragging the Mirror effect on the right onto the storyboard reveals options on the left.

As shown in Figure 7.34, Sonic Foundry's Video Factory has a tab for displaying video filters in the lower left. This example shows the effects of the Wave video, previewed in the lower right. At the top of the screen, you can see the video in the timeline, with no effect.

Figure 7.34
Video Factory's
effects menu.

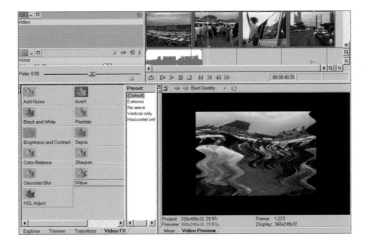

Figure 7.35 displays Video Factory's Add Noise filter. Note the dialog box above the clip. You can adjust noise amount and set the type of noise. You can also vary the noise amounts and style along the video timeline, making the filter a dynamic effect.

Figure 7.35
You need not have the
same amount of effect
throughout the entire
length of a video clip.

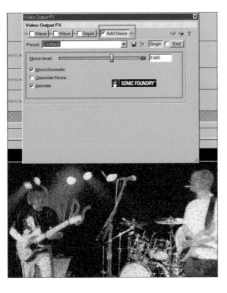

CAUTION

Video filters require lots of CPU power to render and can change your video into something quite unrecognizable if not applied judiciously. For these reasons, video filters should be applied selectively.

CHAPTER 7

Adding a Filter

If you are following along closely with VideoStudio, go ahead and start a video project, inserting a video either in timeline or storyboard mode. I recommend you work through this section using a video clip of no more than five or ten seconds.

As with most video editing programs, VideoStudio provides a menu listing all video filters. Sample thumbnail clips are displayed in the menu, each demonstrating the effects of the filter (Figure 7.36).

Figure 7.36
VideoStudio's effects menu.

To access video filters in VideoStudio, click Storyboard, then click the Media Type drop-down menu on the far right and choose Video Filters. Thumbnails will appear, each displaying the effects of a filter as it would be applied over a few seconds of video. Use the scroll bar on the far right to view all filters. Note: In VideoStudio, filters are accessed only via Storyboard, not through the Effects menu item at the top of the screen.

To add a filter:

1. In the Filter list, click the filter you want to apply.

2. Next, click the variation of the filter that appeals to you.

3. Click the Apply Changes button, and then click a video segment as it appears in the editing area. The segment you click will appear in the Preview screen with the filter applied.

4. To make your editing part of the actual project, press the Play Project button, which renders the newly filtered area.

Editing a Filter

If you are not happy with the default filter settings, you can make adjustments:

▶ **Parameters.** These include effect intensity, color range, orientation, and so forth.

▶ **Timing.** You can specify, for example, if the effect should start at the beginning at full intensity and fade out at the end or if it should start with no effect and build gradually.

To change a filter's parameters, click the Advanced Options button while the filter presets are displayed on the left (Figure 7.37).

Figure 7.37
To edit effect parameters, click the Advanced Options icon.

When the filter's dialog box appears, use the sliders and radio buttons to adjust any available options. These options will vary from filter to filter.

Filter Examples

One very useful filter you'll come across in VideoStudio is the Lighting Filter. In Figure 7.38, a face is shown in the original video with normal lighting. The Lighting Filter initially applies a harsh blue spotlight to the face, then, as shown in the preview frame above the dialog box, the blue fades to a more comfortable direct spot. This is done by using the two keyframes, setting a blue light at the beginning of the video clip, fading it out, and applying a more natural spotlight at the end.

Figure 7.38
A lighting filter that moves from a harsh blue to a softer, non-colored spotlight.

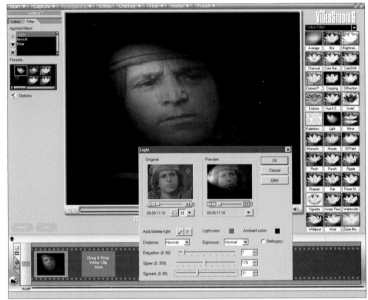

The parameters Elevation, Spread, and Skew can be set for both the beginning and the end. This means you can have a moving spotlight that "circles" around your subject, or a spot that closes in on the face as the clip progresses.

You can also apply many filters at once. In Figure 7.39, two filters are applied to a water skier: a Zoom filter, which exaggerates his motion, and a Star filter, which highlights the skier's trail. In Figure 7.40, you can see that, as the movie progresses, the Zoom effect is decreased and the stars actually follow the skier along his path. This "following" is done in the Star Filter window by dragging the star to a final location at the end of the video.

Figure 7.39
Two filters applied to a
clip in VideoStudio 6.

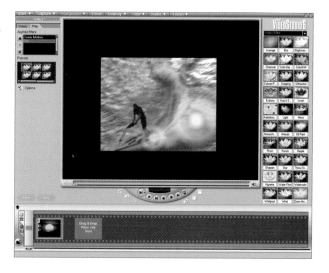

Figure 7.40
The star trails the skier
all the way to the end of
the video.

MediaStudio Filters

Now that you are familiar with how Keyframes work and MediaStudio's dialog boxes for
comparing "before and after" effects, let's look at a few of MediaStudio Pro's video filters. There
are dozens—some more useful than others. I'll just point out a few of the best and leave it to you
to browse through the remainder.

To add a video filter, choose a filter effect from the Production Library and drag it to a video
clip. A dialog box similar to the Moving Path dialog box will appear (Figure 7.41). After you've
previewed and fine-tuned your filter effect, click OK, and the filter will be apparent the next
time you render the clip.

Figure 7.41
Parameters of the Animation Texture filter can change during playback.

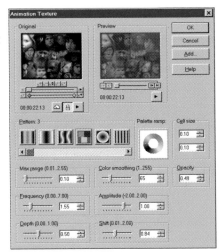

To edit your effect later, click the video clip, choose Ctrl+D, and, when the Video Filters dialog box appears, choose Options. You'll see the dialog box for that specific filter, ready for editing.

TIP

To preview the effect, just drag the playback location I-bar across a few frames of video. You'll see the effect in the preview screen.

Please note that all MediaStudio Pro filters are adjustable. Some filters let you adjust color range, effect intensity, opacity, and so forth. Also, you can add more keyframes, adjusting the filter amount or effect as playback progresses. By default, the effect progresses evenly from the beginning of the clip to its end. Adding keyframes gives you more control over effect intensity over time. You can also abruptly stop and start the effect, displaying a few frames with the effect, then removing it, then adding it again.

Below are examples of seven effects, with "before and after" views shown.

Animation Texture: This filter has many variations. In this example, the filter creates rectangles and varies the color and opacity over time (Figure 7.42).

Figure 7.42
The Animation Texture filter.

Punch: This filter distorts and pushes out the center of the clip (Figure 7.43).

Figure 7.43
The Punch filter.

Hue-Saturation: Varies the color intensity and range over time (Figure 7.44).

Figure 7.44
The Hue-Saturation
filter.

Charcoal: Displaces the pixels adding variable dark strokes (Figure 7.45).

Figure 7.45
The Charcoal filter.

Contour: Displays image outlines using a set of primary colors. This effect is quite interesting when alternated with normal clip footage (Figure 7.46).

Figure 7.46
The Contour filter.

Motion Zoom: all objects in the clip project a forward-moving blurred trail (Figure 7.47).

Figure 7.47
The Motion Zoom filter.

Highlight: Adds richness to dull colors (Figure 7.48).

Figure 7.48
The Highlight filter.

Adding Text to Your Video

Test can be added to video for a variety of purposes, from the purely decorative to the practical—giving directions, aiding with video-based instruction, and displaying titles and credits. Adding text to video is easy. Here's how it's done in Ulead VideoStudio:

1. After adding your video clips, specifying length and transition, click the Title drop-down menu at the top of the screen.

2. Choose Editing from the drop-down menu (Figure 7.49). The options on the left side of the screen change to Text editing options (Figure 7.50). You may add one of the preset Titles from the Title Library on the right side of the screen as previously discussed, or you can create your own text.

Figure 7.49
Add text to a video by clicking the Title menu and choosing Editing.

Figure 7.50
Text editing options will appear on the left.

3. To create your own text, click the Create Title icon at the upper left. A rectangle appears over the video preview area for adding text. The blinking cursor indicates where your text will begin as you start typing.

4. On the left, the Text Editing section has a Font drop-down menu for choosing font type, as well as menus for size and line spacing. Also available are typical font style options such as color, bold, italicize, underline, and justification (Figure 7.51). The Text editing options include a Duration clock for setting text animation length. Your text need not remain on screen for the entire video length.

Figure 7.51
You can edit font style, size, type, and color, as well as alter text animation duration.

5. To set text animation duration, you can type digits into the Duration clock or, after rendering your text, drag the text on the timeline to either shorten or lengthen it (Figure 7.52).

Figure 7.52
Alter text duration by dragging it on the timeline.

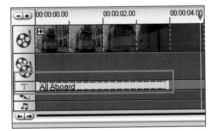

6. Add a shadow or border around your text by clicking the Border & Shadow option button.

7. After you type your text, the Reset and Apply buttons at the bottom left of the screen become active. Click Apply to render your text on the screen, or click Reset to start over.

Text Animation Options

If you leave the text as it is after creating it, your text will appear at the beginning of the clip and remain on-screen for three seconds. However, using the Animation options, you can specify text animation direction and animation length.

1. With the Text options still available, click the Animation Tab at the upper left. Animation options will appear (Figure 7.53).

Figure 7.53
The Text Animation panel.

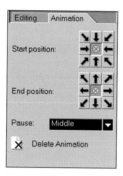

2. Use the Start Position buttons to specify the text animation entry point. Click any button to indicate from where you want the text to enter.
3. Use the End Position buttons to specify text exit point. Click any button to indicate where you want the text to exit.
4. Use the Pause options to indicate how long the text should remain motionless before starting to move towards its exit point.

You can also use a preset text animation from the Animation Library. These animations have a bit of pizzazz that you cannot easily develop on your own with the provided animation tools.

To access the Animation Library, while in Text mode, click the Title drop-down menu at the upper right of the screen and choose Animation. The Library will now display preset animations that you can apply to your existing text just by double-clicking on one. If you want to use text animation, I would strongly recommend using one of the fade-in presets, since text that simply moves in from right or left can look a bit amateurish.

To leave the text editing area, click Storyboard or some other menu option at the top of the screen.

Editing Text

To edit your text, do the following:

1. Click the Title menu button at the top of the screen if you've already left the text editing area.

2. Click the preview window. The text you previously entered will appear, ready to edit.

3. To affect changes to already existing text—to change font, font size, or color, for example—use the mouse cursor to select your text you want to change and then use the Text option on the left to make your edits. It's perfectly fine for individual letters or words to have different text options than their neighbors.

4. Again, click the Apply button, or click Reset if you want to discard your changes.

Crossroads

We've taken a close look at a semi-professional/professional video editing tool. As you can see, once you learn a few basic techniques, it's all up to you and your imagination. Next, you'll learn how to edit your video with special effects. Please note that not all special effects look silly and distracting. You can blend them effectively with regular footage and create something quite memorable.

8

Making Magic: Video Special Effects

Video special effects bring an otherworldliness to your video. Used sparingly, and with a little personal flair, they can be quite nice. They add elements of lighting, shape, or movement that are not quite natural but that can make people sit up and take notice. In this chapter, you'll learn special effect video editing of the following types:

▶ **Masks and Overlays**. Masks and overlays blend your video with another video or image, allowing only a portion of the original to show through. This technology might be used to create a video of a dancer in the clouds or other subject transport tricks. You can also create an illusion of action happening "behind a keyhole." The action can be any video you choose. Using Ulead's Motion Path effect, you can zoom in on the keyhole, moving the action behind it closer. We'll use this technique to create a video of a boy opening a folder of CDs. One CD is "magic," with a video playing inside of it. We'll zoom in on the video so it fills the entire screen. Finally, you'll learn to apply a "painterly" special effect in one segment of a video and use an Image Matte effect to display the rest of the video without the effect (Figure 8.1).

CHAPTER 8

Figure 8.1
Using an alpha channel image to filter only a selected area of a video. Note that the effect applies to the entire video, not just a single frame.

> ▶ **Painting a Video To Life**. We'll use MediaStudio Pro Video Paint to show a video frame gradually emerging as if being painted by a brush. When completed, the actual video appears and the action begins (Figure 8.2).

> ▶ **Adding a 3D Object**. We'll use Ulead's Cool 3D and MediaStudio Pro to apply a moving 3D object over the top of an existing video.

Figure 8.2
Create a video intro that "paints in" the main figure as it begins.

The video effects you'll learn in this chapter can be rendered to an existing video, so you can apply these imaginative tricks to your own video footage. Each of these programs allows you to drag an effect, drawing, or motion path right onto your video or create a "painterly" effect using your own video as a backdrop.

Masks and Overlays

When you download and install MediaStudio Pro, even the trial version, you are provided with tutorials to get you started with these programs. Rather than duplicate those introductory steps, I'd like to show you some very cool and unique effects, techniques that are not quite so obvious from the manual. We'll get started in MediaStudio Pro again, the same program we worked with in the last chapter, and learn about overlays. You'll see how to blend and overlap video clips in creative combinations.

When you create an overlay, you have to determine which part of the video on the lower layer will be visible and which part will be hidden. You are setting up a mask, saying, for example, "Any area of the video on the upper layer that is black should be invisible, and the lower layer video should appear instead of those black areas." Or, you can use a drawing program to create and save a cut-out, then open MediaStudio Pro and put that image with the cut-out on the top layer and add any video you like to the lower layer. Then specify that the lower video should appear in place of the cutout. You can also use MediaStudio Pro's Gray Matte effect to place a video subject "inside" a new environment, for example, in a shroud of mist.

Using MediaStudio Pro, we'll step through four short overlay projects. We will:

> ▶ Place a dancer in a shroud of mist.

> ▶ Place a man smoking a cigarette into a new environment near a waterfall.

> ▶ View a video through a small "keyhole" and zoom in on it; we'll do something similar with a boy holding a folder of CDs.

▶ Apply a painting effect to a video and use an Image Matte to determine that the painting effect should only appear around the edges of the frame.

For the dancer project, we'll use the same video of a dancer from the MediaStudio Pro tutorial on Masking (Figure 8.3). This video is included with the MediaStudio installation files. In the Ulead tutorial, a video of a flamenco dancer filmed against a blue screen is used as an overlay against an entirely different background. By choosing Blue Screen from the Type drop-down menu of the Overlay Options dialog box, the dancer is seen dancing against a new background, the blue screen now being invisible.

Figure 8.3
The blue-screen Dancer video is included with MediaStudio Pro 6.

However, rather than simply repeat that concept, we'll build on it. I'll show you how to display the dancer dancing within clouds and mist, rather than simply punching out the background. This technique adds the component of depth and the illusion of moving through 3D space, rather than simply masking. We can call this a deep mask.

Creating a Deep Mask

A deep mask is great for adding depth and texture to a video. It is quite a remarkable-looking effect, not amateurish. Here's how to create one:

1. Start a new project in MediaStudio Pro and place the video of the dancer on track V1. If the video of the dancer is not available, use any video with the subject against a solid color background. The background need not be blue. We'll use the Overlay Options dialog box to strip out the colored background.

2. Place another video on Va, preferably a video with clouds. Alternately, use a video of a forest, a crowded sidewalk, or some video with various levels of depth (Figure 8.4).

Figure 8.4
The video you place on the Va track will appear behind the masked video, on V1.

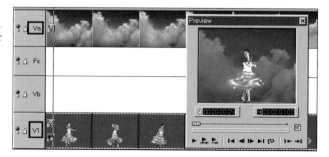

3. Using the Clip Selector tool, click once on a blank track, then click once on the video clip on V1. Then right-click on the V1 video. Choose Overlay Options. The Overlay Options dialog box appears (Figure 8.5). This dialog box will always be used to set masking parameters for your overlay projects. You'll only access it by right clicking on a video on one of the numerical tracks, such as V1, V2, etc.

Figure 8.5
Use the Overlay Options dialog box to specify mask type.

4. The preview window on the left side of the Overlay Options dialog box displays the clip with no masking or blending. The right-side preview window will show the results of your overlay choices.

5. If we were simply replacing the background, we'd choose Blue Screen from the Type drop-down menu on the left side of the dialog box. But we want to blend the Va clip based on the luminosity values (amount of light) of its contents. So, in the Type drop-down menu, choose Gray Key.

6. Click the Invert Overlay checkbox.

7. Make sure the Preview As drop-down menu on the right side of the screen reads Results.

8. Click OK.

If you chose a video clip with density similar to the one I used, the dancer will appear in the mist.

Adding a Second Mask Video

Let's add to this effect, though, by making it more dense. We'll include another misty, cloudy video with a celestial body to complete the effect. Again, in choosing your own video, choose one in which various degrees of depth (Z-pop) can be detected. No brick walls.

1. Add a second overlay video clip to V2, and right-click on it. Choose Overlay Options.

2. Again, choose Gray Key from the Type drop-down menu, and click the Invert Overlay checkbox. This adds another layer of depth to the dancer's movements.

3. Preview your clip by clicking the Play button on the Preview Window (Figure 8.6).

Figure 8.6
Click the Play button to preview your video composition.

CHAPTER 8

To make this video composition look its best, the colors of each clip should be bright, distinct, and enhanced. Bolder colors in each layer make the video's depth more apparent. Let's apply some filters that will enhance your results:

1. Right-click on each video clip, choose Video Filters, and in the Available Filters list of the Video Filters dialog box choose Hue & Saturation.

2. Click Add and then click Options.

3. Drag the Saturation slider to 18.

4. Click OK to apply the filter.

5. Apply this effect to all clips.

6. Using the same technique, apply the Brightness and Contrast filter to each clip, and increase both the Brightness and Contrast by a value of 12.

7. Save this video clip using any name you like, and render the video. You'll enjoy applying this variable masking technique using videos with a variety of lighting and depth qualities.

Working with Alpha Channels

The next project involves editing an image in a graphic editing program such as Paint Shop Pro. When you edit and save an image in just about any digital graphic editing program, the image is saved in three channels, Red, Blue, and Green. Most image editing programs, however, allow you to also save an alpha channel. Alpha channels allow you to specify which portion of an image should be used in a process (such as filters, lighting, and special effects) and which portion will be unaffected. Let's say you open your image and apply a special lighting filter to it. Saving your image with an alpha channel lets you specify that only certain portions of your image should show off the lighting.

My completed example is shown in Figure 8.7. We are using an alpha channel to determine which portions of an image should be invisible, allowing the video behind the image to be seen. MediaStudio Pro lets you layer video clips by simple track positioning. Note that any time you place a video on track Va, it will appear behind a clip on track V1.

Figure 8.7
The smoking man is an alpha channel image that is stationary against the moving video backdrop.

In a nutshell, here's what we'll do:

▶   Use the graphic program's "Magic Wand" tool or other selection tool to separate the main portion of the image from the background, then save the selection as an Alpha Channel. The image should have a background that is easily isolated.

▶ Save the image as a TIF file and specify to save the alpha channel with the image as well. We'll then create a new MediaStudio Pro project and add the image onto the V1 track.

▶ Choose a video that will look good as a background behind the image. We'll use the Overlay Options dialog box to specify the type of Overlay we want to use and choose Alpha Channel.

▶ When we render the project, the video will play back behind the image's subject matter. The image is invisible except for the area you saved as an alpha channel. Of course, the image in the front is still, and the only moving segment is the video in the background.

Creating an Image with an Alpha Channel

The way you create an alpha channel in an image editing program is by simply making a selection and saving the selection as an alpha channel. Figure 8.8 displays the image used in this video project. I chose a face with clear borders, with only white behind it. Using an image with a single background color makes it easy to separate the background from the foreground. You can do this with your graphic program's selection tools, such as the "magic wand" or "lasso." Here's the sequence:

Figure 8.8
The "marching ants" pattern around the white area denotes the selection.

1. First, make your complete selection.
2. Next, invert the selection so that the face is now masked (protected from editing), while the background will be invisible when opened in our MediaStudio Pro project.

3. Finally, save the selection as an alpha channel, as shown in Paint Shop Pro (Figure 8.9).

4. Save the image as a TIF file with "Save Alpha Channel" selected.

Figure 8.9
An alpha channel is simply a saved selection from an image in a program that enables alpha channel saving.

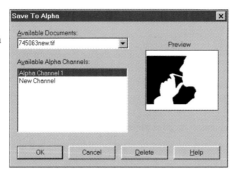

Adding the Alpha Mask to MediaStudio Pro

We'll open MediaStudio Pro and insert our alpha mask image.

1. Starting with a blank project, insert the image onto the V1 track. Using the Clip Selector tool, drag the image a few frames to the right, so it will display for more than a second or two of video.

2. Now, add a video to the Va track. Make the video colorful, with lots of movement. It should invoke a location (Figure 8.10).

Figure 8.10
Add a video to Va, and it appears behind the alpha channel image.

3. Click on a blank track, then click once on the V1 track. Now, right-click on the V1 track, and choose Overlay Options. We'll specify that the program should display the Alpha Channel portion of the image and make the rest invisible.

4. In the Type drop-down menu, choose Alpha Channel. You may also have to click the Inverse Overlay Area checkbox, depending on whether you previously inverted your selection or not (Figure 8.11).

Figure 8.11
Use the Overlay Options
dialog box to choose a
mask type.

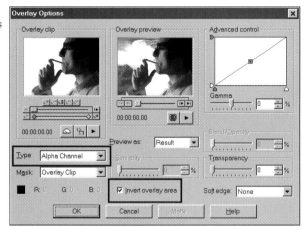

5.   Click OK to close the dialog box. When you render your movie, you'll see the
     image in the foreground, and the video you added to the Va track playing in the
     background.

Creating a Zooming Keyhole Effect

Here's another variation on the Mask and Overlay theme. We'll place a "keyhole" image on the
V1 layer and again place a video with lots of movement on Va. By using MediaStudio Pro's
Motion Path feature, we'll create the illusion of moving closer and peeking inside the keyhole.
We accomplish the "zooming in" effect by making the keyhole image larger as the video
progresses and slightly repositioning it. The complete example is shown in Figure 8.12.

Figure 8.12
The keyhole is a single
alpha channel image,
with a video appearing
behind it.

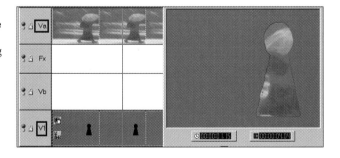

Here's how it's done:

1. First, draw or acquire a drawing with a simple black keyhole and a close-up of a door. Detail is not important, and a "keyhole" can easily be a modified circle and triangle attached top and bottom. Figure 8.13 shows such an image with a selection in Paint Shop Pro.

Figure 8.13
Use any image editing program to cut out a keyhole shape and save to an alpha channel.

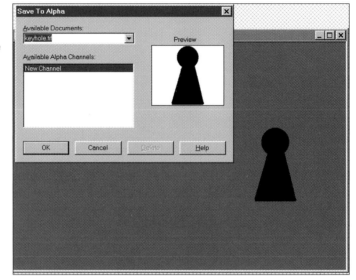

2. Start a new MediaStudio Pro project and place the keyhole image on the V1 track. On the track, drag the image strip to the right so that it lasts for perhaps five or six seconds of viewing time.

3. Insert a video with lots of movement onto the Va track.

Enlarging the Keyhole Image

Now we need to make the keyhole image grow over time, creating the zooming effect.

1. Right-click on the keyhole track and choose Moving Path. The Production Library will appear with the Moving Path selections displayed, each represented by an icon.

2. Click the 2D Basic folder, and on the right side of the Production Library, when the 2D Basic icon appears, drag it to the keyhole track. The Moving Path dialog box will appear. You'll be setting up new Ending Keyframe parameters. Specifically, you want the keyhole image to be about five times as large as it is at the Start Keyframe, and positioned slightly to the left, so that the keyhole appears almost centered when the clip ends, creating the illusion of moving in and peeking into a keyhole to see the video behind it (Figure 8.14). In my example, the starting Keyframe is 635 width × 520 height.

Figure 8.14
The small keyhole as it appears when the video begins.

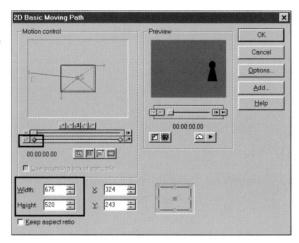

3. In the Moving Path dialog box, click the diamond-shaped icon at the right side of Motion Control path selector. You are now editing the Ending Keyframe, determining the size and position of the image when the clip ends.

4. Type in a size that is between four and five times as large as the start. In my example, the ending size is 2755 width × 2200 height. Position the image slightly to the left. This can be done by clicking on and dragging the ending "E" slightly leftward (Figure 8.15).

5. Click OK to close the dialog box.

CHAPTER 8

Figure 8.15
Use the Moving Path dialog box to enlarge the keyhole at the Ending Keyframe.

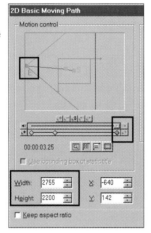

Previewing the Keyhole Project

You're now ready to play back the project, which combines the keyhole image and the movie clip behind it. You may have a little resizing and adjusting to do. Play back the video, and if the keyhole is not quite right, open the Moving Path dialog box again to fine tune the positioning. To again edit the image, right-click on the image and choose Moving Path. The dialog box will appear.

The "Magic CD" Project

In the example shown in Figure 8.16, the video clip with the boy opening the CD case is on the V1 track. The idea is that another video becomes visible as the boy turns to the page with the "magic" CD. The video playing in the background does not appear on the Va track until the boy turns to that page. Obviously, you will not have a video clip just like this one, but by following this example and using your imagination, you can easily come up with ways to create a similar effect in your own work.

Figure 8.16
Create an alpha cutout in the final frame of a video, extract that frame, and zoom in.

The video frame of the "magic" CD with the movie behind it is not a video at all. Rather, it is a single image. The image is saved with an alpha channel. A hole has been cut out exactly the size of the magic CD.

Creating a Single-Frame Image with an Alpha Channel

To create something like what is shown in Figure 8.16, you would do the following:

1. Extract a single frame that you want to gradually enlarge, the frame that will have the movie underneath show through. You'll save that frame as a single image.

2. Open that image in an image editor. Use a selection tool to make a selection around the CD area.

3. Save the selection as an alpha channel (Figure 8.17). Then save the image.

Figure 8.17
The final frame of the CD folder movie with a selection.

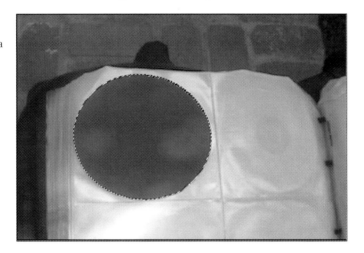

4. Then, when you insert this single image into Media Studio Pro, it will grow, creating the appearance of zooming in. The movie showing through the alpha channel creates the "magic CD effect."

Setting up the Project in MediaStudio Pro

Here's how to set this project up in MediaStudio Pro:

1. After creating and saving the single image, do the following:

2. Open MediaStudio Pro and insert the main movie clip that leads up to the still-image frame.

3. Insert a film clip that appears behind the alpha channel image.

4. After placing your two main video clips into the MediaStudio Pro project, place the single-image at the end of the opening clip. As an overlay clip, the image must be on the V1 track or one of the other numbered tracks.

5. Once you set up the Overlay Option for that single-image clip, the second movie clip will appear behind it (Figure 8.18).

Figure 8.18
Choose Alpha Channel
in the Overlay Options
dialog box.

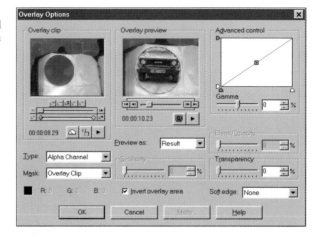

Here's how to set up the Overlay Options:

1. Right-click on the image, and choose Overlay Options. The Overlay Option dialog box will appear.

2. Choose Alpha Channel from the Type drop-down menu, and if need be, check the Invert Overlay Area checkbox. Remember, there must be a movie *behind* the single image, or there will be no peek-through effect to observe.

3. View the effect in the Overlay Preview panel, and click OK to close the dialog box.

4. As we did in the Keyhole example, use the Moving Path dialog box to make the still-image CD picture grow, simulating zooming in.

5. Render your movie to preview the effect.

Limiting Effects with an Alpha Channel

In MediaStudio Pro, you can apply interesting "painterly" effects to your video, but they often cloud detail to such a degree that it obscures your video's contents. The solution is to render your painterly effect to only the edges of the video, while keeping the subject matter in the center unaffected (see Figure 8.1, at the beginning of this chapter). Let's see how this is accomplished using MediaStudio's Image Matte feature.

1. Open a new MediaStudio Pro project and add a video to track Va. The video should have a main character that stays fairly close to the center of the screen.

2. Note the video's measurements and write them down. To check the project's dimension properties, choose File > Project Settings.

3. Duplicate the video onto track V1 by pressing Ctrl and dragging it. You'll now have two identical videos, one on track Va, the other on V1.

Adding the "Painterly" Filter To the Top Clip

Now let's apply a filter to the video on track Va:

1. Apply a Charcoal Video Filter to the video clip on Va. To do this, right-click on the clip and choose Video Filter. When the Video Filter dialog box appears, scroll down to Charcoal, and click Add. This video filter reproduces your video as if it were drawn as a charcoal sketch (Figure 8.19).

Figure 8.19
A separate, unseen alpha image will determine the boundaries of the video filter.

2. Click Options. The Charcoal dialog box appears.
3. The first Keyframe (red diamond-shaped icon) will be selected. We'll apply our options to the entire video, i.e., we won't change them at the End Keyframe.
4. Set Balance to 4, set Stroke Length to 4, and Level to 78.
5. Click OK, then OK again, and the effect will be applied to the video. However, even if you render the video, you'll not see the effect, because the V1 clip does not have the effect applied, and the contents of any clip on V1 are layered above the contents of Va.

We now have a video clip with the charcoal effect applied, and we'll leave our V1 clip without any effect at all. We'll now create an alpha channel image, and use it to specify that the center of the no-effect video will be displayed, while the edges of the video with the effect will also be displayed. This work will be done in an image editor before returning to MediaStudio Pro.

Limiting the Effect with a Cut-Out

Before opening your image editor to make your blank cut-out image, note the dimensions of the video. This example uses a video 640×480. Here's what to do next:

1. Open an image editing program that can save an image with an alpha channel, and create a new, blank image using the dimensions of the video. This will be a mask, and the video will appear underneath it, peeking through.
2. Set the background color to white. When we cut a hole in our image, we want the contrast between the image and background color to be very clear.

3. Fill the image with black. We'll be cutting a hole in this image using white, so black is sure to stand out against it.

4. Using the graphic editing program's Ellipsis or Circle Selection tool, create a large selection near the center of the image encompassing the area where the main character or subject of your video will appear. You'll have to have a pretty clear idea in your mind where the video will be peeking through. The hole you are cutting now is where the video will appear.

5. Press the Delete key or choose Edit > Clear or Edit > Cut. The removed segment will now appear filled with the background color, which should be white. You can now make a mental note that a background that is all white you have saved with an alpha channel (Figure 8.20). The selection markings (the "marching ants" pattern) will remain as you save the image. The selection area—filled with white—is the mask.

Figure 8.20
The alpha image that will protect the main subject from the effects of the filter.

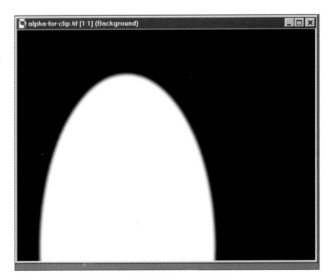

6. We'll save the image, but first we must save the alpha channel. Choose Select > Save Selection, or whatever command directs your graphic editing program to save an image's alpha channel information. You'll be prompted to name the channel. There is no reason to do so. All we'll do in Media Studio Pro is direct the program to its location.

7. Finally, save the image. Note its saved location, because you'll be referring to it in one of Media Studio's dialog boxes.

Inserting the Image as an Image Matte

Now, back in MediaStudio Pro, we can use that alpha channel image to limit how the painterly effect is applied to the entire video:

1. Right-click on the video clip in V1 and choose Overlay Options.

2. When the Overlay Options dialog box appears, choose Alpha Channel in the Type drop-down menu, and choose Image Matte from the Mask drop-down menu.

3. On the right side of the dialog box, you'll see your video display the effects of the mask. The masked portion of the video will display the charcoal effect. If you find that the alpha effect is reversed from what you were expecting, click the Invert Overlay Area checkbox.

4. Click OK to close the dialog box and your video project will be masked. Keep in mind that the mask you added will be applied to all frames of the video.

5. Render the video clip, or drag the Location Indicator I-bar across a small portion of the clip, which will cause the effect to appear in the Preview Window.

Video Paint

Video Paint is a stand-alone program. You do not open it from within the Video Editor. Rather, start it by clicking on the Video Paint icon in the MediaStudio Pro program group in the Start menu. In its simplest application, Video Paint provides painting tools to paint a video canvas with artistic brush strokes (Figure 8.21). You can use watercolor brush styles, oils, charcoals, various pens, and customized strokes that may emulate certain fine artists. In Video Paint, you can paint directly on a canvas (a single frame of video) or create a selection and paint inside that selection. These are some of the most unique and fascinating effects you'll probably have occasion to use. They have not been overused or become cliché quite yet. Use them when you want to make your video look "artistic."

Figure 8.21
MediaStudio Video
Paint blends painterly
strokes with video clips.
Note the video frames
across the bottom of the
screen.

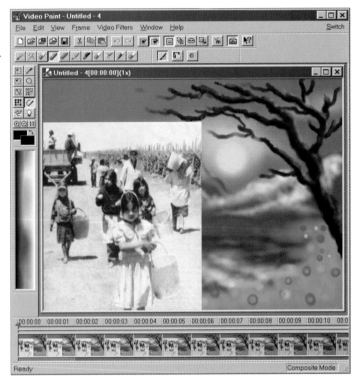

You can paint onto an existing video frame by frame if you wish; however, Video Paint has a
feature, called Power Duplicate, that reproduces your paint strokes over many frames.
Additionally, Video Paint lets you paint with a particular brush stroke, and the image that
emerges will resemble a "painterly" version of your video, rendering your video in, say, oil
paints or charcoal. Let's create a short movie that appears to be painting itself in "real time," as if
a charcoal artist were painting your video to life. The complete project results are shown in
Figure 8.2, and in Media Studio Pro in Figure 8.22.

Figure 8.22
After we create the
painterly video, we'll
fade it into the original
in MediaStudio Pro, so
we'll go back and open
the Media Studio Pro
Video Editor again.

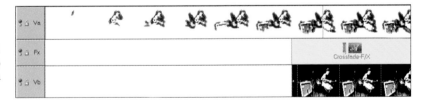

Here's our plan:

1. We'll start a new project in Video Paint, matching the dimensions to the dimensions of the video we want to "paint."

2. Next, we'll choose a paint brush in Video Paint. Video Paint lets you choose a texture for your drawing. This is a pattern that will appear beneath your brush strokes. You can choose the first frame of a video as a texture. As we draw, our video will seem to be appearing beneath our strokes.

3. We'll be recording our painting strokes as a macro, which means our strokes will be saved.

4. Then we'll play back those strokes onto a new, blank frame. We'll specify that the drawing should be played back over a hundred or so frames of video.

5. This "magical" gradual appearance of our video will be saved as a small video, which we can open in MediaStudio Pro. We'll place this "drawn video" clip at the beginning of a project and crossfade it into the actual video. The results will be a video that begins as if it is being painted, then takes off from there.

Drawing Your Video to Life

Let's take the whole project step by step:

1. Choose a video that you would like to duplicate and paint the first frame of, and note its dimensions. You can easily do this by right-clicking on it and choosing the Details tab.

2. Open Video Paint, and create a new project, indicating the same dimensions as the video. Make the video about seven seconds long, and make any other formatting choices you like. When you click OK, you'll see a single blank frame, as well as a row of frames representing your entire movie at the bottom of the screen (Figure 8.23).

Figure 8.23
In Video Paint, you paint onto a blank canvas or existing video.

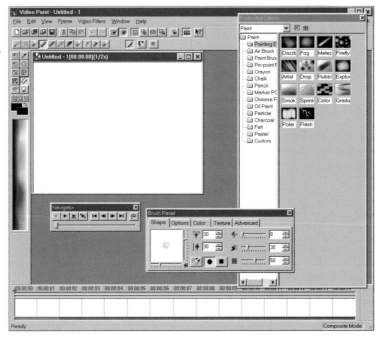

3. Change the background color to white (Choose Frame > Film Color, and click inside the color bar. Choose white from the available colors).

Choosing a Brush Type

Now we have to choose the type of paint effect, or brush type, to render our video in:

1. Click the Painting Tool icon in the toolbox at the left side of the screen.

2. In the Production Library drop-down menu, choose Paint. (If the Production Library is not visible, choose View > Toolbars & Panels, and click the Production Library checkbox.) Icons displaying the different paint options will appear. Each icon represents a painting style.

3. Click the Charcoal drop-down menu in the Paint folder list, and you'll see several charcoal brush styles appear as icons.

4. Click and drag the Gritty Charcoal icon to the new, blank video frame you just created (Figure 8.24). The Brush Panel will appear. If the Brush Panel is not visible, click the Show/Hide Brush Panel icon at the top of the screen.

Figure 8.24
To use the Gritty
Charcoal brush, drag it
onto the canvas.

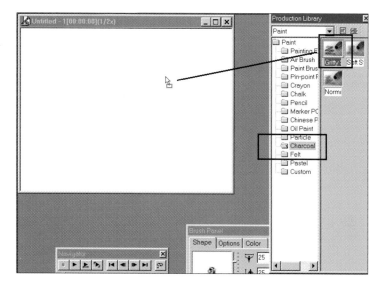

Choosing the Video as Texture

If we were to begin drawing, we would only see a charcoal drawing. We want to set up our
chosen video as the "texture" that appears beneath our strokes. The Brush Panel lets you set up
a texture:

1.   Click the Texture tab of the Brush Panel, and in the Texture Options drop-down
     menu, choose User-Defined. An Open menu will appear, prompting you to
     specify which image or video to use as your texture source (Figure 8.25).

Figure 8.25
Choose a video clip as a
texture to "paint it in"
as an intro video.

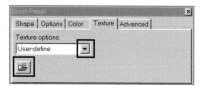

2.   Browse to the video you want to draw with the charcoal. The panel will display
     information about your chosen texture image. Make sure the image you are about
     to draw matches the dimensions of the image or video you are choosing as your
     source, or your drawing will not properly fit the page.

3.   Click Open to choose the image or video. The dialog box will close, and the
     Texture tab will display the first frame of the video you chose as your texture.

Changing the Brush Size

Change the brush size to between 50 and 55 pixels. That's because you don't want to spend all day drawing this image. You are only doing this for a few seconds to show off this special effect before starting the "real" video. To change the brush size, click the Shape tab of the Brush Panel, and type a digit into both the horizontal and vertical brush size fields.

You are now ready to paint your video frame. You'll be recording your strokes, then allowing Video Paint to paint them over many frames of video using the recorded Macro. But before we record, practice a bit.

Drawing in the Single Frame

Draw inside the blank video frame, and see your strokes emerge. You want to especially draw the areas that have a decent amount of worthwhile detail. You don't want to take valuable recording time drawing sky (which will look like nothing when played back). Draw where people's faces or other recognizable shapes will appear.

To undo your practice drawing and get started recording, choose Edit > Undo. Undo enough times to return your video frame back to its original blank state. After a little practice, we're now ready to record.

When you record your strokes, they are saved in a bit of code called a "routine," known as a macro. You can later play back your strokes simply by dragging the macro from the Production Library to a blank frame. The big red "Record" button for macros will only be available if a paintbrush is selected (if the Painting Tool on the toolbox is selected).

Make sure you've practiced your strokes and are confident of the detail you want to reveal while drawing. After you press the red button, your strokes will be recorded:

1. To begin recording a macro, click the red "Record" button at the top of the screen. You'll see a prompt indicating recording will begin.

2. Click OK, and your strokes will be recorded.

3. When you are done recording, click the red button again, and the Add to Library menu appears.

4. Name your macro in the small field to the right, and, in the Annotations box, type in a note to yourself identifying the macro, if need be.

5. Click OK, and your new macro will appear in the Production Library in the Custom subfolder of the Macro list. Your macro will now always be available to you from the Production Library.

Applying Your Macro to the Project

Now you'll apply your macro to a blank video frame and specify that the drawing should be played back across a few seconds of video, not just on one frame. Here's how it's done:

1. Create a new blank video frame with the same dimensions as the first, and make this video about seven seconds long, although you'll only be working directly on frame 1. When the document is created, you'll see rows of video frame icons occupy the bottom of the screen.

2. Locate the macro (if the macro is not visible, click Macro in the drop-down menu on the Production Library, then click the Custom folder).

3. Drag the macro you made to your new blank frame. The Macro Playing Options dialog box will appear (Figure 8.26).

Figure 8.26
You can choose to play back your macro across many frames of video.

CHAPTER 8

Setting Macro Playing Options

You can now specify that your macro should play back over many frames of video, not just as a single image:

1. On the Macro Playing Options dialog box, press the "up" arrow on the Number of frames field so that the maximum number of frames is reached. You want the macro to draw your image across the entire length of this video.

2. As soon as you indicate multiple frames, more Playing Method options will display. Click Progressive, which draws your image from beginning to end, rather than the reverse.

3. Click OK, and you'll see a prompt offering to erase the Undo information in order to save disk space for this operation. Answer any way you wish.

4. After clicking OK, the drawing will begin automatically. The output will probably "strobe" on your screen. Fear not. This only happens when Video Paint is laying down frames. A progress bar at the bottom of the screen moves forward, indicating time remaining in your playback. At this time, Video Paint is rendering. True playback will be much faster.

Playing and Saving Your Creation

To play back and save what you've done, immediately after rendering, choose View > Toolbars & Panels, and click Navigator. Click the Play button on the Navigator. Video Paint will play back your movie, first in the preview window, then in the frame itself. Save your work. What you are doing is saving this project as a Video Paint project.

But you've not created a movie file yet. Let's do that now.

1. Choose File > Video, and choose a movie type, probably an AVI that you would like to use in MediaStudio Pro to complete this project. Note the movie name and location, because you'll momentarily be opening this file in MediaStudio Pro.

2. In the Create Video File dialog box, click the Options button to select movie formatting options.

3. Click OK, and your movie will be created in the location you specify.

Finishing the Project in MediaStudio Pro

We need to combine and blend our drawing film with the original video.

1. Open MediaStudio Pro and create a project with the same dimensions as the movie you created in Video Paint. If you can't locate an option for creating the exact frame size, create a movie with any dimension, then choose File > Customize Frame Size, and indicate the size you want.

2. Import the video you created in Video Paint onto track Va (Insert > Video File), and scroll to view the video clip ending.

3. Import the original video clip you created your Video Paint creation from. Import that video clip onto track Vb (see above Figure 8.22).

4. When inserting the original video onto Vb, overlap the two video clips by two to three seconds.

We don't want these two clips to blend abruptly. Let's add a smooth, gradual crossfade transition. As you may recall, in MediaStudio Pro, transitions are placed on the FX track, right between the Va and Vb tracks.

1. Drag in a crossfade transition. (Choose Window > Production Library, and click Transition Effect in the drop-down menu. Click FX, and drag Crossfade onto the FX track.)

2. Drag the Crossfade transition so that it appears right between the two tracks on Va and Vb. When the Crossfade Transition dialog box appears, you need not make any adjustments.

3. Using the Clip Selection tool, drag the Crossfade transition so that it occupies the entire length of the overlap (Figure 8.27).

Figure 8.27
Create a long crossfade between the painterly video and the original.

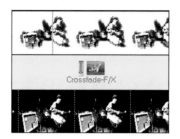

Preview your movie, and you'll see your drawing clip fade into the actual movie. Render the movie if you like the results. I think this is a nice effect to use as opening credits for introducing each character, or for music videos, introducing each musician.

Adding 3D Objects to Your Video

Placing 3D objects and animations into your video adds a new layer of depth because the objects have their own lighting source, and they have reflective surfaces that move through your video in three-dimensional space. In this section, we'll work with a program called Cool 3D by Ulead. Cool 3D is a stand-alone program that creates 3D lettering, objects, and shapes in 3D space. You can export Cool 3D creations into a video editing program and play back your 3D video over your existing video. Ulead Cool 3D can also output to the Flash movie (SWF) format, allowing you to share your video creations with anyone on the Web. With Cool 3D you can create lettering and objects with depth and realism. It's great for logos and special effects or to have the subject matter of your video appear to interact with your 3D objects.

Objects in Ulead Cool 3D begin as shapes or letters (Figure 8.28), or they can be imported from programs like Adobe Illustrator as AI files. This is very helpful if you have a logo created in CorelDRAW or Illustrator that you would like to develop with substance and animate.

Figure 8.28
Adding a shape to a
Ulead Cool 3D project.

At the bottom of the Cool 3D screen are all the styles, lighting effects, shapes, and background images you can apply to your project by simply dragging to the screen (Figure 8.29). Surface textures, motion settings, and even compositions can be applied just by dragging them to the image screen.

Figure 8.29
Dragging a lighting
setting to an object.

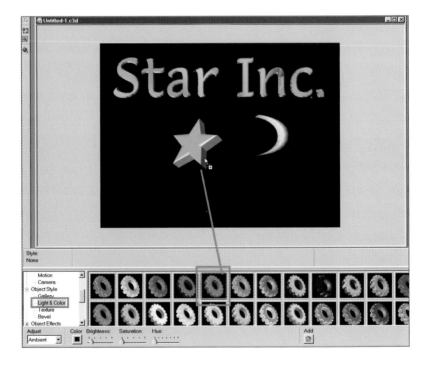

Creating a Cool 3D Project

Let's create a quick flying saucer movie with some text and open it in a video editing program. We'll make it look as though people are watching the flying saucer circle around.

1. Choose File > New, and a new image will appear. The default color is black. Let's change the background color to white.

2. At the lower left of the screen, click the plus sign next to Studio to reveal categories of all kinds (Figure 8.30).

3. Click Backgrounds, and when the Color Cube appears at the lower left of the screen, click it, and choose White. We're doing this so we can get rid of the background entirely when we bring our Cool 3D project into MediaStudio Pro and blend it with an existing video. Later, when you render your AVI movie to take into MediaStudio, you can completely remove the background. Do this by choosing the Compression tab under Options and selecting 32 bit.

Figure 8.30
Accessing the Studio object categories.

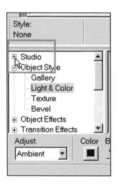

4. Let's increase the image size from 240×320 to a full frame of video: 720×480. Click Image > Dimensions and in the Standard drop-down menu choose 720×480. The image will increase in size. We don't need to change the background color because the video we import into will become the background.

Creating an Object and Adding Motion

Let's add a flying saucer. At the bottom left of the screen, click the Studio plus sign if Studio categories are not already available.

1. Click the Shapes category, and drag a flying saucer onto the upper left of the screen (Figure 8.31).

Figure 8.31
Adding a flying saucer
to the screen.

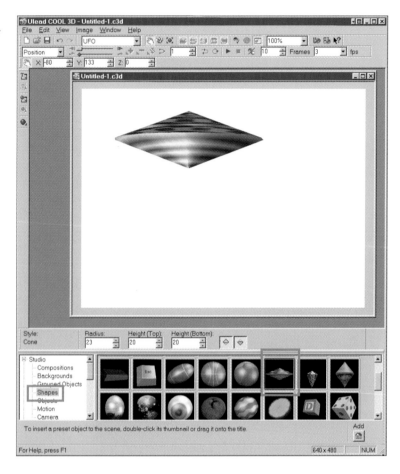

2. Let's make our flying saucer move around the screen a bit. On the lower left, make sure the Shapes main category is still open, and click the Motion category. The thumbnail display on the lower right will show lots of movement examples.

3. Drag the movement example on the far right onto the flying saucer object you just added (Figure 8.32). The movement example we chose creates a circular, back-and-forth motion. The flying saucer will now move according to the setting we just dragged in.

Figure 8.32
Adding a motion preset
to the flying saucer.

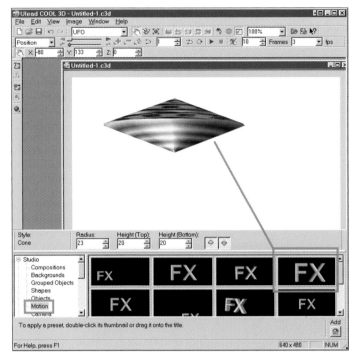

4. To test your motion, click the Play arrow at the upper center of the screen. It will only play once unless you also click the Loop icon, directly to its left.

5. So that our characters don't get seasick watching the flying saucer whiz by when we import the project into a video, let's slow down the frames per second from 15 to 5. Click the fps drop-down menu at the upper left of the screen and choose 5.

There's lots more we could do here. We could add a background, more shapes, stars, and all kinds of objects and color schemes. But instead, let's save our project as a movie, import it into Ulead MediaStudio Pro, and create a little video interaction.

Saving the Project as a Video

To output your Cool 3D project as a video, do the following:

1. Choose File > Create Animation Files > Video Files. After a moment, the Save As Video File save menu will appear.

2. Choose a name, video file type, and location for your video. I am saving this as saucer.avi, and saving it in the same folder as my other video project files.

After saving, you'll see a quick preview of your project played back as a video.

Applying the Video in Media Studio Pro

Next we'll add our Cool 3D project to another movie clip in MediaStudio Pro.

1. Open MediaStudio Pro, and load a video clip of people looking around at something, preferably something up in the air. Load it onto track Va.

2. Insert your video clip from Ulead Cool 3D onto the V1 track—one of the Overlay tracks—and right click on it.

3. From the shortcut menu that appears, choose Overlay Options.

4. When the Overlay dialog box appears, choose Overlay Clip for Mask, and choose Color Key for Type.

5. Using the eyedropper, set your mask color for white just by clicking in the preview area (Figure 8.33). The video will now play back with the white color eliminated entirely.

Figure 8.33
Choosing a mask setting for the Cool 3D overlay video.

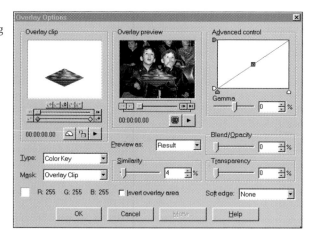

You'll be able to see the flying saucer playing back against the main video (Figure 8.34).

Figure 8.34
The completed project.

Crossroads

Now you've gotten a taste of more advanced video editing, and you even have a few tricks up your sleeve. With the right software, you can create all kinds of special effects with a little patient application. In the next chapter, you'll learn how to apply video skills to the business environment.

9

Making Great Business Videos

A great challenge to any business is letting the world know what they do and how their product or service differs from others. The business process must be explained, either to customers, partners, or new employees. As the owner of a digital video camera, you have a great tool in your hands: the ability to show people in motion, doing and saying things, demonstrating procedures, giving explanations, and describing the steps in a business process. If your business model requires that you show people how to get something done, your digital camcorder can be a great asset. You can film tutorials, interviews, business plan overviews, and even create trade show kiosks using live actors, as well as animation and still photography.

Using Video in Business

What sort of business processes or activities can be enhanced with the use of digital video? Anything that needs to be demonstrated or recorded in motion with visual detail. Here are some examples:

Plant tours: If your company includes a physical plant where production takes place, you take pride in your manufacturing facility, and you want to show its layout. Potential customers, especially volume customers, often like to see just how your products are made. Create a video plant tour showing the important machinery, people at work, products in various stages of completion, quality control, and so forth.

Products in action: Your product's uniqueness may not be evident until potential customers can see it doing something. You can show your product at work from various angles and in various settings. You can develop scenarios that show your product in a favorable light, then storyboard and video those examples.

Web and CD-ROM content: Web-based product displays and demonstrations are a very important business tool, as are providing portable sales material via CD-ROM or DVD. Video material is an essential component of this medium. Fortunately, the newest editing tools easily format video for optimum Web and CD-ROM-based viewing.

Distance learning: Opportunities abound for online classrooms, many of which include video. While large-scale video usage in online classes may not be practical for 56 k modem connections, classes linked with high-speed connections can fully enjoy supplementary video material. Figure 9.1 shows an example of a typical online learning module with video.

Figure 9.1
A video supplements an online chemistry course with in-depth explanations when needed.

Messages to employees: At a large plant, certain important announcements or updates require more than a written memo. They should be given "in person" by the CEO or other top officers. However, in large plants, such a gathering of all employees may not be practical. A videotaped message that can be played back in all departments could be the perfect solution.

Customer training: Your products will work well if they are used correctly. Cut down on customer frustration and calls to technical support by including a video describing exactly how to use your product. Digital video camcorders are great for close-ups, in which you can demonstrate exactly how tricky corners snap into place and how one widget fits into another. Even if users never open the manual, they'll probably pop in the video.

Employee training: You can cut way down on the man hours spent acquainting employees with certain equipment or processes by creating a training video. Skills that multiple employees need to be brought up to speed on can be taught on video.

Inventory: Taking inventory is a time-eating crunch that stresses out employees and slows down sales. Sometimes it's easier to take a slow, moving shot of rows of a particular product line than photograph each product type or model. Using video to keep track of inventory can be a real timesaver.

Business and Industrial Filming: a Unique Endeavor

In previous chapters, we discussed home moviemaking techniques, capturing special moments, creating a video with maximum emotional impact, and so forth. Business filming is different. You have a message, one that you don't mind hammering home a bit, or you have a set of skills that need to be filmed and described precisely. You have a specific goal of getting more customers, clarifying some aspect of your business model, setting your business apart from your competitors, or teaching employees certain skills. So, when you film, you are aiming for clarity, brevity, and directness. Special effects are out. They'll only detract. Humor and playing on emotions should be used sparingly. Here are points to keep in mind when creating a business film:

▶ Business videos should present a unified, polished message. Your presentation should be limited to giving your audience the essentials and a few highlights. Create a chapter or section layout that logically presents your information step-by-step. In each section, restrict your content to images and videos that support that section.

▶ Business and educational videos are often produced as a complete layout. To deliver a message, you'll mix images, text headings, and bulleted lists, as well as videos. A presentation based solely on video may not "hammer home" the message as effectively as a combination of media. Facts are drilled into a viewer when they linger on screen for a few seconds. Thus, the video component of your presentation may be limited to a "talking head," narrator who provides an overview of the subject matter (Figure 9.2) or product close-ups.

Figure 9.2
The CEO introduces a corporate overview with a filmed interview.

▶ File size is a major consideration as well. Video presentations must be portable. The need for mini-movies may be obvious for online viewing, but video uptake from CD-ROMs is often not particularly smooth. This is another reason to incorporate still images when possible and utilize technology that reduces video file size.

CHAPTER 9

► Dovetailing with the last requirement is the need to distribute information in easily digestible portions. Business and education videos are often divided into segments, facilitating smaller file size. Also, a "chapter-based" system makes it easy for viewers to navigate to their interests. Figure 9.3 shows an Adobe Acrobat-based document with videos that make use of Adobe's bookmark layout for easy navigation.

Figure 9.3

This Adobe Acrobat video tutorial employs bookmarks as chapter links.

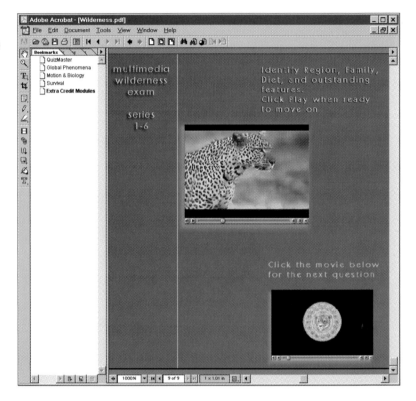

► As a video presentation developer for business or education, you do not want technical barriers erected between you and your potential viewers. Universal distribution is important. You'll want to share your video presentations in formats that are PC, Mac, and UNIX-friendly.

► Another major requirement is interactivity. Viewers may want to navigate your presentation by themselves, fast forwarding and choosing elements of interest. Also, you may want to provide related URLs. A good video layout should include some sort of clickable interface. This chapter will emphasize layouts that promote interactivity.

▶ Narration should be recorded using a high-quality microphone. Check the levels first before a final "take" to make sure the voice is clear and distinct. During final mix-down, do not compress the audio too much. In short, don't undermine your talent with poor audio recording quality.

TIP

When creating your business video layout, keep the following in mind:

Company spokespeople or other onscreen talent should look upbeat. Avoid allowing shadows on faces. However, spokespeople should not look slick and over-rehearsed.

Onscreen text should be limited to a few words at a time. Stick to headings, bullets, and other points of emphasis. Let your video "talking head" express details and embellishments.

Make sure your spokesperson's script is in sync with the on-screen text headings and bullets. Talking heads should repeat any displayed text headings at least once.

Narrators should know their scripts well and have gotten past all the "ums" and "uhs" before filming. A pleasant, well-trained voice helps prevent viewers from reaching for the Stop button out of irritation.

When you film or photograph products, tie off cables and other distracting paraphernalia. Film against a solid-color background, and light the product well. Close-up videos should display exactly what the voice-over is describing.

Putting It All Together

Creating your business video requires the successful execution of several steps. Whether you are making a product demo kiosk or employee training video, similar components will be required:

A clearly defined goal: What should the audience know or be empowered to do after watching your video?

A simple script or storyboard: What scenario(s) would best set the stage for your video's message? A factory floor? A company looking for a solution? An emergency requiring quick intervention? Plot out that sequence of events in a way that best tells your product story from beginning to end.

Props: The product should be displayed often, prominently, and from angles that are the most flattering. Training videos should be as demonstrative as possible. Show everything that will help customers and employees grasp what you want to say.

CHAPTER 9

Environment: Lighting is everything. Shadows and poor lighting will undermine the subject you're trying to feature. Buy, rent, or otherwise commandeer adequate lighting for your project, or move the whole show to a well-lit conference area that will do justice to your presentation. Close-ups require more lighting.

Actors: You'll probably want a corporate talking head with a pleasant demeanor and voice to do introductions as well as present an outline of the entire movie. Then you'll need a techno-wonk to display the product features and activate buzzers and bells while describing what she or he is doing. This way you get the comfort of an easy-to-digest overview as well as someone in a lab coat that really understands this stuff. Don't go out of your way to hire a professional. Earnestness counts more than good looks. Actors with those sonorous radio-announcer voices should be avoided. They can sound annoying and draw attention away from your product or message.

Access to video editing tools: A business video will require a trip to the computer. Editing is necessary. You will want to create titles for each segment, and you'll be cutting segments and moving them elsewhere, incorporating simple transition effects, and adding voice-over. It is here that you'll create several versions of your presentation if needed: one for the Web, another for CD-ROM or DVD, and another for VHS tape.

Planning and Segmentation

As you determine what you want to say with your video, break the content down into segments. Following are two examples.

1. Safely Unpacking Your Widget
2. Setting Up Your Widget for the First Time
3. Using Your Widget
4. Widget Upkeep Tips

The above example follows a simple chronology. You are following the customer's experience with your product during its entire life cycle. On video, this can be quite reassuring, as it conveys that the customer will have your product for a long time.

Here's another example of breaking down the video content into bite-sized chunks:

1. Introduction to Inventory Control
2. How Inventory Control Works
3. Tracking and Marking Inventory
4. Solving Discrepancies
5. Finishing Up

In this example, employees are introduced to a new process in a series of steps that follow their workflow. You have made an overwhelming task sound manageable.

The segments identified above will actually become titles to "chapters" in your video—the breakpoints. You'll introduce a segment with a title, film that segment, close the segment with a conclusion, then display a title for the next segment. With good forethought applied to segmentation, no one will feel overwhelmed by having to digest the totality of the information at one go.

Even industrial films with very few spoken lines leave a lasting impression of your company. Clarity and professionalism count. Take a while to plan things well, as opposed to simply showing up with the video camera and hoping for the best, and you'll be much happier with the results. To this end, here are more planning requirements to consider before filming begins:

> ▶ If necessary, you'll write a short script for each segment, helping viewers stay focused on what you are teaching. You'll also draw out shot-blocking maps for each scene—simple diagrams indicating where camera and actors should be positioned, their exact movements throughout the scene, angles, and close-up requirements.

> ▶ As part of your planning phase, select a filming environment. Keep in mind lighting requirements, as well as the need for minimal noise and interruptions.

> ▶ Finally, select your actors, give them their lines ahead of time, and indicate what actors should wear. At minimum, specify dark or light colors and broad dress style guidelines.

Thinking Ahead

While planning, filming, and editing, always keep the final results in mind. Depending on your goals for your project, each type of presentation has special requirements. Consider and plan ahead for all the various elements your video project will require:

> ▶ Some firms use video to provide a weekly "message from the CEO." This would require nothing more than a simple single-camera video against a complementary backdrop.

> ▶ If you're designing a self-paced overview of classroom material, viewers need a place to click to advance the lesson, answer a question, take the quiz, and so forth. This requires you to plan for user interactivity in your project.

> ▶ Are you designing a self-running "kiosk" video to display at trade shows (Figure 9.4)? Your video needs to frequently display the product name and company contact information. You'll need to superimpose text over the video as it plays back and perhaps display a logo in the corner of the video for the entire duration.

CHAPTER 9

Figure 9.4
An interactive
information kiosk.

> If you're creating tutorial videos that describe specific mechanical or software skills, the output can't be blurry or muddy. Too much compression makes it hard to see details. Rather than compress your project too heavily, shorten the video, replacing some of it with still images, and don't use extreme compression for the remaining video.

Getting It All on Film

After you've planned to the best of your ability, get it all on film. Here are some important pointers:

> Make sure you are filming in a format that your video editor can work with. Check with the editing team for software usage and formatting needs.

> After filming, take a minute to review each shot, and shoot important segments more than once, so you'll have some flexibility when editing. Remember, never show your product in the dark, in a shadow, or in less-than-favorable conditions.

> Actors should state the product and model name clearly and frequently.

> Develop zero tolerance for "umms" and "aahs." Just shoot it again until they get it right. If actors need to simplify their lines in order to get through the script error-free, that's fine, but whatever is said should be said well.

Determining Layout

Your video editing team (which could be you) will determine what software to use for editing. As mentioned above, titles and transitions will be added and mistakes deleted using a video editing program. However, you must also determine the layout, or "package," for presenting your video. For example, the actual footage you shoot may end up being only a portion of your corporate presentation. Perhaps you'll not be ultimately distributing a video but, rather, a slide show in which video is but one component. You can, of course, opt to embed all your titles and bullets and supplemental text inside the actual video, but this can be cumbersome and hard to edit later. Your presentation may work best, then, as one of the following:

▶ A PowerPoint slide show using a corporate template you've previously designed.

▶ An HTML page format that simply links video segments.

▶ An Adobe Acrobat file with embedded QuickTime movies.

▶ Videos linked via a navigational "console," created using Macromedia Flash or Director.

▶ Finally, you could always create the complete project in a video editing program and display the video as a stand-alone document.

Although layout choices abound, let's discuss the pluses and minuses of these five options.

NOTE

One very important consideration when choosing layout is your project's final distribution format. We discuss these choices thoroughly later in the book. However, keep in mind that if your movie will be played back right there at corporate headquarters, on a big, roomy computer hard drive, compression is probably not an issue. If the goal is to create CDs for field use, your final output must be a CD-friendly movie format such as QuickTime with Sorensen compression. If the Web is your goal, you are looking at maximum compression, very small movies, and breaking down the movie into its smallest logical segments for easy Web playback.

PowerPoint

A video presentation could easily be embellished in PowerPoint using text, bullets, and still images. You could insert a video just as you would insert any other object in PowerPoint (Figure 9.5). PowerPoint is on most PCs and most PC users in a corporate environment know how to use it. Thus, editing a PowerPoint video presentation would not require familiarity with video editing programs. It's very easy to add images and text to presentations in PowerPoint.

However, the most portable movie file types, such as QuickTime, can have playback problems in PowerPoint, which prefers the Windows-based AVI format. Also, playing back a PowerPoint presentation with video is very CPU-intensive. PowerPoint presentations are not easily edited for convenient Web display, and they are not a Mac-friendly solution.

CHAPTER 9

PowerPoint Video presentations are great for viewing in a corporate conference room on a powerful computer where portability is not an issue.

Figure 9.5
Adding a movie
to a PowerPoint
presentation.

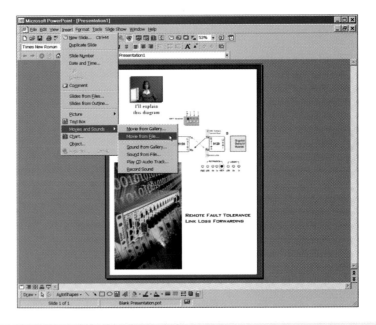

TIP

In a PowerPoint presentation, an inserted video will not begin playing until it's clicked by the viewer. If you want to associate a link with that movie, you'll have to insert an object or text link right beneath it.

NOTE

PowerPoint does have features that bring nice touches to corporate presentations. Let's say you have a movie that begins playback in PowerPoint and you'd like to have text appear midway through the movie playback. You can set up timed text appearances based on events such as mouse clicks. In fact, PowerPoint's animation timing feature can be used to orchestrate a whole series of events triggered by video playback (Figure 9.6). You could add images, hyperlinks, and paragraph text; you could even have files opening and displaying alongside your slide show—all based on how you manipulate timing.

Figure 9.6
Animating a
PowerPoint
presentation.

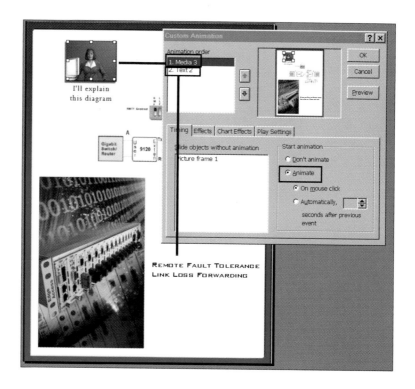

If you choose PowerPoint as your layout program, the following examples of interactivity may be of interest to you. PowerPoint interaction can be used to open stand-alone files. The viewer just clicks the link. As long as the file is where the link expects to find it, and as long as the user's computer knows how to open the file, clicking the link as shown in these figures will open it.

In Figure 9.7, interviewees are discussing a report. Viewers can click the provided link, open the report in question, and follow along more clearly with the interview's content.

Figure 9.7
Using a PowerPoint link
to open a program.

In Figure 9.8, a PowerPoint presentation includes a movie in which, when clicked, a technician explains a diagram. However, when the label "Link Loss Forwarding" below is clicked, a short Flash movie opens in a pop-up window (you can create a link to any file, such as another video that will appear in the viewer's media player, but Flash movies are preferable because they open very quickly).

Figure 9.8
Opening a Flash
movie with a hyperlink
in a PowerPoint
presentation.

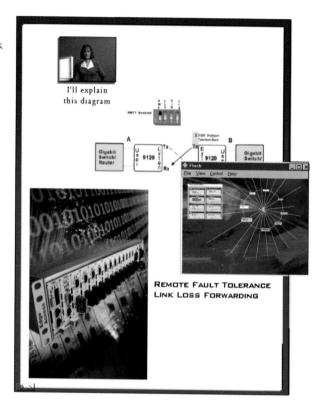

TIP

PowerPoint lets you turn any item on the screen into a link. You can link to
another slide, another presentation, a URL, or any file or program on the
viewer's computer. In this example, the heading "Link Loss Forwarding" is
embedded in the large background picture. However, to make just the heading
itself into a link, draw a rectangle with no fill and no border around the
heading, and associate that invisible rectangle with a link.

HTML

You can easily create a simple HTML page of links with descriptive text that directs viewers to
open each video segment. This would be fast, convenient, and easily undateable. If the movies
are small enough and in the right format, such a presentation could easily be uploaded for Web
viewing or bumped onto a CD-ROM for broad distribution. On the downside, videos would have
to be small and quite compressed and saved in a Web-friendly format. We explore creating video
for the Web later in the book.

CHAPTER 9

Adobe Acrobat

Adobe Acrobat is the primary tool for creating universal documents. It's very easy to embed a QuickTime Video in an Acrobat file, and as long as the movies are transported along with the Acrobat file, the playback is very smooth. Your video presentation can be distributed to its largest possible audience using Adobe Acrobat. However, this solution requires purchasing the Adobe Acrobat program, which is in the mid-$200 range at the moment. Also, the project creator must learn to use the program. Note, too, that Acrobat does not come with presentation backgrounds and familiar layout templates like PowerPoint does.

Macromedia Flash

Everybody likes Flash. It's easy to create backgrounds with buttons that navigate to the various video segments in your presentation. Viewers can easily move from segment to segment. Your presentation can be viewed on the Web or it can easily be transported anywhere. Your presentation will look good, not take up too much disk space, and be quite portable. However, the Flash program must be purchased, and the video project director must see to it that somebody learns it.

Stand-alone Video

Finally, there's the option of allowing the movie to remain a stand-alone video, adding all titling, text, and still images right inside the video editing software. This would involve mastering the editing tools discussed elsewhere in this book. A stand-alone movie has the advantage of simple distribution. You end up with one file, a video, which can be compressed as small as you like and uploaded to a Web site, bumped to a CD-ROM, or left alone on the hard drive uncompressed for optimum playback quality. On the downside is the amount of video editing involved. This option is time-intensive. There'll be no slapping a video clip onto a PowerPoint slide and typing in a title. Nonetheless, once you learn your way around a program like Ulead Media Studio Pro and learn to properly use Cues and other marking techniques, you can get pretty fast at editing. Also, with text and titling embedded right in the video itself, the results will look more professional and be less clunky on playback than other options involving popular layout programs.

A Closer Look: Acrobat and Flash

Two very popular methods for distributing videos in the business world are Adobe Acrobat and Macromedia Flash. These programs create presentations that are attractive, portable, easily navigable, and that allow you to embellish your video with images, links, and text. Note, however, that you'll be spending more money here. The Adobe Acrobat we are discussing is not the free Acrobat reader, but, rather, the actual Adobe Acrobat program. Likewise, Flash costs around $200 and requires a learning curve, although the tutorial below provides a great start. What follows, then, is a walk-through of two popular tools for enhancing your business video's value.

Videos in Adobe Acrobat Documents

You perhaps know of Adobe Acrobat as the online reader used to share documents among viewers, regardless of their computer's operating system. Adobe Acrobat documents can be viewed in the PC, Mac, and UNIX environments. To view a document saved as an Acrobat (PDF) file, one simply makes a trip to the Adobe Web site and downloads and installs the free reader, then opens the file to be viewed.

What is less understood is how documents become Adobe Acrobat files. To create a PDF file, as Acrobat files are frequently called, an author or distributor purchases the Adobe Acrobat program. This program allows a user to convert documents from Word or, for example, into PDF form. Once in PDF form, the documents can be widely distributed.

Adobe Acrobat is an attractive solution for business video layout for a number of reasons. First of all, placing videos inside a PDF file is a single-step process. Once inserted, videos can be moved and resized with the click of a mouse. Also, since PDF files can be multi-page documents, one can easily insert unique videos on several pages, creating links that allow the viewer to navigate between them.

Let's create a quick Adobe Acrobat file with only a single page. (Figure 9.9 shows a completed example.) We'll add a video that will play back when clicked, and we'll add links to URLs as well.

Figure 9.9
An Adobe Acrobat
document with videos.

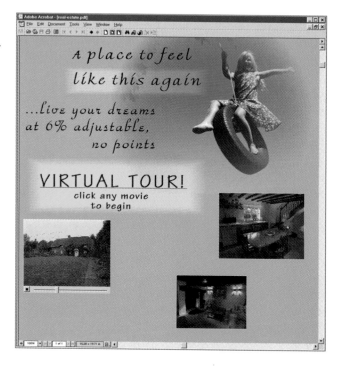

CHAPTER 9

You can open Adobe Acrobat and begin building a document from scratch. For our purposes, we'll just create a page from a single image and add videos and a link.

1. To begin, open Adobe Acrobat and choose File > Import > Image (Figure 9.10). You'll be adding a page created from this image. The image will appear filling the entire screen, although the image size will not be changed. The document magnification is displayed at the lower left.

2. You can now insert a video and position it anywhere you like on the screen. Click the Movie tool on the toolbox on the middle left (see Figure 9.10).

Figure 9.10

Insert an image, then use the Insert Movie tool to draw a rectangle and insert a video.

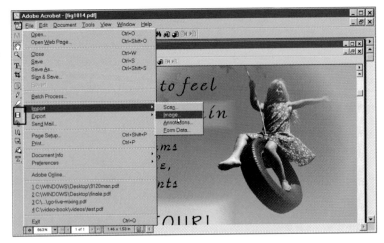

3. Drag a rectangle with the Movie Tool onto the page where you'd like the movie to appear. The movie you will choose will be resized according to the rectangle you now draw, and it will overlay the background.

4. After drawing your rectangle, the Movie Properties dialog box will appear. You'll be prompted to choose a movie and specify its boundary width, if any. Adobe Acrobat can accept AVI and MOV video formats. Using the Movie Properties dialog box, you can specify whether or not the video controller should appear (a Play/Pause/Stop bar). By default, the video you insert will not play back until the viewer clicks it. Once inserted, the movie can be resized and repositioned by clicking and dragging with the Movie tool.

5. Using this same technique, you can insert several movies. Be careful creating multi-movie documents for online viewing, as each additional movie significantly increases loading time.

You can create links in any Adobe Acrobat file. Note that any portion of the image you imported can be made into a link, just by dragging a rectangle anywhere you like with the Link Tool. Here's how it's done:

1. Click the Link Tool on the Adobe Acrobat toolbox on the left side of the screen.

2. Locate the segment in your image that you want to make into a link and drag a rectangle the size and shape of your desired button. The Create Link dialog box appears (Figure 9.11).

Figure 9.11
Creating a link from background text in Adobe Acrobat.

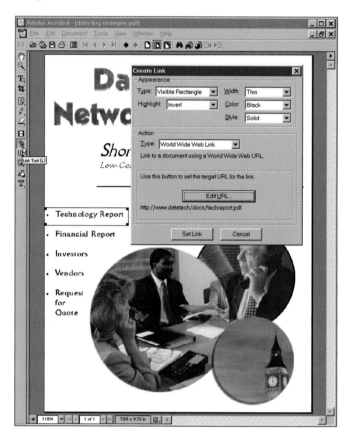

3. Specify link properties, such as rectangle visibility and color, and specify a URL to be opened in a browser when you click the link.

4. Click OK to close the dialog box, and the image area you selected with the Link Tool will now open a URL when clicked.

CHAPTER 9

Creating an Interactive Movie with Macromedia Flash

Just about the best program around for making a multimedia document portable and interactive is Macromedia Flash. In this section, you'll learn how to transform a QuickTime movie into an interactive viewer experience. You'll insert your movie into a Flash background and create buttons that fast-forward the viewer to predetermined points in your movie. Rather than just give people a movie, you're providing an attractive layout that lets viewers navigate it as they wish.

Note that this walk-through will take about forty minutes of your time, and, of course, Macromedia Flash must be installed on your computer. To download the free trial version of Flash, visit the Macromedia Web site: http://www.macromedia.com.

Figure 9.12 displays my complete example.

Figure 9.12
A QuickTime movie
with interactivity added
in Macromedia Flash.

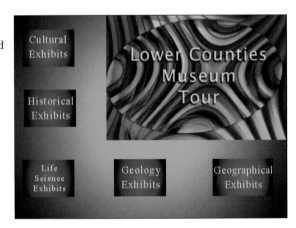

The QuickTime movie at the upper right was created in MediaStudio Pro and divided into sections. The buttons surrounding the video provide links to those sections. When the viewer clicks a button, the movie fast-forwards to that point and begins playing. Let's take a look at how it's done.

NOTE
Flash projects that incorporate QuickTime movies (such as this project) must be exported as QuickTime movies when completed.

Creating a Document Background

Although I used an image that is positioned where the movie appears in later frames, we'll just create a simple gradient color background for this project.

1. Create a new Flash document. The default size is 550×2400 pixels. To alter the size, choose Modify > Page Properties.

2. On the Tools Panel, click the Fill Color square.

3. Click the green fill gradient square at the bottom of the Color Chooser (Figure 9.13).

Figure 9.13
Create a fill by choosing a color from the color cube at the bottom of the Tool Panel.

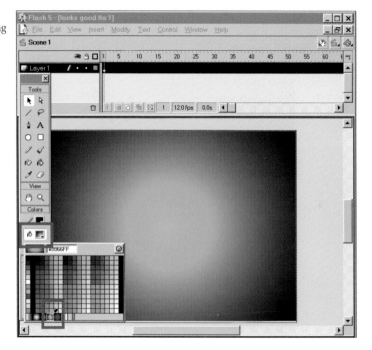

4. On the Tools Panel, choose the Rectangle Tool.

5. Create a rectangle that fits the entire document. The movie background is now a solid green gradient.

In my movie, I created an image that fills the upper right, which is where the movie will appear after the viewer clicks the movie buttons we'll be creating. We need to group this background so we do not inadvertently select a portion of it when adding new elements.

▶ Click the Arrow Tool at the upper left of the Tools Panel, and then click the green background you just made.

▶ Choose Modify > Group.

CHAPTER 9

Naming Layers and Extending Movie Length

We've created this background on Layer 1. We need to access the timeline for Layer 1 and set the movie to extend to the end of the video clip you are going to add. For this reason, it is important before proceeding that you know the length of your QuickTime movie clip.

1. At the top of the screen, near Layer 1, drag the scrollbar at the bottom of the timeline so that the frame number that corresponds to your video length is reached.

2. Click the white or gray frame icon that appears right below your frame number. When clicked, the frame icon will turn blue.

3. Press the F6 key. You'll see a dot on that frame (Figure 9.14). You've just created a Keyframe that extends your background to the last frame of the movie. Now let's add the movie clip.

Figure 9.14
Insert a Keyframe that represents the final frame of your QuickTime movie.

Adding the QuickTime Movie

We are going to import a QuickTime movie, place it on its own layer, and position it at the upper right of the green background. We need to do this on Frame 2, so that the viewer does not see the movie at the very beginning of the presentation.

1. At the bottom of the Layer area, click the plus sign. A new layer is added to the layer list. By default it is named Layer 2. Double-click inside the name Layer 2 and type in Movie (Figure 9.14). You'll now have your layer name so you don't accidentally place the movie on the wrong layer.

2. Click Frame 2 of the Movie layer. You previously used the scroll bar to reach the end of the movie, so you may have to scroll back to the top to see Frame 2.

3. After clicking Frame 2, press F6. You've made a Keyframe at Frame 2. You'll now be able to import the movie to Frame 2 without it just bouncing back to Frame 1 by default.

4. Without clicking anywhere else in the work area, choose File > Import. When the Import dialog box appears, choose QuickTime Movie from the File of Type dropdown menu.

5. Browse to the QuickTime Movie you want to use, and click OK.

6. Position the movie at the upper right of the background so you'll have room to place your buttons. Position simply by dragging with the Arrow tool (the Tool on the upper left of the Toolbox).

7. The only way you'll be able to preview the QuickTime clip you added is by dragging the thin red Location Bar across the frames (scrubbing the movie). You'll see the clip play back.

Creating Buttons

We are now going to make our interactive buttons that, when clicked, will jump ahead to any movie frame you have specified. We'll make them with a blue gradient and add text to identify them.

First, we need a new layer for the button.

1. Click the plus sign beneath the Layers on the left side of the screen. A new Layer will appear.

2. Click inside the new layer and name it Buttons.

3. Click the first frame of Layer 3, which specifies that any item we create will appear on this layer and frame.

Now let's make our button.

1. Click the Fill color icon on the Tool Panel and choose the blue gradient at the bottom of the Color Chooser box.

2. Click the Rectangle Tool and draw a small, button-sized rectangle. You'll be placing text describing the purpose of this link, so leave enough room for your label.

Now you'll add text to the button.

1. After creating your rectangle, click the Text Tool (the "A") and click once inside the rectangle. You'll now be able to add text to your button.

2. Type descriptive text and, before clicking outside the text frame, press Shift+Ctrl and Backspace, which selects the words you just typed.

3. Edit your text by choosing Font style, color, and size on the Character panel. (See Figure 9.15. If you do not see the Character panel, press Ctrl+T.)

CHAPTER 9

Figure 9.15
Set Flash text attributes
with the Character
panel.

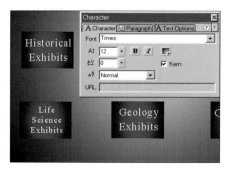

4. Now you have to group the text and the button together so that they can both be made interactive (clickable).

5. Click the text you just created and edited and, while pressing the Shift key, click the blue rectangle as well. Now, choose Modify > Group.

Next we'll add interactivity to the button we created.

Adding Interactivity to the Buttons

Click the button to make sure it is selected and press F8. This accesses the Symbol Properties dialog box. Under Behavior, choose Button. You can now add Actions to this button. We'll make it so when the viewer clicks a button, the video fast forwards to a particular frame. We need to associate an action with this button.

1. Select your button. If the Actions panel is not visible, choose Window > Actions and click the Basic Actions icon so that the little "book" expands to reveal actions (Figure 9.16).

Figure 9.16
Set Actions by clicking
an Action then choosing
parameters.

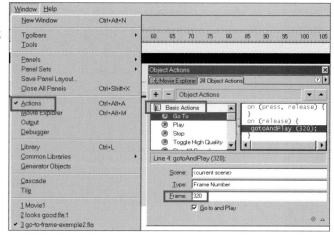

2. Double-click the Go To action. The Action panel expands to reveal choices for that action. We can specify the frame we want to begin playing when the button is clicked.

3. In the Frame field, type in the frame number of your first target segment for playback. Press Enter to lock in your choice (Figure 9.16).

Duplicating the Interactive Button

You've now made one button. To duplicate and edit a copy of this button, do the following:

1. Select the button and press Ctrl+D. You'll have created a second button identical to the first.

2. Reposition the second button and click it.

3. Choose Modify > Ungroup. Choose Modify > Ungroup again, or Break Apart, whichever is available.

4. Click the Text and edit the text label to indicate the next movie segment.

5. Group this second button.

6. Choose F8 and specify a button behavior, indicating it is now a button symbol.

7. Select the button and, on the Actions panel, click the Go to and Play line.

8. Change the Frame number to indicate the second video segment's Go To location.

9. Create and position as many buttons as needed.

NOTE

You need to also create a separate Home button that takes the viewer back to the "top" of the presentation. To do so, create a button called Home, and choose a Go To Action, indicating Frame 1. However, make sure you uncheck Go To And Play. When the user clicks the button, the presentation will rewind and stop, rather than rewind and start up again.

Exporting as QuickTime

Since Flash movies do not display QuickTime movies, you'll need to export your creation as a QuickTime movie. Here's how to do it:

1. First, save your work. Note the folder you've saved into because Flash simply exports your movies to that folder without reminding you where that folder is.

2. Choose File > Publish Settings.

3. When the Publish Settings dialog box appears, click the Formats tab.

4. Uncheck Flash and uncheck HTML.

5. Place a check next to QuickTime.

CHAPTER 9

6. Uncheck Use Default Names. You'll now be able to indicate a meaningful name for your movie.

7. Next to QuickTime, type in a name. You must include the MOV file extension because Flash will not add it for you if you don't.

8. Very importantly, click the QuickTime tab and, under Playback, click Pause At Start.

Publishing Your Movie

You can now publish your movie. You can click the Publish button now, or close the dialog box and, later, click File > Publish.

When you publish this movie, you create a QuickTime video. Click it, and the movie will open in the QuickTime viewer. Since you indicated Pause At Start, the movie will not play until you press one of the buttons. Although the movie opens in the standard QuickTime Viewer, it has interaction. The video is more like a mini-application that responds to the viewer's clicks.

Crossroads

Now that you've learned how videos can play a role in communicating many aspects of your business to the world, we'll move on to another huge medium for sharing videos with others, the Web. In the next chapter, you'll learn about Web-friendly video formats and inserting videos into Web pages with a bit of flair and finesse.

10

Publishing Video on the Web

In this chapter, we'll discuss various approaches to getting your videos up on the Web. The Web is a great vehicle for sharing your movies with the world. Embedding videos in a Web page allows visitors to click through and view your movies freely. You can add videos to your site any time you like and change the selection whenever the idea appeals to you.

You can post quick snippets of family vacations, products in action, artistic presentations, or anything you like. Using Web page design software, your page's design can enhance your video presentation. Background color choice, descriptive text, and images can supplement your video presentation as you see fit.

Note that in this chapter, we won't be building Web pages, but, rather, describing methods for adding a movie to your page. You'll learn about embedding videos in Web pages, Web-friendly options for QuickTime, streaming video options, and creating video links.

Movies created for the Web are a special animal. Web movies must be severely compressed, usually to an obvious degree. Colors will be "averaged," creating a blotchy appearance. Faces and details may be indistinct. Web-based movies are a work of compromise, sacrificing some color depth and clarity in order to have a movie small enough for most viewers to download. Your goal is to create a smooth, downloadable, good-looking movie for Web viewing. In this chapter, you'll especially learn how streaming video helps you have it both ways if at all possible: small size, as well as clarity.

What Makes a Good Web Movie?

A movie that does well on the Web will most often be short and to the point. You'll cut scenes that don't have a quick payoff and opt to show mostly close-ups of main subjects. Showing panoramic, big spaces on Internet video usually doesn't work. In the Web video medium, subtleties tend to get lost.

Here are some basic ground rules for creating Web-based videos.

▶ Before posting your video, take the time to reduce file size, frame rate, color, and audio depth. Movies designed for 56 k modem download should not be larger than 250 k or so, unless you are counting on a very motivated audience. Movies designed for ISDN, DSL, or cable modems should not be more than about 3 MB. These figures are flexible if you use a more advanced streaming technology, which we'll discuss shortly.

▶ Note that movies with fewer colors transmit faster than densely colored films based on complex images. For example, interviews or performances against single-color backdrops transmit nicely.

▶ Avoid the transitions between scenes that you learned about in earlier chapters. Because each frame in a transition is different from its predecessor, transitions greatly add to download time. So, if a movie is destined for the Web, use straight cuts.

▶ Use a frame rate somewhere between six and fifteen per second. Start high and work low. If the high frame rate produces jerky video, then work down two or three frames per second until the video looks somewhat smooth.

▶ Cut ruthlessly. Length is a real issue on the Internet. Resign yourself to the fact that your Web version of this project will cut to the chase much quicker than the CD or tape versions.

▶ Take time to experiment with audio settings. Make your tracks mono, unless your intended audience is on a local intranet with bandwidth to spare. If bandwidth is an issue, it's worth the time to go back and spin a decent-sounding mono mix of your audio track and use that for your Web movie. Also, reduce the audio to 12-bit at 22Hz if you can.

NOTE

Interestingly, video dimensions do not affect download times as negatively as the other factors I've mentioned. If you have a video at 320×240 pixels that you really want to post, but the file size is too large, reducing the dimensions to, say, 160×180 won't make as much difference as you might think.

CHAPTER 10

How Video Works on the Web

The creator of a Web site has two basic chores. One is to design the pages—determining where the images, text, videos, and so forth should appear. The second is to upload those files to a server, the "always on" computer where the Web site and related files can be accessed by visitors. When a Web browser accesses a page, the viewed material is downloaded to and temporarily stored on the browser's computer. For example, if you were to visit a few Web pages, then view your computer's Temporary Internet Files (usually stored beneath the Windows folder), you'd see files representing remnants of the pages you visited. If you cared to look, most files will be very small, representing the images, logos, animated GIFs, and other Web content. However, of all these files that show the footprints of your Web travels, the videos are by far the largest.

The challenge for Web designers has always been to create pages that display content as quickly as possible. For Web browsers with connections at 56 k or slower, viewing a video embedded in a Web page can require more patience than most people possess. Still, multimedia on the Internet is a great thing. Web surfers come to expect it, and Web sites that are able to display good multimedia content (including videos) without huge delays are often pretty popular.

In this chapter, we'll consider a few ways of including videos in your Web creations, using technology that, for example, allows visitors to watch video clips on your site before they are fully downloaded. You'll learn a few bandwidth-sparing techniques and other video-friendly design tips to make for enjoyable online viewing.

Posting Video on the Web

The process of adding a video to a Web page is similar to adding other types of content. With the right Web design program, you'll have an easy time actually inserting videos into a Web page for viewers to log on to your site and enjoy. Most WYSIWYG Web design programs let you drag and drop videos from your video folder right onto your page, or they provide simple commands for doing so. Posting a video on the Web does not require you to be a Web design wizard. Programs particularly friendly to including videos in your Web creations are Macromedia Dreamweaver, Microsoft Front Page, Sausage Software's HotDog Pro, and Adobe GoLive. You can also download trialware and shareware Web design programs from sites like **www.hotfiles.com** and **www.tucows.com**. Please note that not every program that lets you add images and animations to your page will also make it easy to insert videos.

NOTE
WYSIWYG (What You See Is What You Get) Web design programs let you work with a graphic interface. Rather than type in code and learn HTML, you can see your page as you build it just as it will be seen online.

Figure 10.1 shows how easy it is to add a video to a Web page in Dreamweaver, for example. Just drag the video from the Explorer-like folder of Web materials onto the page, and it will appear. Dreamweaver takes care of the required HTML coding for you. Most other popular Web design software provides a similar feature.

Figure 10.1
Inserting a video using a WYSIWYG Web design program.

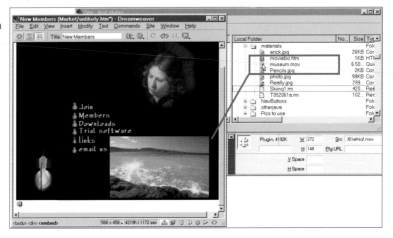

Also, note the solution discussed at the end of the last chapter—the Flash movie interface—can be easily posted on the Web as well.

NOTE

As an alternate to posting your movie on a Web page, several of the programs we discuss let you e-mail your video to any valid e-mail address. Canon Video Home, Ulead VideoStudio, and MGI VideoWave all let you do this. Compressing video to a size small enough for e-mailing is quite a feat. So, some programs require that the recipient of the movie also have installed a small program that will decompress and display the movie once the e-mail is opened and read. This extra step is not too much to undertake if you are sharing videos with a recipient on a regular basis.

Streaming Video

In Chapter 4, we discussed three of the most Web-friendly file types—RM, or RealMedia from RealNetworks; Microsoft's WMV, or Streaming Windows Media; and QuickTime's MOV. Each of these formats supports a technology called streaming.

Streaming allows your online movie to begin playing back before it has completely downloaded. If you simply created a link to an MPEG movie on your page, viewers would have to wait until the entire movie had been transferred to their computer before playback could begin. If you

provide a streaming movie instead, the movie starts running after only a portion has been downloaded, or even as soon as the page appears in a browser. Streaming can also provide a live video feed. In such a case, the visitor is not downloading a movie at all, but, rather, watching a broadcast.

There are two types of streaming technology. The most common and least expensive allows a viewer to begin watching your movie as soon as a portion has been downloaded. Then, as data is transferred according to the connection quality and modem speed, more video will be displayed. In this streaming method, there is no special server set aside just for instantaneous video transfer. Thus, it is called Web server-based, or single-rate streaming.

True streaming requires the Web host to provide a streaming server, also known as a multi-rate server. This is the hardware necessary for a movie to begin playback as soon as a visitor accesses your site. The company hosting your Web site may very well offer a streaming server solution. Feel free to inquire. Streaming servers provide an "intelligent" connection for your movie that not only begins playback as soon as the visitor opens the page, but also adjusts transmission of video data according to Web traffic. The server will always download your movie as fast as the connection will allow, and it will deliver smooth playback even in bad Internet traffic. If Web traffic becomes particularly congested, the server will still try to download data and will not lose the connection. Creating a movie with true streaming technology incurs no special expense. However, paying a Web host to allow access to a streaming server will perhaps more than double your monthly server bill.

RealNetworks RM and Microsoft WMV movies can deliver both types of streaming. There are two ways to create both RealNetwork RM and Microsoft WMV movies. One is to directly export a video project as a Web movie. Editing software such as Ulead VideoStudio and Video Wave let you export your project as either RM or WMV videos (Figure 10.2). You need not purchase a high-end video product just to create streaming content.

<table>
<tr><td>

Figure 10.2

Saving a VideoStudio project as an RM streaming movie.

</td><td>

</td></tr>
</table>

You can also convert an existing movie to a Web movie using RealNetworks' RealProducer or Microsoft's Windows Media Encoder. Since RealProducer and Windows Media Encoder are dedicated streaming movie conversion programs, they offer a few more options than a standard movie editor output menu. Also, RealProducer will create a Web page with your movie, with code that you can copy and paste into any page you like.

Making a RealNetworks Streaming Movie

To convert a video to RM, you can use a video editor or download RealProducer from the RealNetworks Web site. RealProducer can be downloaded free of charge from the RealNetworks Web site: **http://www.realnetworks.com.** The RealProducer converter is updated frequently by RealNetworks, and using a recently downloaded version of RealProducer insures that your RM movie will take full advantage of their latest features and compression options. After downloading and installing RealProducer, you'll be ready to convert a movie.

It's easiest to create a movie with RealProducer by using the Wizard walk-through (Figure 10.3). You are presented with screens that prompt you for output preferences, and the video settings are compiled as you respond. Using the Wizard, you do not directly choose frame rate or audio settings like Hz or bit depth. Nor do you choose a smaller movie dimension than the movie you are converting. Rather, your choices focus on indicating the likely connection speed of your target audience. If you want to directly manipulate numerical settings, use the Options menu at the top of the screen.

Figure 10.3
RealProducer first asks what type of movie you want to create.

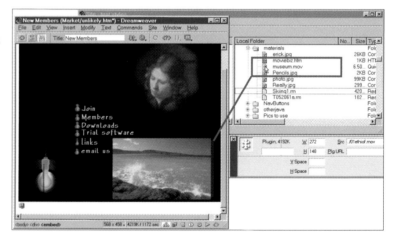

NOTE

Why no direct frame rate selection? Because the whole purpose of streaming is to allow the frame rate to vary based on connection conditions and Internet traffic. Specifying a frame rate would undermine RealMovie's flexibility.

We'll step through a few of RealProducer's most important screens.

1. When you first open RealProducer and start a new session, you'll be prompted to choose a session type (Figure 10.3). You can convert an existing movie or capture data from a device (like a microphone or digital video camera) and save it to disk as an RM file. You can also capture data from a device and send it straight to the Web as a live broadcast.

2. As you step through the screens, you'll be prompted to name your movie, include a description, and indicate a save location. You'll also be prompted to strike a balance between preserving the highest possible image clarity and ensuring that the movie has extra-smooth motion. Your choice depends on the type of movie you are converting (Figure 10.4). Movies with interviews and talking heads need image clarity. Frame jerkiness is not apt to be a problem. However, if your movie has lots of action, such as sports footage, you'll need to keep motion smooth at the expense of a little image clarity. RealProducer lets you make this choice.

Figure 10.4
The Video Quality panel lets you strike a balance between smoothness and clarity.

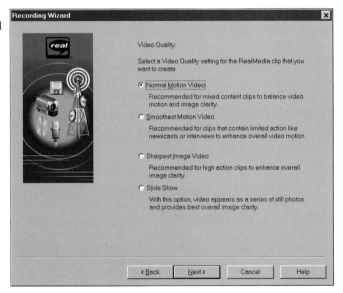

3. You'll also indicate the nature of your movie's audio (largely voice, voice with background music, or largely music). RealProducer will determine the best audio settings based on your movie's requirements. You don't get to manipulate the numbers yourself.

4. You'll be prompted to choose between creating a single-rate or multi-rate movie. A single-rate movie attempts to deliver data at the speed you specify, Internet traffic permitting. Multi-rate movies deliver movie data according to the visitor's connection. You can create several movies; for example, one for slower modems and one for high-speed lines (Figure 10.5).

Figure 10.5
Select the most likely
modem speeds your
audience will be
running at.

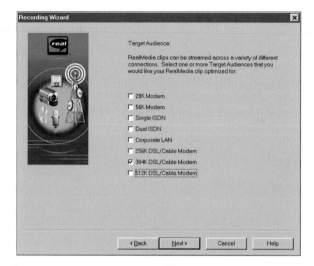

5. After choosing movie settings, you'll see a preview screen that displays your video before and after the RM options are applied (Figure 10.6). To render the movie, press the Start button at the lower left of the screen. When RealProducer has finished rendering the movie, the RM file will already be saved in the specified location.

Figure 10.6
Preview your movie
results by comparing the
original vs. the
compressed version.

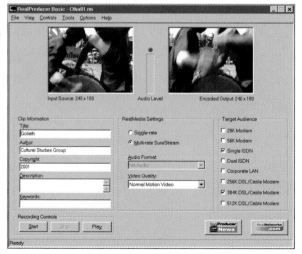

The RM movie will inevitably be a few steps down in quality from the original and will be of smaller dimensions. If desired, use the Audio Format and Video Quality dropdown menu to select new settings, and render the movie again by pressing the Start button. Rendering the movie with your new settings will erase the previous RM and RAM files, unless you specify a new name and location when prompted.

The RM and RAM Files

Note that when RealProducer finalizes video output, the program creates the actual movie (the RM file) and a RAM file. What is a RAM file? The RAM file contains references to the actual movie, and contains an identifier to let the browser know how to process this movie. In order for streaming to occur, when creating your page, you must make a link to this RAM file rather than the RM file itself. The RAM file contains a modified link to the actual movie. When you make arrangements with a Web host to deploy streaming movies, you'll probably be provided exact specifications for creating one using RealProducer or Windows Media Encoder.

Publishing Your RM Movie

RealProducer lets you create a Web page for your movie. Once the page is created, you can copy the code where indicated and paste it into any page of your choice. To create a Web page movie, choose Tools > Web Page from the RealProducer menu; you'll be prompted to specify whether your movie should appear in a pop-up window (a small window that overlays the Web page, usually in a corner) or embedded in the page itself. Note that embedded movies will not be supported by some RealServer Exchange servers, although you can still effectively stream movies even in the absence of a dedicated streaming media server. Check with your Web host for clarification.

Additionally, RealProducer has a Web page publishing tool (Tools > Publish Web Page) that uploads your movie page and related files via FTP and includes all necessary options.

Let me again stress the necessity of making sure that the RAM file, as well as the RM movie itself, is uploaded to your Web host.

Windows Streaming Media

To create Windows Streaming Media movies, Microsoft provides Windows Media Encoder, a free download from **http://www.microsoft.com/windows/windowsmedia/en/default.asp**. Windows Media Encoder converts existing movies to Microsoft's WMV streaming file type, creates a WMV movie from data input from a device such as a video camera or microphone, or creates a live broadcast (Figure 10.7).

CHAPTER 10

Figure 10.7
The Windows Media
Encoder Wizard lets you
specify movie type.

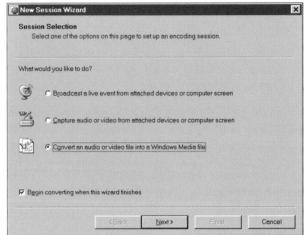

When Windows Media Encoder starts, you'll be prompted to specify settings by walking through a wizard rather than choosing direct numerical values yourself.

For example, you'll specify if a dedicated streaming server will be hosting your site. Your movie will utilize "intelligent streaming" if you choose the streaming Windows Media Server option (rather than the Web server-based option mentioned above). To employ this, your Web host must have Windows Media Server hardware and software installed.

You'll also be prompted to specify your target audience's most likely modem speed and provide an optional movie description. After you select the settings, a preview screen appears and encoding will begin.

When the encoding is finished, you'll be prompted to view the output file (Figure 10.8). The encoding process creates a streaming movie (a WMV file). You'll find the file in the location specified when you finish the encoding. The movie is saved to your hard drive (or uploaded via Webcast) without you having to manually save the file.

Figure 10.8
The Windows Media
Encoder Preview screen.

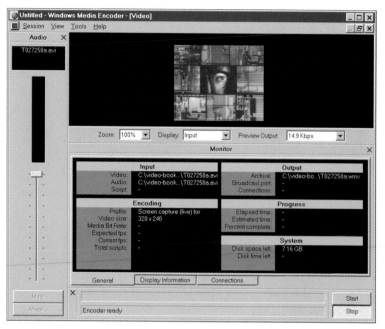

Choosing Movie Output Values Directly

Windows Media Encoder lets you specify numerical settings for your movie rather than answering questions via a wizard. Here's how to set the numerical values yourself:

1. From the main screen, choose New > Session and click the Profile tab.

2. Click the Edit button. From the screens that follow, you can choose modem connection speed, frame rate, audio in bits/Hz, codec type, and even screen dimensions.

3. After setting up a custom profile, it will appear in the Profile list with the others.

The WMV and WVX Files

If you are uploading your movie to a Web host with a Windows Media Server, you have one more step to complete. If you were to simply create a link in a Web page to your WMV file and upload it, the movie would not be streamed when clicked by viewers. You need to create a metafile, a small identifier that indicates that a multimedia server is being used. This file can be created by you and is saved with the file extension WVX or ASX. It is this file that you create a link to on your page. Here's how it's done:

Open a text or HTML editor and type the following:

```
<asx version="3.0">
 <entry>
 <ref href=mms://domainname.com/movie.wmv/>
 </entry>
</asx>
```

In place of "domainname," you would type the actual URL to your movie. Also, rather than movie.wmv, type the real name of the movie you just encoded, using the WMV file extension.

After typing the above, save the file as movie.wvx (again, use the actual name of the movie when naming this file, but use the WVX or ASX file extension).

As you can see, the WVX or ASX file contains a link to the movie itself. When you create the link in your page, create the link to that file, which will open the movie and employ streaming.

Creating a Video Page in Dreamweaver

In this section, I will demonstrate video page creation using Macromedia Dreamweaver, a popular Web site design tool that can be downloaded as thirty-day trialware from **www.macromedia.com**. In my opinion, for Web design, you can't do much better than Dreamweaver. Note that the following discussion has quite a few steps and will mainly be of interest to those wanting to learn video-friendly Web design.

Although this chapter segment can't possibly acquaint you with all the steps required for creating a Dreamweaver Web site, I'll walk you step-by-step through creating a page in Dreamweaver with a movie that behaves as specified. You'll see how easy it is in Dreamweaver to create special effects, and perhaps you'll be inspired to explore the program further. This exercise will also be more effective if you're willing to copy and type a little HTML code that I will provide.

Setting a Video Timer

A primary goal of this Dreamweaver walk-through will be to show you how to incorporate into your Web page a video that will begin playing a specified number of seconds after the visitor has logged on. The movie can suddenly appear at any position in the page, or it can appear first as a still image and then begin playback (Figure 10.9 shows the finished project. The smaller violin image becomes a movie in that exact same position, which begins playing back after a few seconds). This is done by inserting a simple "timer" script that indicates how many seconds playback should be delayed after the viewer clicks your page. A video timer feature can be helpful for a couple of reasons:

> ▶ Delaying video playback allows the viewer time to take in other page content before the movie starts. You'll have more control over the how your material is presented to the viewer.

▶ A delayed start allows time for the movie to "preload," meaning that the movie will be downloaded and ready to play back when the show automatically begins. Since the movie is preloaded, getting ready to play when you've indicated, your viewer will notice less of that annoying "video sputter" that occurs when a video is simultaneously loading and playing.

Figure 10.9
After this page is loaded for a few seconds, a video appears and plays back.

For what follows, you can use any Web-friendly movie type, such as MPEG, MOV, or the streaming content we just discussed. I'll be using a QuickTime movie, and I will explain specifically the options QuickTime provides when displaying QuickTime movies in a Web page. If you have a QuickTime movie available, you may want to use it for this exercise. The movie I'm using in my example is 232×180 pixels, so you may want to choose a clip of similar size.

A still image the same size as the movie is also required. You may recall learning how to extract a single frame from a video. That's what you'll need here, and the first frame is the best for this purpose. To the viewer, it will appear as though the still picture suddenly "came alive" and started moving. For your initial still image, you will want to extract a frame from the movie before you compressed it to a Web-friendly format.

Beginning the Page

Here's how to get started:

1. Create a folder and place both the image and the movie inside it.

2. Next, start Dreamweaver. A blank page appears. This is your Web page, and any content you place in it will appear on the Web when uploaded. The example I'll display here shows a page already populated with images, tables, text, and so forth. However, you can learn this technique just as well using a blank page.

3. Immediately, choose File > Save As, browse to the folder you just created, and save the page inside it. Name the page anything you like.

4. If Dreamweaver prompts you to create a new site using that folder, choose OK and allow Dreamweaver to build the site, which will take only a second or two. We'll not be getting involved in Dreamweaver's site-building capabilities in this instruction.

Inserting a Layer, Image, and Timeline

We can't just put the movie and image on a blank page. It must go inside a mobile box called a Layer.

1. With your blank Dreamweaver page open, choose Insert > Layer (Figure 10.10). My example page is not blank). A rectangular box will appear. This is a layer. You can position it anywhere you like and add content to it, such as images or movies. Click the tiny box in the upper left corner of the layer and drag it anywhere you like. Both our still image and movie will be positioned inside that layer. You need not expand the layer manually to accommodate the contents. It will resize when you insert an item.

Figure 10.10

Adding a Layer to a Dreamweaver page.

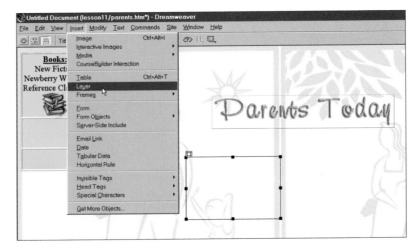

2. Choose Insert > Image. The Select Image Source browse menu will appear. Click the image you saved into the folder, then click the Select button. The image will appear inside the layer.

3. Choose Window > Timelines. Dreamweaver Timelines allows you to set up events that occur after the Web page has been open for a few seconds (Figure 10).

Figure 10.11
Delay the appearance of an event by choosing a later frame on the timeline.

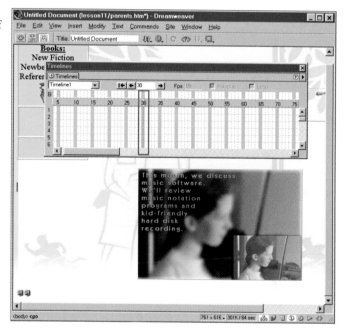

Creating the Video Timer

The Timeline that appears in the Timeline window is a series of frames. Each frame indicates a fraction of a second. We'll be creating an event that occurs on Frame 30. Since, by default, Dreamweaver Timelines count time at 12 frames per second, the event we create will start after the page has been open for 2 1/2 seconds. This is the much-heralded delay interval that gives visitors time to view other elements of your page before the show begins.

To specify what should occur on Frame 30, we need to create a Behavior. Dreamweaver has an extensive menu of preset behaviors. These are really JavaScript commands that allow your Web page to perform tasks that are beyond the capabilities of HTML. We'll access Dreamweaver's Behavior palette and specify that, at Frame 30, the page should begin playing back a movie inside that same layer that currently contains our image.

1. Click the "30" on the top of the timeline (Figure 10.11). The red Location Bar jumps to "30" as well. We've indicated that the event we create will occur 30 frames after the viewer has clicked on the page.

2. Click Frame 30 on the timeline.

3. To access the Behavior Palette, choose Window > Behaviors.

4. Click the plus sign at the upper left of the palette (Figure 10.12).

Figure 10.12
Click the Plus sign on the Behavior Palette to choose a Behavior.

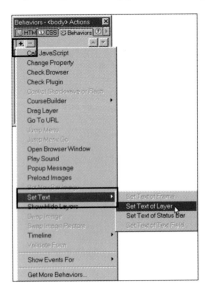

5. When the menu of behaviors appears, choose Set Text > Set Text of Layer. You could use this option to indicate that the layer will simply display a text message when indicated. But we're going to insert a command into the layer instead, a command to display a movie.

6. When a browser opens your movie for playback, it looks for detailed instructions, such as if the video should loop, or if visitors should be able to stop and start the video themselves. We'll include those instructions now. When the Set Text of Layer dialog box appears (Figure 10.13), type the following code into the layer dialog box window:

```
<embed src="mymovie.mov" pluginspage="http://quicktime.apple.com" width="232"
height="180" controller=true loop=true autoplay=true cache=true></embed>
```

Figure 10.13
Type text or code into the Set Text of Layer dialog box.

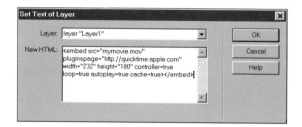

This code is simply a command to play a particular movie using the QuickTime plug-in, at a specified width and height. In a moment, we'll break down the components of this command so you can see the options you have when displaying movies on your Web pages.

If you are following along precisely, type the above code into the Set Text of Layer dialog box. Replace "mymovie.mov" with the name of your own movie. Note the dimensions of my movie: width="232" height="180." Modify these dimensions if your movie is a different size.

Once you type the code into the Set Text of Layer dialog box and click OK, the layer is set to display this text when Frame 30 of the page is reached. In fact, look at the Behavior Palette (As shown in Figure 10.14), and you'll see your commands listed at the top of the Palette: "On Frame 30" and "Set Text of Layer." If you do not see this confirmation, click the blue frame Behavior Indicator on Frame 30 at the top of the Timeline. The Behavior Palette will display the command you just created.

Figure 10.14
The Behavior Palette panel lists your commands.

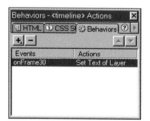

Setting Autoload and Autoplay

Now you have to specify that the Timeline should play back as soon as the page opens:

1. Check the Autoplay box at the top of the Timeline (See Figure 10.11). Dreamweaver adds an OnLoad behavior that plays the timeline immediately upon opening.

2. Make sure the Behavior Palette is still displaying, and click a blank area of your page.

3. Click the plus sign on the Behavior Palette and choose Preload Images from the menu. We're not preloading an image, but we can still use this menu option to preload our movie.

4. When the Preload Images dialog box appears, click the Browse button.

5. When the Browse menu appears, click the Files of Type dropdown menu and choose All Files. Otherwise, your only choice will be picture types.

6. Click the movie you want to preload, and then click Select.

7. Click OK to close the Preload Images dialog box. Your movie will now begin preloading as soon as the page opens in a browser.

8. After closing the dialog boxes, you'll not see the effect in Dreamweaver. You'll have to preview the page in a browser.

Dreamweaver allows you to see how your page will appear and act online before posting it. To view the page in action, press F12, or choose File > Preview in Browser. Dreamweaver will create a temporary page. You'll see the image alone for a few seconds, then you'll see the movie begin playback.

Controlling Online QuickTime Display

In the HTML example above, you may have noticed that the <embed> tag used to insert the QuickTime movie into the page has several detailed instructions, such as "controller," "loop," and so forth. In HTML, when you indicate a basic command, you can also modify that command. These modifiers are called Attributes.

In working with your own QuickTime movies, you can use Attributes to set your display preferences. Very specific Attributes are used to modify each type of HTML tag. In our example, we used the <embed> tag to display our movie. Let's break down this tag and understand its attributes:

<embed> Movies embedded into a Web page do not stream. However, QuickTime employs a plugin that allows the movie to begin displaying before it is fully downloaded. Online QuickTime movies will begin playing back as soon as enough data has been downloaded to get started.

pluginspage=http://quicktime.apple.com This directs the browser to display the movie using the QuickTime plugin.

controller=true This attribute will display the QuickTime controller when playing back the movie. To display no controller, type controller=false.

loop=true This causes the movie to loop.

autoplay=true This causes the movie to begin playback as soon as the movie appears.

cache=true If the movie is cached, visitors who return to this page and again play back the movie will not have to wait for it to download. The movie will be played back from a temporary file that would have been saved onto the user's computer, rather than downloaded again from the server.

To learn more about embedding QuickTime movies in Web pages, visit this site: **http://www.apple.com/quicktime/authoring/embed.html**

Crossroads

You've gotten a short taste of video-friendly Web design tips and how videos can be viewed online. However, it's time to stretch out a little and step away from the computer. In the next chapter, you'll learn about filming family events and memorable occasions and just having fun with your video camera.

CHAPTER 10

11

Special Events, Family Fun, and Educational Projects

Digital video can be a group endeavor. Among family and friends, everyone can have a role and can choose which side of the camera they'd like to be on. Filming and editing a video of a special event would certainly count as "quality time" spent together away from the TV, a way to get everyone to take off their headphones for a few minutes. In this chapter, we'll talk about filming family and commemorative events such as weddings and graduations. Many events are ripe for being filmed, such as athletic events, school plays, and special outings.

We'll also discuss how kids can be involved with creating video projects, jumping in with their own creative ideas and imagination. Finally, we'll discuss creating educational video projects.

Creating a Wedding or Special Event Video

This section shows you techniques for planning, recording, and editing a video that commemorates special events like a wedding, graduation, or an award ceremony. Our example will focus on creating a great wedding video, but the same techniques apply for all special event videos.

Weddings—A wedding or commemoration is a "made for video" event unlike any other, and few documents will be as cherished as your careful work capturing these momentous occasions. It's an honor to be asked to film a wedding. Preparation, practice, and extra set-up time are not too much to ask.

Special Events—Some events happen only once, or so infrequently that you want to make sure your video clearly captures the best moments. Videos of special pageants, parades, award ceremonies, vacations, and birthdays all require a bit of planning. Take along that extra battery and DV cassette, as well as a tripod and extra lighting if you have it. Also, have a backup plan for a change in the weather. When you are filming, be aware of lighting changes—for example, those shifts from indoor to outdoor filming, or filming as evening approaches.

Also, keep in mind that you need not film everything in sequence. The video editing tools you explored in this book make you a master of chronology. You can always film something late in the event and, while editing, move it near the beginning. Film comments and quips throughout the day and later, during editing, splice them together. You can also get creative by filming quick takes of related newspaper or magazine clips to divide your video into segments. There's a lot you can do to make your special event video fresh and unique. And all those special effects and transitions that I told you to avoid while filming for the Web or in professional situations? Well, you can use them now. They are fun, and it's perfectly fine to make your uncle look like he's coming out of a cheeseburger. The point is to get everyone to enjoy themselves.

And, finally, when it comes to filming weddings and special events, think "music." Ask yourself, "What music do I have for this?" Both wedding and special event filming benefit greatly from musical enhancement. Music in video maximizes emotions. When it's time to edit, have lots of songs handy—sad, happy, dramatic, theme-relevant songs and, of course, "favorites."

CAUTION

If someone asks you to film a wedding while your skills are still fresh, don't be afraid to decline. You do want to keep your friends—and your place at the Thanksgiving table. There are good reasons why wedding videographers charge as much as they do for their services. There's added equipment, lots of extra hardware that is specific for wedding videography, as well as experience. However, if filming weddings interests you, ask if you can supplement, not replace, the professional videographer. Why not go along and catch your own footage as well? There are good reasons why this may be desirable to the wedding party. First of all, videographers require time to edit their creations. You can show your footage the next day. Secondly, you'll be sure to capture a few moments that escaped even the most watchful professional eye. Still, though, even in a semi-professional or "friend of the family" videographer role, be prepared to spend more time and energy than you initially imagined.

Planning for the Event

Please note that fail-safe planning is required. The biggest consideration in event and wedding filming is the realization that certain moments are unrepeatable. No one will say, "I do," twice because you still have the video camera set for the outdoor-lighting patio scene and it suddenly occurs to you that the video you just shot indoors will be hopelessly underexposed!

Just as other members of the wedding party will be attending rehearsals, you'll be required to check each filming environment for optimum exposure and sound levels. In Figure 11.1, we see three settings: bright sunlight, a shady garden, and a cloudy late afternoon with evening approaching. Better check that light meter! Note also that special moments will seem to be happening everywhere at once.

Figure 11.1
Plan ahead so you can get optimum quality footage in all environments.

For weddings, you'll have to be everywhere at once, yet remain as unobtrusive as a house plant on the big day. It's really quite a challenging job. As well as the procession and ceremony, you'll be expected to film the following:

- Cake cutting
- Bouquet and garter tossing
- Champagne uncorking and toasts
- First kiss
- Bridesmaids attending the bride
- Mom and Dad's emotional moments
- Driving off in the limo

Make sure you plan adequately for the big day in order to get the right shots. Here are some suggestions for preparing for a wedding day video—most of these suggestions are applicable for all types of special events.

- Spend time talking with the family and best friends—find out what special touches would be most appreciated. For example, favorite songs are a very big deal. Every relationship has songs that mark important milestones, and your video will quadruple in emotional impact if you include a couple of those.
- Plan to interview friends and family members on the day of the event. Ask them to wish the couple well and perhaps share a couple of inside jokes.
- Ask the family to provide a few photos of the bride and groom at various life stages. That's because you may be asked to create a wedding montage with some video footage mixed with slides and text titles. Now that you've read this book, you know how to do those things.
- Double-check the spelling of everyone's names. You'll probably be creating title tracks and maybe even credits.
- Find out if someone else will be taking pictures or if you'll be asked to perform double duty at the wedding and reception.
- Determine the final output format requirement. Do the bride and groom want a VHS tape and/or CD/DVD movie of the event? Also, find out if the wedding families expect wedding footage with a few edits or a production with lots of music overdubs and other production effects.

CHAPTER 11

Filming the Event

Here are points to keep in mind at film-time, when it's too late to run back to the house to grab forgotten gear and you can finally enjoy the results of all your careful planning.

▶ A wedding video really shines when filmed with a more expensive 3-chip camcorder. As you may recall, 3-chip digital camcorders use three-color sensing chips for capturing colors. The results are that faces and flowers are brighter and the day just looks fresher.

▶ During the ceremony, have the groom wear a wireless microphone if at all possible (it won't work with the bride—too much fabric). Later, no one will be straining to hear the big words.

▶ Film a little bit of everything, especially if you'll be assembling a montage later. Get lots of unique footage. Capture all the quiet moments, loud moments, tears, laughter, smoldering glances, and everything candid and unplanned (Figure 11.2) as well as all the major moments. Make sure the camera is never too far away from immediate family members.

Figure 11.2
You'll have to film a little of everything on a wedding day.

▶ If at all possible, consider using two videographers. You'll get more footage, and you won't have quite so much running around to do. This, of course, requires two camcorders, and the two of you should make sure you are using similar settings while filming. One videographer can focus on close-ups and ceremony specifics, while another can get more of "the long view," filming the audience, arrivals, conversations, and so forth.

NOTE

You may want to review Chapter 5's discussion about camera angles, contrasting foreground/background, and subject framing. Also, go back to Chapter 3 and review how to use field of focus to your advantage. These are very important wedding video considerations.

▶ If you want to be Hero of the Year, get enough footage to create a "When They First Met" video in which you interview friends, family, and the couple to give a bit of chronology. ("When Sarah first went out with Michael, we thought she'd never stay with him.")

▶ Take the time to gather encouraging words from mentors, friends, and family.

Getting these various angles, clips, and topics will make your special event video fabulous. You will have so much material for your video editing tools that you can create things like "almost broke up" sequences and "true love" sequences, interspersing them with the actual event in a meaningful manner. A great event video will be more appreciated than any set of dishes or matching quilts. After all, you have a digital camcorder, and you have talent!

Including Music in Special Event Videos

While filming your special event footage, especially a wedding, remember that you'll have tracks for adding voice and music. Remember what your video editing software is capable of. You can drag a music clip along the video timeline and position its starting and ending point anywhere you like. You'll be able to fade one song into another and end a song just when the video transitions. Music, narrative overdubs, and songs are components you can pop in and out as needed to enhance your project. Think of them as modules that you can mix and move as you like.

Figure 11.3 shows an example of adding audio tracks to wedding video clips. Two synchronized audio transitions are highlighted. In the first, a song begins playing when the video transition begins. In the second, one song fades into another. The fade is complete when the final video clip begins playback.

Figure 11.3
Adding audio to video clips in a wedding video.

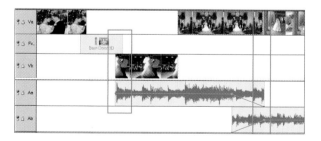

CHAPTER 11

NOTE

During the editing phase, review Chapters 6 through 8 to create text titles, transitions, blending still images and video, and music cross fades. Avoid transitions and special effects that distract.

Kids and Digital Video

Kids can have a blast with digital video. They can be involved in many ways. Tap into their imaginations and let them come up with ideas. They can also act in their projects, be behind the camera with supervision, and even help with editing decisions. We'll talk about the pros and cons of kids actually doing the filming, as well as ideas that kids can run with and develop any way they like.

There's a world of difference between letting kids get involved and having them hold the camera and actually do the filming. Children under twelve can participate in a video project by planning it, acting in it, even editing it—but all of that is a far cry from handling the camera. Filming with a video camera requires a lot of visual coordination and dexterity as well as the continual realization that the object in your hand is worth more than half the average biweekly paycheck. For such reasons, I would recommend that only adults and older, responsible children actually handle the camera.

The ideas that follow are ways that kids can experience the magic of the camera. Beginning with this bag of tricks, kids can actually be inspired to compose stories and come up with a script or two. Filming with kids should be fun, and a bit of mayhem should be tolerated. Spontaneity is not hard to come by with kids, and films that capture the unexpected are always fun to watch. So, with that in mind, be flexible, just allow the scene to unfold, and enjoy the following ideas.

TIP

The amount of explanation and direction you must provide for the children you are filming with depends on how much they can understand. Younger kids may really not understand what you are doing until they see it on film. Tell them what will appear on-screen later, even though they don't see it now. Take the time to explain steps so that their actions on the camera look less tentative and like they are really engaged.

NOTE

Since many of the projects below involve replacing on-screen subjects with new characters while the camera is stopped, the projects described below are best filmed with a tripod. You'll want to avoid giveaway camera movements that shift viewing angle while you fuss with props.

The Disappearing Trick

Here's a classic "disappearing object" film trick (Figure 11.4). Turn a kid into a magician. It's easy. The scene below requires two children, a stage aid, a magic wand, and a large teddy bear or similar-sized object. You'll be filming a child in the chair then replacing the child with the teddy bear.

Figure 11.4
By stopping the camera, you can rearrange onscreen objects for special effects.

Here's how it's done:

1. Create a scene with a single chair and a child holding a magic wand standing next to the chair.

2. Place a second child in the chair; this is the child who will disappear.

3. Tell the standing child that when she waves the magic wand, the camera will make it look as though the child in the chair will change into a teddy bear. Instruct the standing child to wave the wand toward the sitting child and to stop her motion when the wand is level with the sitting child.

4. Tell the child with the wand to hold her position after the camera stops—to hold it until after the sitting child leaves and is replaced by the teddy bear. If the child is young, make these instructions very clear before filming.

5. Prepare the child sitting in the chair to act as though he is about to disappear when the standing child waves the wand.

6. Film an introduction announcing that a great magician is about to perform.

7. Tell the children that once the camera begins rolling, the wand should be waved. Announce, "Rolling!" and begin filming.

8. Stop filming about a half second after the wave of the wand, and do not allow the camera to move. Remind the child to keep the wand in the same position.

9. Direct the sitting child to leave, being careful not to bump the chair, and ask a stagehand to place the teddy bear on the chair.

10. Tell the standing child that when you resume filming, she is to move her arm back up to its previous position. Say, "Rolling," and begin filming.

11. When the magic wand has been raised, continue filming for about a second, then stop.

You are finished with the essential filming of this project. You may add titles or extra opening and closing content if you like. When you play this back for the kids, they are sure to get a charge out of it.

NOTE
Remember that kids are small and can get swallowed up in a larger-than-necessary scene frame. Take care that the scene not extend much beyond the height of the standing child's head. When filming, don't leave much blank horizontal space. You may have to film from a kneeling position to avoid visual distortion caused by the camera-subject height differences.

CAUTION
The preciseness of the above directions lets you know how important it is to be clear with little kids, or they'll make no connection between what they are doing with the camera and what they'll later see on screen.

The Magic Tree Trick

In this scene, a child who walks toward a tree from the right changes into a different child as he emerges from behind the tree toward the left. To add more visual bafflement, while the camera is not filming, replace the walk-on child who is standing behind the tree with a third child. The effect is that child 2 is seen walking behind the tree where child 1 "disappeared," and only child 3 emerged, the first two children having disappeared entirely.

This scene requires at least three or four children and a tree large enough to completely hide a child who walks behind it. To make my instructions clearer, I'll refer to each child with a number, child 1 through 4.

1. Set your scene so that the camera has the tree in focus, with seven or eight feet free on both the left and right sides of the tree. You'll want to film close enough to make it obvious that children are disappearing, but not so close that telltale disappearing shoulders and forearms are obvious when you replace children behind the tree.

2. With the camera rolling, have child 1 walk behind the tree. Direct the child to stop walking behind the tree and be totally invisible to the other side, where the filming is taking place.

3. Stop the camera and replace child 1 with child 2.

4. With the camera rolling, have child 2 walk out from behind the tree towards the left, and, simultaneously, have child 3 walk towards the tree, behind it, from the right. Direct child 3 to completely "hide" from the camera's view once he or she is positioned behind the tree.

5. Stop the camera and replace child 3 with child 4.

6. With the camera rolling, have child 4 walk away from the tree towards the left, and simultaneously direct child 2 to walk towards the tree from the right and hide behind it.

7. Repeat the above steps, mixing up the children so that the sequence does not become predictable.

8. After a couple rotations of this, you are finished filming. This will elicit lots of laughs on playback. To add to the effect, in a video editing program, make a copy of the film clip and reverse it, and sequence it to begin right as the first clip ends. You'll then see the kids walk backwards, but still away and towards the tree.

Creating a Faux Entrance

Here's how to make a faux entrance screen, in which the action seems to be taking place inside a famous movie set or arcade (Figure 11.5) when, in reality, everyone's in the living room. This is done by utilizing a quick film clip or still image of a famous location, then zooming in on some sort of performance by your actors.

Figure 11.5
A faux entrance from
the exterior to interior of
an event venue.

The camera moves in closer (you learned to do these false zooms in Chapter 8, or you could actually zoom). The camera then fades into the action scene with your actors. In the example shown in Figure 11.5, the band seems to be performing inside the world-famous Hollywood Palladium. Obviously, one would only use such trickery for entertainment value.

Video Drawing Tools

Young children can add more of their own creative touches to videos through the use of video drawing tools such as CG Infinity, which is included with MediaStudio Pro. Despite its hi-tech name, the program is a lot of fun for kids.

Video editing *per se* can be intimidating and technical. In most video editing programs, the interfaces for adding text and "Hi, Grandma" messages to videos is rather small. I don't think the experience of typing and adding the message would be particularly satisfying to anyone under the age of ten or so. But there is one program that comes with Ulead MediaStudio Pro that allows drag-and-drop object manipulation. Kids can insert moving suns and animals and furniture and make clouds jump over the moon and such, all right on top of the family vacation video (Figure 11.6). You can do this with CG Infinity, the text animation program that is part of MediaStudio Pro, mentioned in Chapter 8. This creative outlet may indeed be satisfying for young children because the interface is large enough to really see the video being edited.

Figure 11.6
CG Infinity provides video editing tools that can be fun for fairly young children.

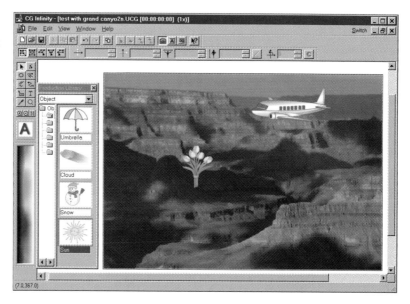

After children add their drawings on top of the video, playback is immediate at the click of a button. The animations you can add to the video are easily inserted and moved. They look pleasantly cartoonish, and the movement path is built right into the object as soon as it is dragged onto the screen. Even young kids can quickly get the idea that their cartoons produce their own movements against the backdrop movement of the video. To a young child, this concept is a heck of a mouthful to describe, but you don't have to. Just let them do it.

Educational Video Projects

Digital video is a natural enhancement to school projects and other educational endeavors. With digital video, you can create a living record of all types of events. Later, you can add voiceover, supplementary archival clips, still images, transitions, and all kinds of material to supplement and enhance your footage. Here are a few examples.

Creating Time-Lapse Movies

Creating timed exposure videos of natural phenomenon can be very educational for kids. You can film a sequence of events that takes hours and compress it into a few minutes of video. This is great for sunsets, scudding clouds, lightning and other nocturnal sky phenomenon, and seedlings sprouting from a plant dish.

The best way to involve children in this sort of filming is to set the camcorder on a tripod in position to occasionally film an event as it gradually unfolds. There are devices that can automate film exposure cycles, but that doesn't promote child participation.

A video of a gradual sunset, as in the example shown in Figure 11.7, requires filming a few seconds of sky every minute or two, just enough to make the change in the sky gradual and smooth.

Figure 11.7
A time-lapse sunset video.

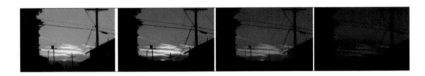

In contrast, filming a seedling gradually bloom in a plant dish requires a few seconds of video every three or four hours for a couple of days during daylight.

For a very gradual but fascinating time-lapse filming experience, the kids could film a home being built, stage by stage. In video playback, the kids could watch the construction unfold, starting with the foundation, scaffolding, drywall, paint and awnings, all the way up to final landscaping. To make playback more fun, speed it up significantly. The jerkiness of multiple viewpoints and workers popping in and out would just seem like part of the effect. Required filming would be a few seconds every two or three days, throughout the whole process. Of course, you'd have to use the tripod and mark your camera's orientation and placement exactly. Otherwise, you'd be stuck leaving your camcorder in the same position for days and days.

NOTE
By using a tripod to ensure no changes in position, the viewer won't be distracted by camera movements. You can't do too much in the editing phase to smooth out the transitions, because any cutting you may do will probably just make the transition look choppier. In some editing programs, you can increase frame speed, which helps blend transitions.

Nature Films

You can create a great movie by taking your camcorder along on a wilderness trail, wildlife reserve visit (Figure 11.8), or to a hidden natural environment not so far away. Film anything of interest, then later supplement the footage with research from books and the Web, still images, and voiceover. Use titles and transitions to create natural "chapter" breaks in your film. If the first trip was rewarding, venture elsewhere and get even more footage.

Figure 11.8
A video project developed from a wildlife reserve visit.

Local Documentary

Think you know your town? Its history? Who settled here and why? What is happening in your town that can shed a little light on its origins? All these questions are worth exploring with your video camera. This is a great project for children, since people are often quite happy to give all kinds of colorful information to children that they'd keep to themselves around other adults. After you get basic footage, interview families with roots in your town and visit the library to get a little more background. Expressed with a little drama and effective sequencing, a local documentary can be quite fascinating (Figure 11.9).

Figure 11.9
Footage from a local documentary.

A Day in the Life of...

OK, so the teacher gave a frighteningly open-ended assignment: "Come back with something the class would really love. Just be creative." Well, there's "Why my older brother likes Nine Inch Nails" or, perhaps, a trip to a public institution with a video camera. How about "A day in the life of a fireman," or "What happens at the zoo after the people go home?" Many academic projects, great and small, can be supplemented by digital video.

Crossroads

So you've learned how to have a little fun with your digital camcorder, how to capture important family moments, and how to turn it loose with the kids for their educational projects. Next, you'll learn how to distribute your video projects in their final forms. You'll see there are many ways to share your creativity with the world.

12

Exporting and Organizing Videos

After your movie is edited and ready to go, you need to make decisions about exporting it. Those decisions will be based on the format and type of equipment in which your final videos will be viewed. In this chapter, we'll learn about exporting your video to mediums such as CD, DVD, DV tape, VCR, the Web, and hard drive playback. We'll also cover the Ulead DVD Movie Factory, a wonderful option that lets you save multiple projects on DVD or a CD playable on a typical commercial DVD player. Finally, we'll consider video-friendly thumbnail-viewing programs. After you've created many projects, or have acquired lots of video clips used to create projects, you'll need an organizational tool to keep track of your work and resources.

Outputting Video

The following sections define your choices for modifying movie formats and compression choices to match the output medium you have in mind. When we're finished, you'll have no trouble choosing a movie format and compression type that suits your playback needs.

Common Output Formats

Below are descriptions of your basic export choices and information about the unique characteristics of each. Most of the video editing programs discussed in this book (especially Ulead VideoStudio and MediaStudio Pro) allow you to output your movie in one of the formats listed below. You'll be able to access each of these as part of the basic movie export options in your program of choice.

AVI: Native format for Windows computers. Used for playing back movies from a hard drive. AVI files can only be played back on a Windows-based PC. However, they can be played back on just about any Windows-based PC without regard for version. As long as you chose one of the Indeo compression options when saving your movie, you can be pretty sure that any Windows user can play back your movie without having to make a trip to a download site first.

CHAPTER 12

QuickTime: Native format for Macintosh computers, but considered top choice for cross-platform use. Compresses well into CD-playable configuration. If your video is 8-bit color (256 colors), a palette can be assigned to ensure common colors no matter what equipment the movie is played back on. Using special QuickTime authoring tools, you can create video applications (with links and timing) with QuickTime layers. You can easily create progressive download movies to generate a type of Web streaming video. When saving as QuickTime, you can add special streaming features that make Web-based movie viewing go more smoothly. For example, you can add a "hint track" to a movie, as shown in Figure 12.1. This process adds special, unseen streaming content that QuickTime requires for progressive playback. On the downside, users will have to have QuickTime installed on their computer to play back your movie. QuickTime is very common. All Macintosh computers have the QuickTime player pre-installed. PC users will undoubtedly come across an invitation to install the QuickTime Movie Player when they visit any media-enriched site on the Web. Otherwise, viewers of your QuickTime movie can visit **www.QuickTime.com** and take a minute or two to download and install the player.

Figure 12.1
Selecting a "hinted" movie option while formatting a QuickTime movie.

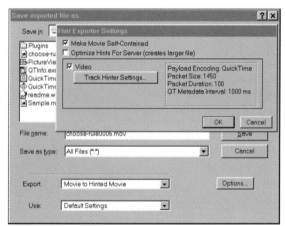

VCR Cassette: To record onto a VCR, use the digital camcorder as an intermediary device. The digital camcorder is necessary to reformat the movie to VCR type and quality. You don't need to record onto the digital camcorder, just use it as a go-between. To do so, connect out from your computer to the digital camcorder via FireWire card. Then connect out from digital camcorder to the VCR using S-video or standard A/V cable. You can then record using the VCR while playing the video on your computer. First, choose the "Record to VCR" option on your video editing software's output settings, and review the "Output Options" section below, as some options relate to TV monitor playback. Then, after plugging in the cables as described, just press record on your VCR recorder and begin playing back your movie in your video editing software.

DV Cassette: Recording your edited movie back onto your DV cassette is usually just a matter of playing back the movie in the video editing program while your digital video camera is recording. Most video editing programs have a feature for playing back your project in real time (Figure 12.2 shows VideoStudio's feature) while sending full-quality video out through your FireWire cable into your digital camcorder. Please note that if a video project will be recorded back onto a DV cassette, there is no need for more compression or other space-saving adjustments. That's because video must be compressed quite a bit to jump from DV cassette to computer, but not the other way around.

Figure 12.2
Ulead VideoStudio's Timeline Playback feature, which records directly to DV tape.

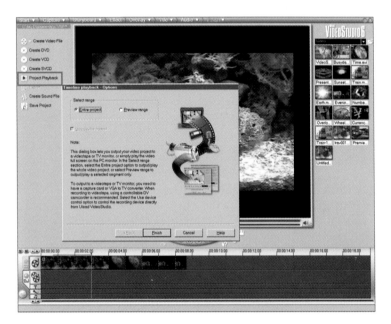

MPEG: A very compressible format for Web viewing. MPEG provides lots of choices to facilitate fast loading, such as keyframe-based compression and variable bit depth for video color. You can control color bit depth and adjust the number of unique colors used in the movie, allowing for faster viewing.

NOTE

In compression programs, be careful when reducing bit depth. Doing so doesn't noticeably depreciate videos with large, single-color blocks, but it will reduce the quality of any gradient fills and flesh tones.

CHAPTER 12

MPEG with SVCD Compression: DVD movies cannot be generated from just any old video. SVCD-compressed MPEG is the compression and format that should be used. When you generate a DVD using programs like DV MovieFactory, the program automatically first creates an MPEG movie with SVCD compression. You can, however, manually compress your MPEG with SVCD compression if you think you'll be making a DVD from it later. We'll explore using the DVD MovieFactory in greater detail later in this chapter.

RM: RealMedia streaming movie type. RM utilizes a large variety of compression techniques to optimize Internet file loading. Streaming technology allows playback of video before it has finished downloading. If a special server is used, playback commences as soon as the viewer opens the video's Web page. Please see Chapter 10 for a detailed discussion about Internet-friendly video formats, of which RealMedia is one of the best. You'll see this option as one of the standard "Export Movie" options in your video editing software.

WMV: Windows Streaming Media movie. WMV also utilizes a variety of compression techniques to optimize Internet file loading. Streaming technology allows playback of video before it has finished downloading. If a special server is used, playback commences as soon as the viewer opens the video's Web page. Please see Chapter 10's discussion about Internet-friendly video formats. You'll see this option as one of the standard "Export Movie" options in your video editing software.

DVD: Some video editing programs provide special output options for creating DVD-compatible movies. A DVD creation tool can divide a movie into scenes. Movies with scene divisions can be stored on a DVD and accessed with the DVD player's remote handset (Figure 12.3). Creating a movie for DVD allows you to maintain very high quality. There's no need to shorten or use special compression other than compression that the DVD-creation process employs. Of course, only viewers with DVD players will be able to see your movie.

Figure 12.3
A DVD movie menu built from a video project.

Output Options

No matter which format you select, when it comes to outputting your video, there are certain choices you'll have to make that will affect the quality and playability of your video in the various output formats. Choices you make determine the quality of the video and the type of equipment it can be played on, such as a television, Windows-based PC, Mac computer, the Internet, or all of the above. Most video editing programs discussed in this book give you plenty of video output options. You'll not be stuck with a movie you can't easily export.

Below are the options you'll typically see in "Save as Type" dialog boxes when outputting video.

▶ **Audio Sample Rate/Bit Rate:** When you create your final video output, the output options you choose will determine how much information to keep and how much to discard. The idea is to get rid of as much as you can, keeping the file size down, but also keep enough digital information so that the movie still looks and sounds good. One way to trim a little excess file size from your final movie is reducing the audio sample rate. If your movie can do without some of its audio information, the final file size will be a little smaller. But, if you reduce sampling too much, the sound will suffer. So, movies in which music plays a significant role should not have sample rates reduced below 44.4 kHz, unless they are destined for the Web (Figure 12.4). For Web viewing, reduce the audio to mono and avoid compressing music at less than a 22 kHz sample rate. If your movie is bound for CD-ROM, DVD, or a hard drive, saving space is not a primary issue, so go ahead and keep your audio sampling rate at 44.4 kHz.

Figure 12.4
Choosing audio track export settings.

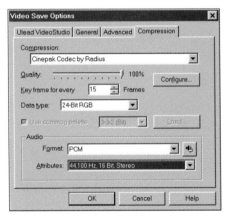

▶ **Interlacing:** Videos to be played back on VCRs should be saved with interlacing, a requirement for viewing on a television monitor. You need not use interlacing if your audience will be viewing your video from a computer monitor.

CHAPTER 12

▶ **Frames or Fields:** Choose Fields if the movie will be played back on a television. On television, a single frame of video is built using interlacing, where "Field A" represents odd lines used to create a frame and "Field B" represents even lines. In video, two fields combine to create a single frame. Choose Frames for all other playback options.

▶ **Add Keyframes:** When you are about finished editing your movie, some movie editors let you indicate which frames should be keyframes. You should designate as keyframes those frames in your video that have lots of action or camera movement of some type. When you designate a frame as a keyframe, you are indicating that the compression should go easy on that section of video. (The compression scheme will know when the action ends. It just needs you to tell it where the action begins.) If you are going to be severely compressing your movie, such as for Web viewing, you should take the time to go into your movie and add keyframes at the action points. Indicate a high-action movie segment with a keyframe and it will be spared the harshest compression (Figure 12.5). Clicking the Add Keyframes option merely tells the compression program to go ahead and use those keyframes you previously set up in your movie. Deselect Add Keyframes and the keyframes you indicated in your movie will be ignored here.

Figure 12.5
Setting up compression keyframes

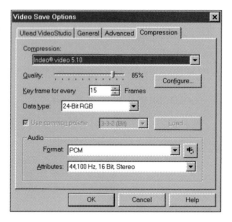

▶ **Frame Rate:** Slower frame rates create movies that are faster to download. That's because if, for example, only twelve frames are used to create one second of video, the output will be much smaller than if twenty-nine frames are used to create the same second of video. Compression schemes allow you to specify a frame rate and remove frames deemed less significant to the action. However, if you remove too many frames, the movie will appear jerky.

▶ **Interleave Audio and Video:** Interleaving lets you specify proportionally how much video data should be delivered before a portion of audio data is delivered. If you see actors talking a split-second before or after you hear their voice, you can raise the proportional amount of audio data delivery from the default values.

▶ **Recompress:** Select this option only if you want to again compress a previously compressed movie. Keep in mind that each time you compress a video, you are removing more quality from it. With dual compression, more colors will be approximated, rather than reproduced. Audio will be sampled less frequently, resulting in poor sound. Select this option only if you need maximum compression and are only secondarily concerned about quality.

Common Compression Schemes

Following are some of the most popular compression choices and their uses. Some compression schemes are automatically associated with a video file type; for example, Indeo compression always goes with AVI files. However, you can choose a compression scheme yourself is you want more control over file size and quality. For example, if you allow your program to choose the compression option for you, then you notice your movie size is too large for your purposes, you can try again. Save your movie again, but, this time, go into your compression options and play with the sliders a bit and see what you can do about that file size.

You'll see these options as you move through the Video Output dialog boxes in your video editing program. In most programs, the options below just present themselves by clicking Next. In other programs, you'll see a button labeled "Options," or "Configure."

▶ **Indeo:** A very efficient compression scheme, Indeo creates high-quality movies. It's often used for AVI videos and movies distributed for hard drive playback. Note: Viewers must have the version of Indeo compression for playback on their computers that corresponds with the version you used to compress it. If the same version is not found, the viewer's movie player will attempt to establish an Internet connection and download the correct compression version, installing it as unobtrusively as possible.

▶ **Cinepak:** Accommodates slow transfer rates, making this a popular compression type for CD-ROM and slow hard drives.

▶ **Sorensen:** Very popular for compressing movies for CD-ROM playback.

▶ **MPEG:** Provides a large array of compression options for optimizing Web playback.

▶ **SVCD:** Compression required for DVDs and CDs to be played on DVDs. You'll have the option to compress your movie small enough to be played back on a CD configured for DVD playback, or you can configure it for full DVD playback. That last option will only be helpful to you if you have access to a DVD recorder.

CHAPTER 12

▶ **DivX:** A compression technology facilitating large video transfer on high-speed modems. Using a specification very similar to MPEG 4, full-screen movies are delivered at an amazingly small file size. DivX is popular for compressing and distributing DVD full-length videos and "theatre screen" dimension movies. Note that improvements in the DivX spec are always in the works and that newer versions of DivX are often not compatible with older versions.

Compression Options

Following are some compression options common to most compression types and suggestions about when you may want to employ them. Keep in mind that not every situation calls for increasing compression. If you are saving your movie as a DVD, you have the luxury of optimum quality, full-sized video playback. Similarly, if the movie you create will be hanging around on your hard drive (or someone else's) and will be played back on your computer's movie player, there's no need to grab every last ounce of possible compression. However, if you are making a movie for the Web and find that, despite your best efforts, you just can't get the movie small enough, export your movie again, but this time, dig deeper into the compression options and see what you can change.

▶ **Quality Slider:** Most compression formats provide a slider allowing you to set general video quality, measured in percentage. Higher numbers result in larger file size and better quality. Default quality for most video compression is fifty percent.

▶ **Data Type:** Specifies video color bit depth, which determines the number of colors used. Normal video is 24-bit, or 16 million colors. Reducing bit depth to 8-bit, or 256 colors, decreases file size, but areas of complex color will translate very poorly. Reduce bit depth if your video is largely drawings or cartoons or contains large areas of flat color. Not all compression types allow you to reduce color bit depth. Specifically, QuickTime does, as does MPEG.

▶ **Data Rate:** Some compression schemes let you specify an ideal data rate for your movie. CD-ROM drives often boast data rate transfers in the 6 MB per second range. However, video requires sustained data transfer, whereas most manufacturers report a peak transfer rate in their literature. I'd recommend setting data transfer rates for playback on newer CD-ROM drives at 1 MB per second and older drives at 300 k per second. Hard drives can usually sustain a data transfer rate of 3 to 6 MB per second. Manufacturers of hardware will howl that I am not giving them full credit for the machine's capabilities. However, it's better to shoot for lower-than-ideal data uptake rates rather than create a movie that starts skipping frames half-way through.

▶ **Keyframe Every:** Specifies Keyframe frequency. The compression scheme calculates and displays all colors in a Keyframe. In non-Keyframe frames, only the colors that have changed dramatically since the previous Keyframe are calculated. For example, to have the program completely calculate all colors used in one out of fifteen frames, specify a Keyframe every fifteen frames.

Creating DVD Movies, Step-by-Step

You'll now learn how to create a DVD directly from your video editing program. You don't need a DVD recorder to do this. Rather, you can format your movie directly onto a CD, but do so in DVD format. You'll be playing back your DVD-formatted CD on a software DVD player, not a CD-ROM drive. DVD burners let you create full-length movies as DVDs. However, using software such as DVD MovieFactory, you can create shorter movies in the DVD format and burn them with regular CD burners—to be played back in a software DVD player.

Note that there is currently no suitable program that will start with a project in a video editing program and burn onto CD for normal CD-ROM playback. Successfully playing back a CD-ROM movie depends greatly on your CD-ROM player and other factors related to the playback computer. Because of the considerable disparity in CD-ROM playback specifications from unit to unit, recording a movie onto a CD-ROM with good CD playback quality guaranteed is not very feasible.

However, you can record straight from your project right onto DVD and record onto your CD-ROM recorder as if it were a DVD. The DVD specification is hefty enough that you are guaranteed a good playback experience in a DVD player. There will be no jerkiness or dropped frames. That said, you will need special DVD burning software like Ulead's DVD MovieFactory. This is a great tool for introducing yourself to the world of DVD authoring. DVD MovieFactory also gives you the option to save in two other formats if your project's length won't fit in DVD format: VCD, which holds approximately 74 minutes of video (best for long projects), and SVCD, which will hold approximately 35 minutes of video. Although we'll be working directly with Ulead's DVD MovieFactory, the menu setup and multiple project capacity is similar to what you'll find with other DVD tools.

The Ulead DVD MovieFactory converts existing MPEG movies to a DVD format. Simultaneously, a DVD or DVD-compatible CD is created, while the movie and necessary support files are added to this specially formatted CD or DVD (if you happen to have a DVD recorder on your computer). While the movie and CD are properly formatted, additional support files are also placed on the CD or DVD.

NOTE
The Ulead DVD MovieFactory represents a very specific approach to DVD movie creation. Most certainly, other video editing programs will offer similar add-ons, including DVD-making capabilities, in later software releases.

In both MediaStudio Pro and VideoStudio there are three steps to creating DVD movies:

1. An existing movie is converted to MPEG with SVCD compression.
2. That movie is converted to DVD format, marked with clickable "scenes" that viewers can use to navigate your movie via remote control.
3. The movie and support files are burned onto a CD or DVD using your existing software and hardware. All of the above steps take place using the simple DVD MovieFactory wizard, which features at most six thumbnails. You'll be done in no time.

CHAPTER 12

In the following example, we'll use Ulead VideoStudio 6 to burn a DVD-compatible CD. Let's get started:

Reformatting the Existing Movie

To begin, choose a project you want converted to DVD and load it into VideoStudio 6. Please note that the final output will be a high-quality movie played back on top equipment. Pick a large movie with good color that shows your best work. It'll be played back full-screen, and you'll not have to worry about jerky playback or blotchy compressed color. You're with the big boys now.

1. After loading the movie, click Finish, which lets you access movie format export options.

2. At the top of the screen, click the dropdown arrow next to the Create Video File button, and choose MPEG as the file type (DVD recording requires this initial conversion step before proceeding). Name your movie. You'll be saving the current movie as a new, separate file.

3. Click Options on the Save As dialog box. When the four-tab MPEG options dialog box appears, make any changes you like, then click the Compression tab.

4. On the Compression Tab, click the Media Type drop-down menu and choose NTSC SVCD (Figure 12.6).

Figure 12.6
Saving an MPEG movie with NTSC SVCD compression.

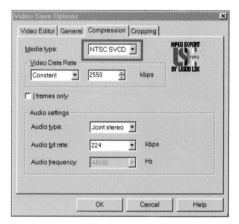

 NOTE
European versions of the plug-in will offer PAL SVCD or Secam SVCD format choices in geographical locations that use those formats.

5. Click OK to close the dialog box and begin export. The movie will be converted to MPEG with the specified compression type. The green progress bar on the main screen will indicate conversion progress. It will take a while.

Note that nothing you've done so far involves opening the DVD MovieFactory menus. You'll do that next. After the movie is finished converting, you'll be ready to begin part two.

NOTE

You can't convert the movie then later burn a DVD-compatible CD. The DVD MovieFactory executes dual processes that must be done simultaneously. Note also that the DVD MovieFactory does not store DVD movies on your hard drive. You're burning right onto the DVD disk.

Creating the DVD Files and Disk Format

Here's how to create the DVD:

1. If the movie you just created begins playing back in the VideoStudio main screen, you can use this movie to make your DVD. If not, locate the encoded video file in the video library and click the Export button.

2. At this point, you should place a CD or DVD in your recorder, if you've not done so already.

3. If you are not already there, click the arrow next to Finish at the upper right of the screen. Then, choose Create DVD, VCD, or SVCD, depending on the medium you are recording onto (Figure 12.7).

Figure 12.7
Exporting a movie using the DVD MovieFactory.

CHAPTER 12

4. After the Ulead DVD MovieFactory option appears, click the Export Video Clip
    arrow on the left. The DVD Wizard will open, initially displaying a screen
    indicating the name of the file that will be created, its size, and its save location.
    You cannot adjust these options. After viewing this screen, click Next. The Add
    Scene dialog box will appear.

Adding Scenes to Your DVD

Here's where you add thumbnails that represent starting-point movie scenes. These thumbnails
represent segments of your video. You are essentially allowing viewers to fast-forward to points
you choose and play back from there. The thumbnails display the first frame of that segment.
You can also import a new video project into your DVD, thus combining video projects onto a
single DVD presentation.

▶ On the left of the Add Scene dialog box is the movie you are exporting, as well
   as a control panel for fast-forwarding to different parts of the movie and selecting
   scenes (Figure 12.8). Note that with Ulead DVD MovieFactory, you can not only
   include segments of your current project, but also clips from other videos and
   projects as well.

Figure 12.8
The Add Scene
dialog box.

▶ On the right is a thumbnail list displaying the opening frames of the scenes you
   will select for the DVD project.

Later, when the DVD is viewed by the user, the same opening screen thumbnail view appears.
However, the viewer will see them presented in an attractive interface, not a list. By remote
control, the user will click any thumbnail view, and movie playback will begin from that scene.
Your job right now is to fast forward through your movie and add scenes to the thumbnail list.

Of course, the first scene you'd want to add is the beginning of the movie. The plug-in adds that automatically. Scene one, then, appears at the upper right of the screen as thumbnail one.

To add scenes, do the following:

1. Use the Next Scene arrow at the lower right of the control panel below the movie preview, or use the location indicator to "scrub" forward and locate the beginning of a scene you want to add.

2. When the preview screen displays the frames that you want to be the beginning of your new scene, click the Add button. That scene is added to the thumbnail list on the right.

3. Continue adding as many scenes as you like. The DVD MovieFactory will continue to add thumbnails for scenes. You can also check the box in the top right to add an Intro Video file that will play before the menu appears.

4. When you are finished adding scenes, click Next. The Select Menu Template dialog box appears.

Selecting a Background

Your DVD presentation is part of the creative process. You're creating an interface, or a console, for viewers to choose which project or project segment to view. The background you choose or import should reflect the nature of your project. Viewers will return to it often, using that ol' remote control to flip back and forth just as if you had given them a whole new set of TV channels to play with.

In the Select Menu Template dialog box, you can choose a backdrop for the movie scene thumbnails (Figure 12.9).

Figure 12.9
The Select Menu
Template dialog box.

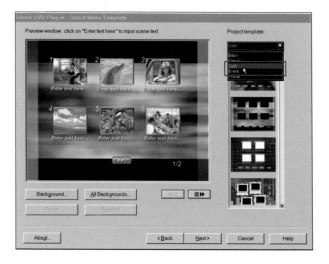

CHAPTER 12

▶ The left side of the screen displays your thumbnails as they would appear in a template. This backdrop is what the DVD user will see when the DVD (or CD) is inserted into the drive. Note that if you have added more than six scenes, the plug-in adds additional pages to accommodate all your thumbnails.

▶ The right side of the screen allows you to choose templates from a drop-down menu. Displayed in Figure 12.9 is one of the "Cool" templates.

You can add a short text label to each thumbnail, indicating to the viewer the content of each scene. Note the Forward arrow near the bottom of the preview. You'll see this if you have more than six thumbnails. The arrow indicates a new page of thumbnails that the user can access. At this time, click the arrow to add text headings to those additional pages.

Seeing What the Audience Sees

Click Next, and the Playback Simulation dialog box appears (Figure 12.10):

Figure 12.10
The Playback
Simulation dialog box.

▶ The left screen displays the DVD selection screen as the viewer would see it.

▶ The right screen shows a typical DVD remote control. Here you can click the digits and buttons to simulate the user's experience navigating your movie. To make adjustments to your scenes, labels, or sequence, use the Back arrows to return to previous screens.

When you are happy with the layout, click Next to confirm your CD-ROM or DVD burning options.

Burning the DVD/CD

Use the Determine Output Options Settings dialog box to specify where the working files should be created and confirm driver choice for your recordable device. You're getting ready to actually make your CD. Depending on the speed of your CD or DVD recorder, the burning process could take a while.

When you are ready to begin creating the CD or DVD, click Next. The Finish screen will appear. Two progress bars will appear. The top progress bar indicates remaining time until all DVD creation related tasks are completed. The bottom bar indicates CD or DVD burning progress.

After the tasks are completed, you can remove the disk from the recorder. It is ready to be viewed on a DVD player.

Archiving and Organizing Your Movies

As clips and projects begin to multiply on your hard drive, you may be wondering what you can do with them all. Perhaps you've looked at the file sizes of your raw footage and noticed some are larger than a gigabyte. What will you do with those files? They are too large to store on recordable CD. A gigabyte video would span across two CDs, or ten 100MB Zip disks, if you could find software that could reliably archive a video file across multiple disks.

CAUTION

Currently, reliable software that can span files across recordable CD-ROM drives is very hard to come by. The newest version of WinZip will do this, if you have a recordable CD-ROM drive. However, reading a CD-ROM spanned file and unzipping it is not always problem-free. This leaves you in the position of requiring a backup for your backup, which rather defeats the purpose.

We have two situations to tackle here. One was just mentioned above—finding a way to off-load those huge video "source" files and free up some disk space on your computer again. The other is determining which video clips you'd like to keep on hand for other projects. Some footage is just nice to have around to carve up and borrow clips from and use as needed. The files you want to keep on hand require an archival system, which we will deal with below. However, off-loading and saving source video files larger than a gigabyte is quite a task.

CHAPTER 12

Storing Oversize Source Files

Saving options for such large files are somewhat limited. There are four possible solutions.

▶ Cut your source video into clips small enough for each to fit on a recordable CD (600 MB or so. Don't try to overstuff the CD).

▶ Acquire a portable hard drive or extra hard drive for saving your large source videos.

▶ Acquire a recordable DVD drive, which would provide you with nearly 5 GB of storage space per disk.

▶ Delete the source videos, since they are simply a replica of what exists on your digital camcorder's DV tape. Perhaps it's too much trouble to maintain a computerized duplicate of what safely exists on your DV tape anyway.

Archiving Clips for Later Use

Let's discuss how to archive completed projects and video clips you'll want to again use for later projects:

After you've acquired lots of video clips and finished a few projects, you'll need ways to locate them quickly. You'll want to quickly scour your hard drive and pull out a clip to be used in your newest creative endeavor. One system would be to create a thumbnail archive, in which you could view your video clips as individual thumbnails. You could view many clips at a glance. Find one you like? Boom. Click it, and drag it onto MediaStudio Pro or some video editing program that supports drag and drop for video clips. As soon as you've recorded lots of video projects and amassed a library of clips, you'll appreciate having gone to the trouble to be organized from the start. A thumbnail viewing program is a good answer.

There are many types of thumbnail programs. However, you need one that can view videos as thumbnails. Not every thumbnail viewing program can display AVI, MOV, or MPEG files (the largest files and, thus, the movies most likely to need archiving onto CD or DVD). Also, some thumbnail programs will display thumbnails of certain movie types but not others. For example, if your thumbnail program views AVI file thumbnails but most of your movies are QuickTime, you'll still be left guessing about your QuickTime movie content until you open them up.

There is one thumbnail program that displays a picture of each movie in a folder as soon as that folder is clicked. It's Ulead PhotoExplorer, and it runs pretty automatically. Here's how it works:

After installing PhotoExplorer, start the program. Inside the program, you'll notice your hard drive mapped out as an Explorer-like menu of folders. Click a folder and, without doing anything else, PhotoExplorer begins displaying the thumbnail of the first frame of every movie in that folder (Figure 12.11).

Figure 12.11
Ulead PhotoExplorer
displaying a folder full
of video clips.

Getting each thumbnail in a folder displayed may take a few minutes, depending on how many movies are in it. You can then scroll through the thumbnails and get an idea regarding which movies are in that folder. Right-click on a thumbnail to view more information about the movie, and, of course, click on a movie to view it in a movie viewer.

Using a thumbnail view of many movies at once, you can initiate group actions, such as selecting many movies at once and saving them to a CD or to a secondary hard drive. Like most thumbnail programs, PhotoExplorer lets you copy and move any file using drag and drop operations. What's more, you can drag a clip from PhotoExplorer right onto a movie editor such as MediaStudio Pro.

A Final Word

Well, that's it, you made it through. This book covers a lot of ground, and there's much material you may not have caught the first time around. As your skills grow, return to the book to check out the sections on advanced video editing, and when someone asks you to film a wedding or concert, or to create a trade show video, you know you've got something to turn to. Happy videography. Remember to have fun. It will show.

CHAPTER 12

Index

C

G

H

I

K

INDEX

INDEX

W

MUSKA & LIPMAN

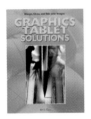

We want to hear from you.

We are interested in your ideas and comments. When you provide us the feedback, we'll add you to our monthly announcement list if you wish so you can hear about new books. We won't sell or share your personal information with anyone.

Tell us what you think of this book—what you like and what you don't like or what you would like to see changed.

Let us know what other books you would like to see from Muska & Lipman. You are a valuable resource for us.

Visit our Web site to submit your feedback:

http://www.muskalipman.com/feedback.html

Or send us a letter with your feedback at:
Muska & Lipman Publishing
P.O. Box 8225
Cincinnati, Ohio 45208-8225